The Books
OF Enoch A.I.

A collection of eight A.I. enhanced books of Enoch

By AJ Carapezza

Contents

In realms of light and realms of dark, A tale unfolds, both fierce and stark. Of Heaven's glory, a celestial sight, And Hell's abyss, where shadows ignite.

Holy angels, with wings unfurled, Radiant beings, in grace they twirl. Their souls ablaze, with divine fire, Guiding mortals, lifting them higher.

In golden halls, a heavenly choir sings, A symphony of love, that forever rings. Their halos gleaming, a radiant crown, A paradise eternal, where peace is found.

But beyond the realms of ethereal grace, Lies the realm of darkness, a sinister space. Unholy fallen angels, their wings once pure, Now tainted and twisted, their hearts obscure.

Satan, the embodiment of pride and deceit, A fallen angel, his power complete. His minions, the giants of wrath and despair, Ravaging souls, in a relentless warfare.

They clash and clash, in battles untold, Wielding their might, as stories unfold. Good versus evil, a cosmic strife, As Heaven defends its gift of life.

Yet, amidst the chaos, hope persists, For in every soul, a light exists. God's love, a beacon, forever strong, Redeeming hearts, righting every wrong.

For even in darkness, a chance to mend, To embrace the light, and to ascend. In the tapestry of existence, a sacred dance, A battle for souls, a second chance.

So let us choose wisely, with hearts laid bare, To nurture goodness, compassion to share. For Heaven and Hell are but reflections of choice, And our destiny's echo, in each silent voice.

Introduction

What are the angels' names mentioned in the King James Bible? From Genesis through Revelation, angels are mentioned close to 300 times. But only a handful are ever named. The reason why is because there are missing books from the Holy Bible. This is a collection of one such book, The Book Of Enoch. Enoch the great-grandfather of Noah, one of God's most loved humans, god granted him more knowledge than almost any of his most holy angels. This is the lost story of the angels and of the knowledge God bestowed upon Enoch.

Nephilim Land of Giants

The world's most important authors have confirmed these tales of giants, gods, and islands of Crete. Pliny, Strabo, Plutarch, Diodorus Siculus, and Plato. In addition to these historical stories by some of the world's most reputable authorities, there is science with real-life enormous bones found on Crete. In fact, the largest bones ever unearthed were uncovered on this island, which may prove it was the Land of Giants.

Apocrypha Texts

Of the 14 texts that make up the Apocrypha (from Greek apokryptein, "to hide away"), in biblical literature, works outside an accepted canon of scripture. One of the most significant non-canonical apocryphal writings is The Book of Enoch, an ancient Hebrew apocalyptic religious scripture that undoubtedly had a significant impact on early Christian ideas, notably Gnostic ones. The scriptures, which are dated to between 300 and 200 BC, are traditionally attributed to Enoch (Noah's great-grandfather). Enoch revealed ideas such as the coming of a Messiah, Resurrection, a Final Judgment, and a Heavenly Kingdom on Earth through hallucinatory visions of heaven and hell, angels, and devils. The Bible also tells the story of the Watchers' fall, who were the angels who gave birth to the Nephilim, angel-human hybrids. This information is interspersed with quasi-scientific tangents on geographical concepts, cosmology, astronomy, and meteorology.

Mention of Angels in KJV Bible

We see them called "angels of God" (Luke 12:8), "sons of God" (Job 1:6), "sons of the mighty" (Psalm 89:6), "heavenly host" (Psalm 148:2; 1 Kings 22:19), "holy ones" (Psalm 89:5), "holy watchers" (Daniel 4:13), "rulers" (Daniel 10:13), and "heavenly beings" (Psalm 29:1). Yet very few are ever called by name. Of the hundreds of angelic references, only four have shared names, with one implied.

Angels mentioned by name in KJV Bible

Archangel Michael, Gabriel, Lucifer, and Abaddon the destroyer are named throughout the Bible. Four angels are named out of hundreds of thousands. Ever wondered why? Why just four when Christian theology relies on angels? The most popular version of the Bible, the King James Bible, lacks manuscripts. These manuscripts were confirmed in the Dead Sea Scrolls found in 1946 at the Qumran Caves dating back to the second century.

Translation of M. S. to The Book Of Enoch

Over time the M. S. have been translated and turned into multiple books. Enoch, Noah's great-great grandfather, is

4

captured in three volumes. His story is the story of the angels—holy and fallen. I hope you appreciate my translation of these volumes of Enoch, enriched for the first time by artificial intelligence A.I. and hundreds of original pictures, which I developed to graphically depict the incredible story of Enoch.

History of The Book Of Enoch

A lot of religious organizations, particularly conservative Christians, see the Bible as the inspired, inerrant Word of God. This doctrinal position affirms that the Bible is unlike all other books or collections of works in that it is free of error due to having been given by the inspiration of God, and that it is profitable for doctrine, for reproof, for correction, and for instruction in righteousness—so that the man of God may be perfect and fully equipped for all good works (2 Timothy 3:16, 17). The Book of Enoch is an ancient Jewish religious work, attributed by tradition to Enoch, the great-grandfather of Noah, which played a crucial role in forming the worldview of the New Testament authors. These authors were not only familiar with it but also quoted it in Jude 1:14–15, where it is attributed to "Enoch the Seventh from Adam" (1 En 60:8). No other text can claim the same unique authority. The group that first acquired and analyzed the Dead Sea Scrolls also used the text. While some churches today include Enoch in the biblical canon (for example, the Ethiopian Orthodox Tewahedo Church and the Eritrean Orthodox Tewahedo Church), other Christian denominations and scholars only accept it as having historical or theological non-canonical interest. Enoch is frequently used or assigned as supplemental material within academic settings to help students and scholars discover or better understand the cultural and historical context of the early Christ. When it says,

"God, who at various times and in various ways spoke in time past unto the fathers by the prophets" (Heb. 1:1), the Book of Enoch gives commentators important insight into what many ancient Jews and early Christians believed. For those who are unfamiliar with 1 Enoch, it is the ancient apocalyptic literary work commonly (but inaccurately) referred to as the Book of Enoch. Most academics concur that the book of 1 Enoch was first written in Aramaic, maybe as early as the third century B.C. The Dead Sea Scrolls contain some of the book's earliest fragments, which date to around the second century B.C. This sets the book in the midst of the Intertestamental Period, also known as the Second Temple Period, which runs from approximately 500 B.C. to 70 A.D. The more academic term (Second Temple Period) will be used in this book. Many readers will remember that the Genesis 6:4–6:6 account of the sons of God (Hebrew: beney ha-elohim) entering into the daughters of men is expanded in the Watcher story of 1 Enoch. As a result, the preferred Enochian name (among others) for the divine sons of God is Watchers. Understand that the Enochian language is the "Langued of the Angels". The Book of Enoch in my opinion should be included in the Holy Bible and will be a crucial supplementary tool for aiding serious scholars and students in their study of the Bible.

Origins of M. S. translated into The Books Of Enoch

The origins of the last three remaining books of Enoch. The M. S. translated and gave birth to; The Book of the Secrets of Enoch, The Book of Enoch the Watchers and The Book of Enoch.

The manuscripts from slavonic scripts, The Book of Enoch's Slavonic redaction, which is now being translated into English and for the first time being enhanced by using artificial intelligence, has mostly been preserved in two forms. They are translations from Greek and Slovic manuscripts.

A M. S. was found in the Public Library of Belgrade in the year 1886 by Professor Sokolov of Moscow. The spelling used in this recension of the Bulgarian language dates from the middle Bulgarian period. This M. S. was most likely written in the sixteenth century. It details the Deluge, the birth of Melchizedek, and the priesthood of Methuselah and Nir.

The M. S., which dates to the second half of the seventeenth century, is included in a collection of miscellanies called Shornih that also contains saints' biographies and other theological treatises. Mr. A. Popov published this article in the University of Filmore's Transactions of the His/ori cal and Archaeological Society, vol. iii. (Moscow Unfortunately, it is extremely corrupt in many places. The present text is based on it, but where it is corrupt, efforts have been made to substitute a more reliable text from another M. S.

There is a Serbian redaction that was published by Nova kovié in the sixteenth volume of the literary magazine Starine (Agra-m, M.), as well as a reduced and incomplete reduction of the text that is known to have three M. S. Any readings of this M. S. are really intriguing.

A M. S. from the seventeenth century that is in the custody of Mr. E. Barsov of Moscow. It is from the sixteenth century and is cited as B.

Additionally, Pypin's Memorials of Old Russian Literature (HaMHTHImE crapuHHofi pyccrcofieeparypsi) and Tikhonravov's Memorials of Russian Apocryphal Literature (HaMHTHmcn orpeq Hofi pyccrcofim eparypsr) contain parts of the Book of Enoch. We can tell that these late texts are simply copies of much earlier ones that have long since vanished because of references and quotations found in early Slavonic literature. Tikhonravov mentions a M.S. from the fourteenth century in this way.

BOOK OF THE WATCHERS A.I.
Section I: Chapters I-XXXVI

1.1 These are the words of the blessing of Enoch, which blessed the chosen and upright who must be present on the appointed day of hardship to remove all the wicked and impious.

1.2 Enoch began his story: There was a virtuous man whose eyes were opened by the Lord, and he saw a Holy vision in the Heavens, which the Angels showed me. I heard everything from them and understood what I saw—not for this generation, but for a future generation.

I spoke about the Chosen and told a parable: The Holy and Great One will come out of his house.

1.4 The Eternal God will appear on Mount Sinai with his Host and in his power from Heaven.

1.5 The Watchers will quake and all will be scared, shuddering to the ends of the world.

1.6 High mountains and hills will quake and melt like wax in a flame.

1.7 The earth will sink, everything on it will be destroyed, and all will be judged, including the virtuous.

1.8 For the righteous, He will make peace, protect the Chosen, and show kindness.

They'll flourish and be blessed under God's light.

1.9 And behold, He comes with ten thousand Holy Ones to judge them, slay the impious, and contend with all flesh about everything the sinners and impious have done and wrought against Him.

2.1 Consider how the lights in the sky rise and set in order, at their proper times, and do not deviate from their law.

2.2 Look at the planet from beginning to finish and see that God's work doesn't alter.

2.3 Consider summer and winter, when clouds, dew, and rain cover the planet.

3.1 Notice how all the trees are withered and stripped of their leaves, except for the fourteen trees that keep their old foliage for two or three years.

4.1 Recall summer's beginning, when the Sun is above it. You seek refuge and shade since the Sun's heat scorches the land, and you cannot walk on it or a rock.

5.1 Consider the trees' green leaves and fruit. Understand everything and see how He Who Lives Forever crafted these things for you.

5.2 And how His works are before Him each year, and all His works serve Him and do not vary; but as God has determined, everything is done.

5.3 Consider how seas and rivers cooperate.

You haven't kept the Lord's Law. But you transgressed and spoke haughty and harsh words against his majesty with your dirty tongue. You heartless! No peace!

5.5 This will plague your days and ruin your life. The eternal curse will increase and you will not be pardoned.

5.6 You will curse the virtuous forever. They'll curse sinners eternally.

5.7 The chosen will inherit the earth with light, pleasure, and peace. You, impious, will be cursed.

5.8 The chosen will survive and never do wrong again when wisdom is imparted. Wise people are humble.

5.9 They will never sin again, never be judged, and never die of wrath. They'll reach their lifespan. All their days will be filled with joy and peace.

6.1 When men increased, they had lovely daughters.

6.2 The Heavenly Angels saw them and wanted them. "Come, let us choose wives from men's children and have children," they urged.

"I fear that you may not wish this deed to be done and that I alone will pay for this great sin," stated Semyaza, their leader.

"Let us all swear an oath and bind one another with curses, so not to alter this plan, but to carry out this plan effectively," they replied.

6.5 They swore and cursed each other.

6.6 Two hundred came down on Ardis, Mount Hermon's top. On Hermon, they cursed and swore.

Their leaders' names are:

Semyaza, their leader, Urakiba (Araqiel), Rameel, Kokabiel, Tamiel, Ramiel, Daniel, Ezeqiel, Baraqiel, Asael, Armaros, Batariel, Ananel, Zaqiel, Samsiel, Satariel, Turiel, Yomiel, Sariel. (Chs 8 & 69)

6.8 These lead the two hundred Angels and everyone else.

7.1 Each chooses a wife. They left. promiscuous with them. They taught them spells and roots and tree chopping.

7.2 They had giants. Three thousand cubits tall.

7.3 These consumed men's labor till they could not survive.

7.4 The giants attacked to eat men.

7.5 They sinned against birds, animals, reptiles, and fish, devouring each other's flesh and drinking their blood.

7.6 Then Earth protested about lawbreakers.

8.1 Azazel instructed men to build swords, daggers, shields, and breastplates. He showed them how to make bracelets, jewelry, eye makeup, eyelid beautification, the most expensive stones, and all kinds of colored dyes. World altered.

8.2 Impiety and adultery led them astray and corrupted their ways.

8.3 Amezarak taught spellcasters and root cutters, Armaros spell release, Baraqiel astrologers, Kokabiel portents, Tamiel astrology, and Asradel moon route.

8.4 When men were destroyed, they cried out to Heaven.

9.1 Michael, Gabriel, Suriel, and Uriel looked down from Heaven and witnessed all the blood and evil on Earth.

9.2 "Let the devastated Earth cry out, up to the Gate of Heaven," they urged.

9.3 Oh Holy Ones of Heaven, the souls of humanity cry out, "Bring our complaint before the Most High."

9.4 They called their King "Lord of Lords, God of Gods, King of Kings!" Your majestic throne is blessed and praised throughout history!

9.5 You created everything and controlled everything. You can see everything, and nothing is concealed from you.

9.6 Azazel hath taught all earthly evil and divulged Heaven's eternal secrets.

9.7 Semyaza, whom you are given power to dominate over others, has cast spells.

9.8 They entered the daughters of men, slept with them, became filthy, and revealed these transgressions.

9.9 Women bore giants, filling the Earth with blood and iniquity.

9.10 Now behold, the souls that have died cry out and moan towards the Gate of Heaven, and their grief has ascended, and they cannot go out because of the sin on earth.

9.11 You know everything before it happens and what concerns each of them. You're silent. What should we do about them?"

10.1 The Most High, the Great and Holy One, spoke and dispatched Arsyalalyur to the son of Lamech, saying,

10.2 "Say to him in my name; hide yourself! Show him the conclusion, which will kill the world. A global deluge will destroy everything.

10.3 Now tell him to escape and his children to survive for the whole Earth."

10.4 The Lord ordered Raphael to bind Azazel and hurl him into darkness. Split Dudael's desert and throw him there.

10.5 And cover him with jagged stones and darkness. Keep him forever. Cover his face to block light.

10.6 for the Great Day of Judgment.

10.7 Restore the Earth the Angels destroyed. Declare Earth's regeneration. I will rebuild the Earth so that the Watchers' knowledge won't harm all men.

10.8 "Azazel's teaching has ruined the whole Earth; and against him write: ALL SIN."

10.9 The Lord told Gabriel, "Proceed against the bastards, reprobates, and sons of fornicators." Kill the sons of fornicators and Watchers. Send them out, let them fight, and let them die.

10.10 They will petition you, but the petitioners will achieve nothing because they hope for eternal life and five hundred years apiece.

10.11 The Lord told Michael, "Go, notify Semyaza and the others with him, who have mingled with the women to corrupt themselves with them in all their uncleanness.

10.12 When all their sons kill one other and observe the destruction of their loved ones, tie them for seventy generations under the hills of the earth until the day of their judgment and consummation, until the eternal judgment is completed.

10.13 They will take them to the Abyss of Fire, where they will be tortured and imprisoned forever.

10.14 Semyaza shall be burned and destroyed with them, bound for all generations.

10.15 Destroy all lustful spirits and

Watcher sons because they mistreated mankind.

10.16 Eliminate evil by eradicating wrong.

10.17 The righteous will now be humble and survive to beget many. They shall peacefully complete their youth and sabbaths.

10.18 In those days, the whole world will be tilled in righteousness, planted with trees, and blessed.

10.19 They shall plant vines and attractive trees on it. The vine planted on it will produce abundant fruit, and every seed sown on it will generate a thousand, and each measure of olives will provide ten baths of oil.

10.20 You purify the earth from all injustice, wickedness, sin, impiety, and uncleanness.

10.21 All men will be righteous, and all countries will serve, bless, and worship me.

10.22 And the Earth will be cleaned from all corruption, sin, anger, and suffering, and I will never again pour a flood upon it for all generations.

11.1 In those days, I will open the Heavenly Storehouses of Blessing to send them.

down on Earth, men's effort, and toil.

11.2 Peace and truth shall last forever.

12.1 Enoch disappeared, and no one knew where he was or what occurred.

12.2 His life was spent among the Holy Ones and Watchers.

12.3 Enoch blessed the Great Lord and King of Eternity.

Enoch the scribe, the Watchers called to me:

12.4 Enoch, upright scribe.

Go and inform the Watchers of Heaven, who have abandoned the High Heaven and the Holy Eternal Place, defiled themselves with women, and taken wives like men, becoming utterly corrupt on earth.

12.5 Since they won't celebrate their sons, they won't experience peace or forgiveness on Earth.

12.6 They will witness the murder of their loved ones and the death of their sons. They won't have mercy or tranquility."

13.1 "You will not have peace," Enoch told Azazel. You're bound by a harsh sentence.

13.2 "Because of the wrong you taught and all the works of blasphemy, wrong, and sin you showed to men, you will have neither rest nor mercy nor the granting of any petitions."

13.3 I then addressed them all, and they were frightened and trembling.

13.4 They begged me to type out a petition so they may gain forgiveness and take it to the Lord in Heaven.

13.5 Because of their misdeeds, they could no longer speak or look to Heaven.

13.6 Then I wrote down their petition and supplication on their spirits, their deeds, and their request for absolution and forbearance.

13.7 I went to Dan, southwest of Hermon, and sat by the Dan River, reading their plea until I fell asleep.

13.8 A dream came to me, and visions fell upon me, and I saw a vision of wrath—that I should speak to the sons of Heaven and reprove them.

13.9 I woke up and went to them, and they were all sitting together mourning in Ubelseyael, between Lebanon and Senir, with their faces covered.

13.10 I told them about my dreams and chastised the Watchers of Heaven.

14.1 As the Holy and Great One commanded in that vision, this book contains righteousness and reproof for the Watchers from Eternity.

14.2 I saw in my sleep what I shall now say, with my flesh tongue and breath, which the Great One has given men in the mouth to speak and understand.

14.3 He created me to reprove the Watchers, the sons of Heaven, as He created and appointed men to learn the word of knowledge.

14.4 I typed up your petition, but in my vision, it appeared that your petition would not be granted for all eternity; total judgment has been decided against you, and you will not have peace.

14.5 You will never ascend into Heaven again, and you will remain on Earth forever.

14.6 Before this, you will see the annihilation of your beloved sons, who will be slain before you.

14.7 Your plea for them and yourself will be denied. While you mourn and beg, you say nothing from my words.

In the image, clouds and mist called me. Stars and lightning accelerated me.

In the vision, winds flew me, lifted me, and accelerated me.

14.9 I continued till I reached a hailstone wall ringed by a tongue of fire, which scared me.

14.10 I entered the tongue of fire and arrived near a gigantic hailstone house with a mosaic wall and a snow floor.

14.11 Its roof was like the stars and lightning, with flaming cherubim and a watery sky.

14.12 Its wall and door were blazing.

14.13 I entered that house, which was hot as fire and frigid as snow, with no life or joy. I shook with fear.

14.14 I fell on my face, trembling.

14.15 In the vision, I saw a grander home with all its doors open, built of a tongue of fire.

14.16 It was so glorious and large that I cannot express it.

14.17 Its floor, lightning, stars, and roof were all fire.

14.18 I saw a high throne with ice-like walls, cherubim, and the Sun.

14.19 Fire streamed from behind the high throne, making it impossible to see.

14.20 The Great in Glory sat on it, and his raiment was brighter than the Sun and whiter as snow.

14.21 No angel could enter, and no fleshly creature could stare at His Honoured and Praised Face.

14.22 A sea of fire surrounded Him, and a big fire stood in front of Him. No one approached Him. Ten thousand times ten thousand stood before Him yet He needed no Holy Council.

14.23 His Holy Ones never left Him by night or day.

14.24 While trembling, I covered my face. "Come here, Enoch," the Lord said.

14.25 He carried me to the door. I glanced, face down.

15.1 He said, "Hear!" Righteous Enoch, do not fear.

righteous scribe. Listen to me.

15.2 Tell the Watchers of Heaven, who sent you to petition, that you should petition for mankind, not men for you.

15.3 Why have you abandoned the High, Holy, and Eternal Heaven, lain with women, become filthy with the daughters of mankind, taken wives for yourselves, done as the sons of the earth, and borne enormous sons?

15.4 You were spiritual, holy, and everlasting, but you became unclean upon women, begot children through flesh, lusted after men's blood, and produced flesh and blood, like they do, who die and are destroyed.

15.5 I give men spouses to spread seed in them, have offspring, and execute acts on Earth.

15.6 You were once spiritual, living an endless, immortal life for all generations.

15.7 I did not arrange brides for you since the spiritual ones live in Heaven.

15.8 Now, the giants produced from body and flesh shall be termed Evil Spirits and live on Earth.

15.9 Since they were created by the Holy

Watchers, wicked spirits came out of their flesh.

Evil spirits, named "Spirits of the Evil Ones," will roam Earth.

15.10 The Spirits of Heaven live in Heaven, but Earth-born spirits live on Earth.

15.11 The giants' spirits sin, battle, break the Earth, and create grief. They never eat, thirst, or be seen.

15.12 Because they sprung from them during slaughter and ruin, these spirits will rise against men and women.

16.1 The giants' flesh will be destroyed before the Judgment after their spirits go. Thus, they will be eliminated till the Great Consummation, upon the Great Age, the Watchers, and the impious ones."

16.2 To the Watchers, who sent you to pray for them, who were once in Heaven:

16.3 "You were in Heaven but its mysteries had not yet been revealed to you; and a worthless mystery you knew.

In your heartlessness, you told women. This mystery increases evil on Earth."

16.4 Say "You will not have peace."

17.1 They led me to a place where they were like fire and could transform into men.

17.2 They carried me to a stormy mountain whose summit approached Heaven.

17.3 I saw illuminated regions, thunder in the outermost extremities, a bow of fire, arrows and their quivers, a sword of fire, and all the lightning flashes in its depths.

17.4 They carried me to the Water of Life and the Fire of the 7 West, which receives every Sunset.

17.5 I found a river of fire that runs like water into the west-facing Great Sea.

17.6 I saw all the huge rivers and reached the huge Darkness, where all flesh walks.

17.7 I saw the Mountains of Winter Darkness and the area where all the deeps pour out.

17.8 I saw all Earth's river outlets and the depths.

18.1 I saw the Earth's foundations and the storehouses of all the winds.

18.2 I saw Earth's cornerstone. I observed the four winds supporting Earth and heaven.

18.3 The Pillars of Heaven are the winds, which stretch the height of Heaven.

18.4 I saw the winds that rotate the sky and set the Sun and stars.

18.5 I witnessed the Angels' pathways and Earth's winds that support clouds. I glimpsed Heaven's firmament at Earth's end.

18.6 I traveled south, and it was scorching day and night, where there were seven mountains of valuable stones, three east and three south.

18.7 Those facing east were of colored stone, pearl, and healing stone, while those facing south were red stone.

18.8 The middle one reached Heaven, like the Lord's stibium throne, and the top was sapphire.

18.9 I observed a raging fire and everything in the mountains.

18.10 I saw where the seas gathered beyond the broad earth.

18.11 I saw a deep earthly chasm with pillars of heavenly fire and falling blazing pillars of Heaven, which were unfathomable in height and depth.

18.12 Beyond this gap, I saw a desert with no water, birds, or sky.

18.13 I saw seven awful lights like burning mountains.

18.14 Like a spirit interrogating me, the Angel said: "This is the place of the end of Heaven and Earth; this is the prison for the Stars and Host of Heaven.

18.15 The stars that roll over the fire disobeyed the Lord from the start because they didn't rise at the right time.

18.16 He was furious and tied them until their wickedness was finished in the Year of Mystery.

19

.1 Uriel told me, "The spirits of the Angels who were promiscuous with women will stand here; and they, assuming many forms, made men unclean and will lead men astray so that they sacrifice to demons as gods. They will wait until the great judgment day to be judged and destroyed.

19.2 Their spouses, having misled the Angels of Heaven, will become peaceful."

19.3 Only I, Enoch, witnessed the end of all.

20

.1 These are the Holy Angels who guard.

20.2 Uriel, the Holy Angel of Spirits of Men.

20.3 Raguel, a Holy Angel who avenges the world and lights.

20.4 Michael, one of the Holy Angels, is in charge of the nation and the best of humanity.

20.5 Saraqael, a Holy Angel, oversees men's sinful spirits.

20.6 Gabriel, a Holy Angel, oversees the Serpents, Garden, and Cherubim.

21

.1 I visited an empty place.

21.2 I saw a dreadful thing, neither heaven nor earth, but a desert, prepared and terrible.

21.3 Seven Stars of Heaven, linked together like mountains, burned like fire.

21.4 "For what sin have they been bound, and why have they been thrown here?"

21.5 The Holy Angel Uriel, who guided me, asked, "Enoch, about whom do you ask?" Who are you interested in?

21.6 These stars disobeyed the Lord Most High and have been imprisoned here for ten thousand ages, the number of their sins.

21.7 Then I went somewhere worse. I witnessed a terrible fire. The place had a gap going into the abyss, filled with gigantic pillars of fire that fell; I couldn't see its magnitude or source.

21.8 "How terrible this place is, and how painful to look at!"

Uriel, a Holy Angel accompanying me, replied. He replied, "Enoch, why do you have such fear and terror because of this terrible place and before this pain?"

"This place is the Angels' prison," he told me.

22

.1 From there, he showed me a large, high mountain, a rough rock, and four magnificent sites in the west.

22.2 Inside was deep, wide, and smooth. That glides well and looks dark!

22.3 Raphael, one of the Holy Angels with me, replied: "These beautiful places are there to gather the spirits, the souls of the dead."

They were meant to gather human souls.

22.4 They created these places to detain them until the Day of Judgment and their set period, which will be long, until the dreadful judgment falls upon them.

22.5 I witnessed the dead sons of men complain to Heaven.

22.6 I asked Raphael, my angel, "Whose is this spirit, whose voice thus reaches Heaven and complains?"

22.7 He replied, "This spirit came out of Abel, whom Cain, his brother, killed." He will whine about him until his offspring are wiped out from the Earth and from among men."

22.8 "Why is one separated from another?" I questioned about him and judgment on everyone.

22.9 "These three places were made to separate the spirits of the dead," he replied. The source of water and light have separated the noble souls.

22.10 Sinners who die and are buried in the soil without judgment have a place too.

22.11 Their souls will be divided for this immense anguish until the immense Day of Judgment, Punishment, and anguish for cursers forever and of retribution on their souls. He'll bind them there forever. Since creation, He is.

22.12 Thus, a place has been set apart for the souls of those who complain and report their death in the sinners' days.

22.13 Thus, a place has been made for the souls of sinners, who will live among the sinners. Their souls will not die on judgment day or rise from here."

22.14 "Blessed be my Lord, the Lord of Glory and Righteousness, who rules everything forever," I said.

23.1 I then traveled west to the ends of the Earth.

23.2 I saw a fire that burned and ran without stopping, day or night, in the same way.

23.3 "What is this that never rests?"

23.4 Raguel, one of the Holy Angels accompanying me, replied: "This burning fire, whose course you saw towards the west, is the fire of all the Lights of Heaven."

24.1 From there, he showed me a day-and-night-burning mountain.

24.2 I approached and saw seven lovely mountains. All were precious, stunning, and unique stones.

Three east, three south, and deep, rocky valleys, none of which were close to each other.

24.3 In the middle of these was a seventh mountain with aromatic plants surrounding it.

24.4 One of them was a tree I had never smelled, and none of the others were like it.

24.5 Its leaves, blossoms, and wood never wither, and its aroma is incomparable. Its fruit tastes like palm date bunches.

"Behold, this beautiful tree!" Beautiful, nice leaves, and wonderful fruit."

24.6 Michael, one of the Holy and Honoured Angels who was with me and in command of them,

25.1 said, "Enoch, why do you ask me about the fragrance of this tree, and why do you inquire to learn?"

25.2 Enoch replied, "I want to know everything, but especially this tree."

25.3 He said, "This high mountain, which you saw, whose summit is like the Throne of the Lord, is the throne where the Holy and Great One, the Lord of Glory, the Eternal King, will sit when he comes down to visit the Earth for good.

25.4 The upright and meek will receive this magnificent and fragrant tree, which no creature of flesh may touch until the great judgment, when he will take vengeance on all and bring everything to a climax forever.

25.5 The chosen shall live off its fruit, planted in a holy spot near the home of the Lord, the Eternal King, to the north.

25.6 They will be joyful and pleased in the Holy place. They will absorb its scent and live long like your forebears. They will not suffer sorrow, agony, toil, or punishment."

25.7 I blessed the Lord of Glory, the Eternal King, since he has prepared such things for righteous men, created them, and promised to provide them.

26.1 I traveled to the center of the land and observed a blessed, well-watered region with living branches that sprang from a cut-down tree.

26.2 I saw a holy mountain and water flowing south under it to the east.

26.3 I noticed another mountain of the same height to the east, and between them was a deep, narrow valley with a stream.

26.4 To the west of this one was a lesser mountain with a valley between them. Other deep, dry valleys ended the three mountains.

26.5 All the valleys were deep, narrow, and hard rock with trees.

26.6 The rock and valley astonished me.

27.1 "What is the purpose of this blessed land, which is completely full of trees, and this accursed valley in the middle of them?"

27.2 Raphael, one of the Holy Angels accompanying me, replied: "This accursed valley is for people who are condemned forever.

All who slander the Lord and His Glory shall be brought here. Here they shall be gathered and judged.

27.3 In the end, the righteous will witness their judgment forever. The merciful will bless the Eternal King here.

27.4 "In the days of their judgment, they will bless Him because of His mercy, according to their lot."

27.5 I blessed the Lord of Glory, addressed Him, and recalled His grandeur as appropriate.

28.1 I proceeded east to the middle of the wilderness mountain and saw only desert.

28.2 However, this seed grew trees and water poured over it.

28.3 The northwest-flowing river sprayed and misted from all sides.

29.1 I left the wilderness and headed east of this mountain.

29.2 I saw Trees of Judgment, notably incense and myrrh jars, and they were different.

30.1 Above it, above these, above the eastern mountains, and not far away, I saw another region, valleys of water like that which does not fail.

30.2 A magnificent tree smelled like mastic.

I smelled cinnamon near these valleys. I headed east past those valleys.

31.1 I saw another mountain with trees, water, and styrax and galbanum nectar.

31.2 I noticed another mountain with aloe trees and firm almond-like fruit.

31.3 This fruit smells better than any other.

32.1 After these fragrances, I looked north and saw seven mountains of exquisite nard and aromatic cinnamon and pepper trees.

32.2 I crossed the Red Sea, the Angel Zotiel, and the peaks of those mountains to the east.

32.3 I entered the Garden of Righteousness and saw many large, sweet-smelling, beautiful, and wonderful Trees of Wisdom, from which people eat and gain much wisdom.

32.4 Like the carob tree, its fruit is lovely bunches of grapes on a vine, and its smell extends far.

32.5 "This tree is beautiful!"
It's gorgeous!"

32.6 The Holy Angel Raphael, who was with me, replied: "This is the Tree of Wisdom, from which your ancient father and ancient mother, who were before you, ate and learned wisdom; and their eyes were opened, and they knew that they were naked. They fled the garden."

33.1 From then, I journeyed to the ends of the earth and observed enormous animals and birds with diverse forms, beauty, and calls.

33.2 To the east of these animals, I beheld the ends of Earth, where Heaven resides, and the wide Gates of Heaven.

33.3 I counted the Gates from which the stars of Heaven came and wrote down all their outlets, one by one, according to their number. The Angel Uriel showed me their names according to their constellations, places, times, and months.

33.4 He wrote down their names, rules, and functions and showed me everything.

34.1 From there, I travelled north to the ends of the Earth and beheld a wonderful wonder.

34.2 Three Gates of Heaven let north winds out, bringing cold, hail, hoarfrost, snow, fog, and rain.

34.3 One Gate blows for good, while the other two Gates blow with might, bringing misery to the world.

35.1 From there, I traveled west to the ends of the Earth and saw three more as I saw in the east.

open as many Gates as outlets.

36.1 From then, I walked south to the ends of the Earth and witnessed three Gates of Heaven open, releasing the south wind, mist, rain, and wind.

36.2 From then, I proceeded east of Heaven's ends and saw the three eastern Gates open and lesser Gates above them.

36.3 The stars of Heaven pass through these smaller Gates and head west following the path revealed to them.

36.4 When I saw, I blessed, and I will always bless the Lord of Glory, who has fashioned Great and Glorious Wonders to display the magnificence of His Work to His Angels and the souls of humanity so they can praise Him. So all His creatures could behold His Power, worship His Hands, and bless Him eternally!

Chapters XXXVII–XXXI
The Parables

37.1 Enoch, the son of Jared, Malalel, Cainan, Enosh, Seth, and Adam, had the vision of wisdom in his second vision.

37.2 This begins my words of wisdom. "To those who dwell on dry ground: Hear, you men of old, and see, those who come after; the words of the Holy One, which I will speak, in front of the Lord of Spirits."

37.3 "It would have been better to say these things before, but from those who come after, we will not withhold the beginning of wisdom."

37.4 The Lord of Spirits has never given me such wisdom. My knowledge, the Lord of Spirits' wish, and my eternal life.

37.5 After receiving the three parables, I shouted to the dry earth dwellers:

38.1

When the righteous appear and sinners are condemned and expelled from the dry earth.

38.2 The Righteous One appears before the selected righteous, whose actions are assessed by the Lord of Spirits. When the pious and chosen on dry ground see light. Sinners live where? Where will the Lord of Spirits deniers rest? They should have never been born.

38.3 When the secrets of the righteous are exposed, sinners will be judged and the impious expelled from the righteous and selected.

38.4 From then on, earthly rulers will be weak. The Lord of the Spirits' light will shine on the Holy, righteous, and selected, so they won't be able to see them.

38.5 The virtuous and Holy will then defeat the powerful kingdoms.

38.6 After death, no one can seek the Lord of Spirits.

39.1 In these days, the selected and holy children will descend from heaven and their progeny will become one with humans.

39.2 Enoch got books of rage and uproar. The Lord of Spirits promises them no mercy.

39.3 Clouds and a storm wind transported me from the earth to the end of Heaven.

39.4 I saw another vision of the Righteous Dwelling and Holy Resting Places.

39.5 There my eyes beheld their residence with the Angels and their resting places with the Holy Ones, and they were begging, supplicating, and praying for the sons of men; righteousness poured in front of them like water, and mercy like dew on the ground. It's always with them.

39.6 In those days, my eyes saw the Place of the Chosen Ones of Righteousness and Faith. There will be righteousness in their days, and the righteous and chosen will be without number in front of him forever and ever.

39.7 I saw their home under the wings of the Lord of Spirits, and all the righteous and selected gleamed in front of him like fire. They blessed and thanked the Lord of Spirits. He will uphold righteousness and truth.

39.8 I wanted to live there, and my soul craved for it. The Lord of Spirits had decided my fate.

39.9 In those days, I blessed and praised the Lord of Spirits, as he has designed me for blessing and praise.

39.10 I gazed at that location and blessed him, saying, "Blessed is He, and may He be blessed from the beginning and forever!"

39.11 He is infinite. He knew the world before it was made, even for future generations.

39.12 Those who do not sleep bless you and stand before Your Glory, blessing, praising, and exalting, crying, "Holy, Holy, Holy, Lord of Spirits; he fills the earth with spirits."

39.13 I saw all the non-sleepers standing in front of Him, blessing and exclaiming, "Blessed are you, and blessed is the name of the Lord, forever and ever!"

39.14 My face became unrecognizable.

40.1 Then I saw a thousand thousands and ten thousand times ten thousand! Countless people stood before the Lord of Spirits' Glory.

40.2 I looked, and on the four sides of the Lord of Spirits, I saw four figures, distinct from those who were there. The Angel who went with me revealed their names and taught me all the secrets.

40.3 I heard the four figures singing praises to the Lord of Glory.

40.4 The first voice blesses the Lord of Spirits eternally.

40.5 The second voice blessed the Chosen One and the chosen depend on the Lord of Spirits.

40.6 The third voice petitioned and pleaded for people who live on dry land and pray to the Lord of Spirits.

40.7 The fourth voice drove away the Satans and prevented them from accusing those on high ground before the Lord of Spirits.

40.8 Then I questioned the Angel of Peace, who walked with me and showed me everything secret: "Who are those four figures, whom I have seen, and whose words I have heard and written down?"

40.9 "This first one is Holy Michael, the merciful and long-suffering," he told me. Raphael, the second, oversees all ailments and wounds of humans. Holy Gabriel, the third, controls all powers. Phanuel oversees repentance and eternal life's hope."

40.10 These are the four Lord Most High Angels and the four voices I heard in those days.

41.1 After this, I saw all Heaven's mysteries, how the Kingdom is divided, and how men's deeds are weighed in the Balance.

41.2 I saw the Dwelling of the Chosen and the Resting Places of the Holy, and all the sinners who deny the Lord of Spirits were driven out. The Lord of Spirits' retribution forced them to leave.

41.3 I saw lightning and thunder secrets there. I witnessed where the winds, clouds, and dew come from, and how they are distributed to blow over the earth. From there, earth dust is drenched.

41.4 I saw locked storehouses from which the winds are distributed, and the storehouses of hail, mist, and clouds; and its cloud stayed over the land from the beginning of the creation.

41.5 I saw the Sun and Moon Chambers, where they go out and return. Their triumphant return and how one is honored more than the other. And their glorious route, which they never change. Their oath and loyalty.

41.6 The Lord of Spirits commands the Sun to go out first and complete its trip, and his Name endures eternally.

41.7 The Moon's hidden and visible path continues at that place by day and night. One stands opposite the other in front of the Lord of Spirits, giving thanks and singing praise.

41.8 The Sun rotates for blessings and curses. The Moon's route is for virtuous light but darkness for sinners. In the name of the Lord, who divided light and darkness, divided men's spirits, and established the righteous spirits.

41.9 Because the judge sees and judges all, no angel or power can hinder.

42.1 Wisdom lived in Heaven.

42.2 Wisdom went out to live among men but found no place, so she returned to her place and sat with the angels.

42.3 Iniquity came out of her chambers, found those she did not seek, and dwelt among them, like rain in the desert and dew on the parched ground.

43.1 I saw lightning and stars again,
and He called them all by their names, and they obeyed Him.

43.2 The Balance of Righteousness weighs them according to their brightness, width, and appearance day. And how their revolutions make lightning, and how they preserve trust with each other.

43.3 "What are these?" I asked the Angel who revealed the secret to me.

43.4 He told me, "Their likeness, the Lord of Spirits has shown to you; these are the names of the righteous who dwell on the dry ground and believe in the name of the Lord of Spirits forever."

44.1 I also witnessed some stars rise
and become lightning but cannot lose their form.

45.1 The Second Parable. About those
who dispute the Holy Ones' Dwelling and Lord of Spirits' Name.

45.2 Sinners who defy the Lord of Spirits shall be kept until the Day of Affliction and Distress and will not ascend into Heaven or come to earth.

45.3 The Chosen One will choose their works on that day. Their resting places will be endless, and seeing My Chosen One and others who call on My Holy and Glorious Name will strengthen their souls.

45.4 I will make Heaven an eternal blessing and light and dwell My Chosen One among them on that day.

45.5 I will bless the dry ground and make My Chosen Ones dwell on it, but sinners and evildoers will not tread on it.

45.6 "I have seen and satisfied with peace My Righteous Ones, and have placed them in front of Me; but for the sinners My Judgement draws near so that I may destroy them from the face of the earth."

46.1 I saw a "Head of Days" with a
white woolly head. With him was a man with the grace of a Holy Angel.

46.2 I asked one of the Holy Angels, who went with me and showed me all the mysteries, about that Son of Man—who he was, where he came from, and why he went with the Head of Days.

46.3 "This is the Son of Man who has righteousness and dwells with righteousness," he said. He will unveil all secret treasures since the Lord of Spirits has selected him and his uprightness has surpassed all others in front of the Lord of Spirits forever.

46.4 This Son of Man, whom you have seen, will rouse the kings and powerful from their resting places, the strong from their thrones, and the sinners from their teeth.

46.5 He will depose the kings from their thrones and kingdoms because they do not exalt, laud, or humbly acknowledge where their reign came from.

46.6 He will strike down the strong and fill them with disgrace, darkness, and vermin. They cannot rise from their graves because they do not magnify the Lord of Spirits.

46.7 They judge the stars of heaven, lift their hands against the Most High, trample the dry earth, and dwell on it. Their deeds are iniquitous, their authority comes from their wealth, their faith is in their hand-made gods, and they deny the Lord of Spirits.

46.8 They will be expelled from his congregation and the devout who trust in the Lord of Spirits.

47.1 In those days, the righteous' prayers and blood will have ascended to the Lord of Spirits.

47.2 In these days, the Holy Ones in Heaven will unite with one voice to supplicate, pray, praise, offer thanks, and bless in the name of the Lord of Spirits. because of righteous bloodshed. "And because of the prayer of the righteous, so that it may not cease in front of the Lord of Spirits, so that justice may be done to them, and that their patience may not have to last forever."

47.3 In those days, I saw the Head of Days sit down on the Throne of his Glory and open the Books of the Living, and all His Host, which live in the Heavens above, and his Council stood before him.

47.4 The Holy Ones rejoiced because the number of righteousness had been reached, the righteous had been heard, and the Lord of Spirits had not required their blood.

48.1 In that region I saw an unlimited stream of righteousness and many springs of wisdom encircled it, and all the thirsty drank from them and were filled with wisdom, and they lived with the Righteous, Holy, and Chosen.

48.2 In the presence of the Lord of Spirits, the Son of Man was named and presented to the Head of Days.

48.3 The Lord of Spirits called his name before the Sun, constellations, and stars were created.

48.4 He will be a staff for the righteous and holy to lean on and not fall, the Light of the Nations, and the hope of the grieving.

48.5 All people who live on dry ground will fall down and worship him, blessing, praising, and celebrating the Lord of Spirits with psalms.

48.6 He was chosen and hidden before the world was created and eternally.

48.7 But the wisdom of the Lord of Spirits has shown him to the Holy and the righteous, for he has protected their lot because they loathe and reject this world of evil. They hated all its actions in the name of the Lord of Spirits. He saves them and takes their life.

48.8 The monarchs of the Earth and the powerful who own the dry earth will have downcast faces because of their works because they will not save themselves in their pain and suffering.

48.9 I will give them to my chosen ones, who will burn them in front of the righteous and sink them in front of the Holy, leaving no trace.

48.10 On the day of their anguish, the earth will rest and they will fall down before him and not rise. For rejecting the Lord of Spirits and his Messiah, no one will raise them. Bless the Spirit Lord!

49.1 Wisdom is like water and glory will never fail before Him.

49.2 He is powerful in all the mysteries of righteousness, and iniquity will fade away like a shadow and have no existence; for the Chosen One stands in front of the Lord of Spirits, and His Glory is forever and His Power for all generations.

49.3 He has the spirit of wisdom, intellect, knowledge, power, and righteousness.

49.4 He will judge the secrets, and no one will be able to speak empty words in front of him since he was chosen by the Lord of Spirits.

50.1 The Holy and the selected shall get the Light of Days and glory and honor in those days.

50.2 On the day of trouble, misfortune will be piled over sinners, but the righteous will win in the Name of the Lord of Spirits and He will show this to others to repent and renounce their works.

50.3 The Lord of Spirits will have mercy on them and save them in His Name.

50.4 He is righteous in His judgment, and sin shall be eliminated in front of His Glory.

"From then on," says the Lord of Spirits.

51.1 In those days, Earth will return what was given to it, and Sheol will return what it received. Destruction will pay.

51.2 He will choose the Righteous and Holy from among them since the day of salvation is approaching.

51.3 The Lord of Spirits appointed and honored the Chosen One, who would sit on his throne and speak all the Secrets of Wisdom.

51.4 In those days, mountains will leap like rams and hills will skip like milk-satisfied lambs, and all will become angels in heaven.

51.5 When the Chosen One rises and the earth rejoices, their faces will gleam with delight. The pious and chosen shall live on it.

52.1 After those days, I was swept off by a whirlwind and brought to the west, where I had seen all the visions of the secret.

52.2 I saw the secrets of Heaven—everything that would happen on Earth—in a mountain of iron, copper, silver, gold, soft metal, and lead.

52.3 I questioned the Angel accompanying me, "What are these things I have seen in secret?"

52.4 "All these things you have seen serve the authority of His Messiah, so that he may be strong and powerful on Earth," he stated.

52.5 The Angel of Peace said, "Wait a little and you will see, and everything which is secret, which the Lord of Spirits has established, will be disclosed to you.

52.6 You saw the mountains of iron, copper, silver, gold, soft metal, and lead. Like wax before fire, these will be weak under the Chosen One's feet.

52.7 In those days, neither money nor metal will save men; they will be unable to flee.

52.8 There will be no iron for war or armor, bronze, tin, or lead.

52.9 When the Chosen One arrives before the Lord of Spirits, these will be destroyed.

53.1 I saw a vast valley with an open mouth. All those who live on dry ground, and the sea, and the islands will send him gifts and offerings, but that deep valley will not fill.

53.2 Their hands commit evil, and everything the righteous toil, the sinners evilly devour; and thus the sinners will be eliminated from before the Lord of Spirits and expelled from His Earth forever and ever.

53.3 I saw the Angels of Punishment gathering Satan's tools.

53.4 I asked the Angel of Peace, who

accompanied me, "These instruments—for whom are they preparing them?"

53.5 "They are preparing these for the kings and powerful of this Earth to destroy them," he added.

53.6 The Righteous and Chosen One will then cause the house of his congregation to appear, and they will not be impeded in the name of the Lord of Spirits.

53.7 "In front of him these mountains will not be firm like the earth, and the hills will be like a spring of water; and the righteous will have rest from the ill-treatment of sinners."

54.1 I turned and saw a deep valley with fire.

54.2 They flung kings and powerful into that valley.

54.3 I watched them make heavy iron chains for them there.

54.4 I asked the Angel of Peace, who was accompanying me, "Who are these chain instruments for?"

54.5 He told me, "These are being prepared for the forces of Azazel, so that they may take them and toss them into the lowest portion of hell; and they will cover their jaws with jagged stones, as the Lord of Spirits directed.

54.6 Michael, Gabriel, Raphael, and Phanuel shall seize them on that great day. And toss them into the furnace of scorching fire on that day, so that the Lord of Spirits may take vengeance on them for their wrongdoing in becoming Satan's minions and leading the dry ground's inhabitants astray.

54.7 The Lord of Spirits' punishment will end, and all the water storehouses above and below will open.

54.8 All waters will join the sky-high floods.

Male water is above the sky and female water is below.

54.9 All who live on dry land and beneath the heavens shall be wiped away.

54.10 "And they will acknowledge their iniquity on Earth and be destroyed."

55.1 The Head of Days repented, saying, "I have destroyed all those who dwell upon the dry ground for no reason."

55.2 He swore by His Great Name: "From now on I will not act like this towards all those who reside upon the dry earth. As long as Heaven is above the Earth, I will set a sign in Heaven as a pledge of trust.

55.3 This follows my order. "My wrath and anger will remain upon them when I want to take hold of them with the hands of the Angels on the day of distress and pain," says the Lord, the Lord of Spirits.

55.4 "You powerful kings of the dry ground will have to watch my Chosen." One sits on the throne of My Glory and judges Azazel and his allies and hosts in the Name of the Lord of Spirits."

56.1 I saw the Angels of Punishment carrying iron and bronze chains.

56.2 I asked the Angel of Peace, who accompanied me, "To whom are those holding the chains going?"

56.3 "Each to his own chosen ones, and to their beloved ones," he said.

56.4 That valley will be filled with their selected and cherished ones, and their life and leading astray will be over.

56.5 The angels will gather and attack the Parthians and Medes from the east. They will stir up the kings so that a troubling spirit will descend upon them and drive them off their thrones. They will come out like lions from their lairs and like hungry wolves in their flocks.

56.6 They will go up and tramp on the Land of My Chosen Ones, turning it into a trodden pathway.

56.7 However, the City of My Righteous Ones will hinder their horses, cause slaughter among themselves, and strengthen their right hand. Until there are enough dead, a man will not admit to knowing his neighbor, brother, father, or mother. Their punishment will not be in vain.

56.8 "Sheol will open its mouth and swallow up the sinners in front of the chosen."

57.1 After this, I saw another host of chariots with men on them coming from the east and west, to the south.

57.2 Their chariots were heard. The Holy Ones watched from Heaven as the Pillars of the Earth were rocked.

One day, the sound was heard everywhere.

57.3 All shall bow before the Lord of Spirits. Second parable concludes.

58.1 I began The Third Parable. The Righteous and The Chosen.

58.2 Blessed are the pious and chosen— your lot will be wonderful!

58.3 The righteous will be in the light of the Sun and selected in eternal life. Their life and the Holy's will never cease.

58.4 They will seek light and discover justice with the Lord of Spirits. Peace to the righteous with the World Lord!

58.5 After this, the Holy will be told to seek the secrets of righteousness and faith in Heaven, since it has become brilliant as the Sun, on the dry earth and all darkness has faded away.

58.6 Because darkness will have been eliminated, there will be constant brightness. The light and uprightness shall stay before the Lord of Spirits forever.

59.1 In those days, my eyes witnessed the mysteries of lightning flashes, lights, and their regulations. They flash for blessings or curses as the Lord of Spirits chooses.

59.2 I observed how thunder crashes in Heaven and how it's heard.

They showed me the houses of the dry ground and the sound of thunder, for peace, blessing, or cursing, according to the Lord of Spirits.

59.3 After this, I learned all about lightning and lights. Blessings and satisfaction flash before me.

60.1 In Enoch's fiftieth year, seventh month, fourteenth day that was.

Then, I saw the Heaven of Heavens tremble violently and the Host of the Most High and the Angels, a thousand thousands and ten thousand times ten thousand, exceedingly upset.

60.2 Then I saw the Head of Days on his splendor throne with the angels and righteous around him.

60.3 Fear gripped me, my loins crumpled, and I fell on my face.

60.4 And the Holy Michael dispatched another Holy Angel, one of the Holy Angels, and he elevated me, and my spirit returned, for I had been unable to endure the sight of that host, the disturbance, and the shaking of Heaven.

60.5 The Holy Michael said, "What sight has disturbed you like this?

He has shown mercy and long suffering to those who live on dry land till today.

60.6 The Lord of Spirits has prepared a Day, Power, Punishment, and Judgment for those who worship the Righteous Judgment, for those who refuse it, and for those who take His name in vain. They selected a covenant, the offenders a visitation."

60.7 On that day, Leviathan, a female monster, will be separated from the other and live in the sea's depths above the springs.

60.8 Behemoth fills Dendayn, a vast desert east of the Garden where the chosen and virtuous live, with his breast. Where my great-grandfather, sixth from Adam, was received.

60.9 I begged the other Angel to show me the power of those creatures, how they were divided one day and hurled into the sea and the desert, respectively.

60.10 "Son of man, you here wish to know what is secret," he continued.

60.11 The other Angel talked to me, the one who traveled with me and showed me what is secret; what is first and last in Heaven, in the heights, under the dry earth, in the depths, at the Ends of Heaven, at the Foundations of Heaven, and in the Storehouses of the Winds.

60.12 Spirit distribution and weighing. How springs and winds are counted by spirit strength. Moonlight power. Named star divisions. How all divisions are made.

60.13 Thunderfall according to location. Lightning divisions to flash. Its hosts obey fast.

60.14 Thunder has waiting intervals. Thunder and lightning are related but distinct. They walk together by spirit.

60.15 When lightning flashes, thunder roars, and the spirit calms it and divides equally between them since the storehouse of their occurrence is like sand. Each is restrained by a rein, turned back by the spirit, and propelled forward according to the number of Earth's regions at the right time.

60.16 The sea's manly and strong soul turns it back with a rein, drives it ahead, and scatters it among all the mountains of the Earth.

60.17 Hoarfrost has its own Angel, and hail has a good Angel.

60.18 Because of its might, the snow's spirit has withdrawn, and its ice is like smoke.

60.19 The mist spirit's storeroom is an angel, and its course is magnificent in light and darkness, winter and summer.

60.20 The dew spirit lives at the extremities of Heaven and is connected to rain storehouses. Its clouds, winter, and summer course. The mist clouds share.

60.21 Angels unlock the storehouse and bring forth the rain spirit when it moves. It joins all the water on the dry ground when it is dispersed over it.(......)

60.22 The waters are food from the Most High in Heaven for those who live on dry ground.
The Angels know the rain's measure.

60.23 I beheld these toward the Garden of Righteousness.

60.24 The Angel of Peace told me, "These two monsters, prepared in accordance with the greatness of the Lord, will feed them the Punishment of the Lord. Mothers and children will die together.

60.25 The Lord of Spirits' retribution will stay on them so it doesn't go to waste. Then His mercy and patience will judge."

61.1 In those days, those Angels received long cords and wings flew north.

61.2 I asked the Angel, "Why did they take the long cords and go?" "They went to measure," he said.

61.3 The Angel who went with me said, "These will bring the measurements and ropes of the righteous to the righteous, that they may rely on the name of the Lord of Spirits forever.

61.4 The chosen will live with the chosen, and these measurements will enhance faith and righteousness.

61.5 These measures will expose all the secrets of the depths of the Earth and those who were destroyed by the desert, fish, and animals, so they can return and rely on the Day of the Chosen One. The Lord of Spirits cannot annihilate anyone."

61.6 The heavens received a command, power, one voice, and a fire-like radiance.

61.7 They blessed, exalted, and wisely praised Him before everything. They spoke and lived wisely.

61.8 The Lord of Spirits placed the Chosen One on his splendor seat, and he will judge all the Holy ones in Heaven above and measure their actions in the Balance.

61.9 When he lifts his face to judge their secret ways according to the word of the Lord of Spirits, and their path according to the Righteous Judgment of the Lord Most High, they will all speak with one voice and bless, praise, exalt, and glorify the Lord of Spirits.

61.10 And he will call all the Host of the Heavens and all the Holy Ones above, and the Host of the Lord, the Cherubim, Seraphim, and Ophannim, and all the Angels of Power and all the Angels of the Principalities, and the Chosen One, and the other host that is upon the dry ground and over the water, on that Day.

61.11 They will raise one voice and bless, thank, glorify, and exalt in the spirit of faith, wisdom, patience, mercy, justice, peace, and goodness. They will all say, "Blessed is He, and blessed be the name of the Lord of Spirits forever."

61.12 Heaven's Unsleeping shall bless him. His Holy Ones in Heaven, all the selected ones in the Garden of Life, and every spirit able to honor, praise, exalt, and hallow your Holy Name shall bless Him. All flesh will praise and bless your Name forever.

61.13 The Lord of Spirits is merciful and long-suffering, and he has revealed to the righteous and the chosen all his works and forces, as many as he has made.

62.1 "Open your eyes and raise your horns if you are able to acknowledge the Chosen One," the Lord commanded the kings, great, exalted, and earth dwellers.

62.2 The Lord of Spirits sat on His Throne of Glory, and the spirit of righteousness was poured forth on him. His word kills all sinners and lawless, and they are annihilated in front of him.

62.3 On that Day, all the kings, mighty, exalted, and earthly rulers will stand up and behold how he sits on the Throne of His Glory. The virtuous are judged righteously before him, and no empty word is spoken.

62.4 They will suffer like a woman in labor, who struggles to give birth when her child enters the womb.

62.5 One half of them will look at the other and be afraid, cast down their faces, and feel sorrow when they see that son of a woman seated on the throne of His Glory.

62.6 The powerful monarchs and those who rule the earth will bless and worship Him who rules everything unseen.

62.7 The Most High kept the Son of Man hidden and exposed him only to the selected.

62.8 The Holy and the chosen will be seeded and all the chosen will appear before him on that day.

62.9 And all the mighty kings, the elevated, and those who rule the dry ground will bow down before him, on their faces, and worship; and they will fix their hopes on that Son of Man, beg him, and petition for mercy.

62.10 But the Lord of Spirits will force them to leave Him, and their faces will be shamed and darkened.

62.11 The Angels of Punishment will take them to punish them for harming His offspring and chosen ones.

62.12 The righteous and His chosen ones will exult over them because the Lord of Spirits' anger and sword will be drunk with them.

62.13 The virtuous and chosen will be saved on that Day and will never see the faces of sinners and lawless again.

62.14 The Lord of Spirits will rule over them, and with that Son of Man they will live, eat, sleep, and rise forever.

62.15 The righteous and selected will have risen from the earth, stopped crying, and put on the Garment of Life.

62.16 This will be a Garment of Life from the Lord of Spirits, and your clothes and splendor will not fail before him.

63.1 In those days, the powerful monarchs of the dry ground will beg the Angels of His Punishment, to whom they have been handed over, for a little reprieve. To worship and confess their sins before the Lord of Spirits.

63.2 They will bless and praise the Lord of Spirits, saying, "Blessed be the Lord of Spirits, and the Lord of Kings, and the Lord of the Mighty, and the Lord of the Rich, and the Lord of Glory, and the Lord of Wisdom!

63.3 You reveal all secrets, and your strength lasts forever and your grandeur is eternal. Your secrets and justice are uncountable.

63.4 We recognize we should thank and bless the Lord of Kings and the King of all Kings."

63.5 They will say, "Would that we might be given a respite, so that we might praise, thank, and bless him, and make our confession in front of His Glory.

63.6 We crave for a reprieve but cannot find it; we are driven off but cannot acquire it; and the light has passed away from before us, and darkness will be our home forever.

63.7 We have not confessed before him, praised the Lord of Kings, or praised the Lord for all his deeds, but our hopes have been on the sceptre of our reign and splendor.

63.8 On the day of our misery and distress, he does not save us, and we find no respite to declare that our Lord is loyal in all his doings, judgements, and justice, and that his judgments show no respect for persons.

63.9 "All our works and sins have been counted exactly, and we pass away from him."

63.10 They will reply, "Our souls are sated with possessions gained through iniquity, but they do not prevent our going down into the flames of the torment of Sheol."

63.11 After this, their faces will be black and shameful before that Son of Man, and they will be driven away. The sword shall live among them, before Him.

63.12 The Lord of Spirits declares, "This is the Law and the Judgment for the mighty, the kings, the exalted, and those who possess the dry ground, in front of the Lord of Spirits."

64.1 Other figures were hidden there.

64.2 Angelic voice stating, "These are the Angels who came down from Heaven onto the Earth and revealed what is secret to the sons of men, and led them astray, so that they committed sin."

65.1 Noah saw the Earth skewed and its catastrophe nigh.

65.2 He left there and screamed out to his great-grandfather Enoch, saying three times in a harsh voice, "Hear me, hear me!"

65.3 He asked him, "Tell me what is happening on Earth, that the Earth is so afflicted and shaken, lest I be destroyed with it!"

65.4 I sank to my knees after a big disruption on Earth and a voice from Heaven.

65.5 My great-grandfather Enoch came, stood beside me, and asked me: "Why did you call out to me, with such bitter wailing and weeping?

65.6 The Lord has ordered the dry-ground dwellers to die this way. For they have learned all the secrets of the Angels, all the wrongdoings of the satans, all their secret power, and all the might of those who practice magic arts, enchantments, and molten pictures for the entire Earth.

65.7 And how earth dust produces silver and soft metal.

65.8 Lead and tin are not formed from the earth like the former; they are produced by a spring and distributed by an Angel who stands in it.

65.9 After this, my great grandfather Enoch took my hand, elevated me, and said, "Go, for I have asked the Lord of

Spirits about this disturbance on the earth."

65.10 He told me, "Because of their iniquity, their judgment has been completed, and they will no longer be counted before me; because of the sorceries they have searched out and learned, the Earth and those who dwell upon it will be destroyed.

65.11 But for you, my son, the Lord of Spirits knows that you are pure and innocent of this disgrace concerning the secrets.

65.12 He has fixed your name among the Holy and will keep you from those who dwell on the dry ground, and he has intended your offspring in righteousness to be rulers and for great honors. Your progeny will produce an endless stream of the Righteous and Holy.

66.1 After this, he showed me the Angels of Punishment, who were ready to release all the water forces under the earth to judge and destroy all people who live on dry ground.

66.2 The Lord of Spirits ordered the approaching Angels to maintain watch and not raise their hands, as they controlled the water forces.

66.3 I left Enoch.

67.1 In those days, the Lord spoke to me: "Noah, behold; your lot has risen up before me, a lot without reproach, a lot of love and uprightness.

67.2 Now the Angels are building a wooden structure, and when they finish, I'll hold it and protect it. Change will occur to fill the dry ground.

67.3 I will set your offspring before me forever and spread those who reside with you across the dry ground. I will not test them again on Earth, but they will be blessed and increase on dry ground in the name of the Lord."

67.4 And they will seal up those Angels who revealed iniquity in that burning valley my great grandfather Enoch had shown me in the west, among the mountains of gold, silver, iron, soft metal, and tin.

67.5 I noticed that valley with a lot of water heaving.

67.6 The fiery molten metal and commotion caused the waters in that region to smell like sulfur. That valley of Angels, who misled men, burns underground.

67.7 And in the valleys of that same area, rivers of fire will chastise those Angels who led the dry ground astray.

67.8 Those waters will serve the kings, the great, the elevated, and those who live on dry land for soul and body healing and spirit punishment. For rejecting the Lord of Spirits, their lustful spirits will be punished in their bodies. They suffer daily yet don't believe in Him.

67.9 As their bodies burn, their spirits will alter forever, for the Lord of Spirits cannot tolerate idle talk.

67.10 Because they trust in their bodies but deny the Lord's spirit, judgment will fall on them.

67.11 When those Angels are punished, the temperature of those springs of water will alter, and when they rise, the water will become frigid.

"This judgment, with which the Angels are judged, is a testimony for the kings and the mighty who possess the dry ground," said the Holy Michael.

67.13 "These waters of judgment heal the kings' bodies and satisfy their lust, but they do not see or believe that they will change and become a fire that burns forever."

68.1 After this, my great grandfather Enoch explained all the mysteries in a book and put them together in the Book of Parables.

68.2 On that day, the Holy Michael replied to Raphael: "The power of the spirit seizes me and makes me tremble

25

because of the harshness of the Angels' judgment. Who can survive the severe sentence that has been administered and before which they melt with fear?"

68.3 The Holy Michael spoke to Raphael again: "Who would not soften his heart over it, and whose mind would not be disturbed by this word? Judgment has fallen on those they led out like this."

68.4 When he stood before the Lord of Spirits, the Holy Michael told Raphael, "I will not take their part under the eye of the Lord, for the Lord of Spirits is angry with them, because they act as if they were the Lord.

68.5 Because of this, the concealed judgment will fall on them forever, as no other Angel or man will receive their lot.

69

.1 After this judgment, I will terrify them and make them tremble because they have shown this to others.

69.2 And behold, the names of those Angels: Semyaza (Azza), Artaqifa, Armen, Kokabiel, Turiel, Ramiel, Daniel, Nuqael, Baraqiel, Azazel, Armaros, Batriel, Basasael, Ananel, Turiel, Samsiel, Yetarel, and the eighteenth.

69.3 These are their Angels' leaders of hundreds, fifties, and tens.

69.4 The first is Yequn, who led all the offspring of the Holy Angels down onto the dry ground and through the daughters of men.

69.5 The second is Asbeel, who deceived the offspring of the Holy Angels into corrupting their bodies with women.

69.6 Gadreel, the third, dealt all the mortal strokes to men.

He misled Eve. He showed the sons of men the shield, armor, sword for slaughter, and all the deadly weapons.

69.7 From his hand they have gone out against the dry earth dwellers forever and ever.

69.8 Penemue, the fourth, taught humans bitter and sweet and all their wisdom.

69.9 He taught men to write with ink and paper, and many have gone astray from eternity to eternity and today.

69.10 Men were not made to write their religion in ink.

69.11 For men were made no differently from the Angels, so that they may remain righteous and clean, and death, which destroys everything, would not have touched them; but with this knowledge of theirs they are being destroyed and through this power death consumes them.

69.12 Kasdeyae, the fifth, showed men all the wicked strokes of spirits and demons, even those that miscarry the embryo in the womb. The soul-attacking serpent bite. Midday blows and the strong serpent's son.

69.13 Kesbeel, the oath chief, showed the Holy ones the oath when he lived in splendor. Named Beqa.

69.14 This one told the Holy Michael to show him the secret name so they might mention it in the oath, so that those who showed the sons of men everything secret shuddered before that name and oath.

69.15 This oath is strong and powerful, and Akae gave it to the Holy Michael.

69.16 These mysteries of this oath are strong, and Heaven was suspended before the world was created and forever.

69.17 It created the earth on water, and from the mountains' dark recesses pour magnificent rivers from the world's creation and forever.

69.18 Through that oath, the sea was created, and as its foundation, he placed the sand for the period of rage, and it does not go beyond it from the creation of the world and forever.

69.19 That oath made the deeps steadfast, and they stand in their place from the beginning of the world and forever.

69.20 Through that pledge, the Sun and

Moon follow their command from the creation of the world and forever.

69.21 He calls their names and they answer him, from the creation of the world and forever.

69.22 Also the spirits of water, winds, and all breezes, and their pathways, according to all the spirit groupings.

69.23 The storehouses of thunder, lightning, hail, hoarfrost, mist, rain, and dew are maintained.

69.24 They confess, thank, and sing praises to the Lord of Spirits. They give thanks, laud, and exalt the Lord of Spirits forever in their food.

69.25 This oath keeps them secure and on course.

69.26 Because the Son of Man's name was revealed, they rejoiced and blessed, praised, and exalted.

69.27 He sat on the Throne of His Glory and gave the Son of Man the entire judgment, causing sinners to perish from the Earth.

69.28 Those who misled the world will be chained and imprisoned in the assembly-place of their ruin, and all their efforts will vanish.

69.29 Nothing corruptible will remain. For that Son of Man has appeared and sat on the Throne of His Glory, and everything bad will pass away in front of Him, and his word will be strong before the Lord of Spirits.

70.1 After this, his name was lifted from the dry ground to the presence of that Son of Man and the Lord of Spirits while he was alive.

70.2 He was hoisted on the spirit chariots, and his name disappeared from them.

70.3 From that day, I was not reckoned among them, and He positioned me between two winds, between the north and the west, where the Angels took the cords to measure my spot for the selected and righteous.

70.4 I saw the First Fathers and righteous who lived there from the beginning.

71.1 After this, my spirit went to Heaven. I Saw the sons of the Holy Angels treading on fire with white robes and snow-like faces.

71.2 I saw two rivers of fire that gleamed like hyacinths, and I fell on my face before the Lord of Spirits.

71.3 The Archangel Michael seized my right hand and elevated me, leading me to all the secrets of mercy and righteousness.

71.4 He revealed the mysteries of the Ends of Heaven and the Storehouses of the Stars and Lights from below the Holy Ones.

71.5 The Spirit transported Enoch to the Highest Heaven, and I beheld something made of crystal stones and tongues of living fire in the centre of that Light.

71.6 My spirit saw a circle of fire around that dwelling, with rivers of living fire on its four sides.

71.7 The Seraphim, Cherubim, and Ophannim, who never sleep, guarded the Throne of His Glory.

71.8 I saw uncountable angels surrounding the house. Michael, Raphael, Gabriel, Phanuel, and the Heavenly Angels entered and left that dwelling.

71.9 Michael, Raphael, Gabriel, Phanuel, and countless Holy Angels without number emerged from that abode.

71.10 And the Head of Days, his head white and pure as wool and his robes incomprehensible.

71.11 I fell on my face, my body melted, and my spirit was transformed. I shouted out in a loud voice, in the spirit of power, and blessed, praised, and exalted.

71.12 That Head of Days liked my blessings.

71.13 The Head of Days came with Michael, Gabriel, Raphael, and Phanuel with thousands and tens of thousands of Angels.

71.14 That Angel came to me and greeted me with his voice, saying, "You are the son of man who was born to righteousness and righteousness remains over you and the righteousness of the Head of Days will not leave you."

71.15 He told me, "He proclaims peace to you in the name of the world to come, for from there peace has come out from the creation of the world and so you will have it forever and ever and ever.

71.16 Because righteousness will never forsake you, all will follow you. They will live and work with you forever.

71.17 And so there will be a length of days with that Son of Man, and the righteous will enjoy peace and an upright way in the name of the Lord of Spirits, forever and ever."

Section I I I. Chapters LXXII-LXXXII The Book of the Heavenly Luminaries

72.1 Heaven's Lights Revolution Book.

Each according to class, according to their reign, months, names, and origins. That Uriel, my Holy Angel leader, showed me. He showed me all their regulations, just as they are, for each year of the world and forever, till the new creation will last forever.

72.2 The First Law of Lights. The Sun rises in the east and sets in the west.

72.3 I saw six Gates from which the Sun rises and six Gates in which it sets, the Moon rising and setting in those Gates, and the leaders of the stars with those they lead. Six are in the east, six in the west, and many windows are to the south and north of those Gates.

72.4 First comes the Sun, whose disc is like Heaven's and is full of brightness and warmth.

72.5 The wind blows the chariots on which it ascends, and the Sun goes down, returns through the north to reach the east, and is led to the suitable Gate and shines in the sky.

72.6 In the first 30 months, it rises via the fourth of the six east-facing Gates, the big Gate.

72.7 The fourth Gate, through which the Sun rises in the first month, has twelve window-openings that emit flames when opened.

72.8 The Sun rises in Heaven, goes out via the fourth Gate for thirty days, and sets in the west of Heaven at the fourth Gate.

72.9 Until the thirtieth morning, the day grows longer and the night shorter.

72.10 On that day, the day is double the night, and the night is eight parts.

72.11 For thirty mornings, the Sun rises from the fourth Gate, sets in it, and returns to the fifth Gate in the east.

72.12 The day lengthens by two parts to eleven parts, and the night shortens to seven parts.

72.13 Because of its sign, the Sun returns east and rises and sets in the sixth Gate for thirty-one mornings.

72.14 On that day, the day is double the night and twelve parts long, while the night is six parts short.

72.15 The Sun rises to shorten the day and lengthen the night, returns to the east, arrives to the sixth Gate, rises from it, and sets for thirty mornings.

72.16 After thirty mornings, the day shortens by one part, making it eleven parts and the night seven.

72.17 The Sun leaves the west by that sixth Gate, proceeds east, rises in the fifth Gate for thirty mornings, and sets in the fifth Gate in the west.

72.18 On that day, the day shortens by two parts, making it ten parts and the night eight.

72.19 The Sun rises from that fifth Gate, sets in the fifth Gate in the west, and rises in the fourth Gate for thirty-one mornings because of its sign.

72.20 On that day, day and night are equal in length, and each has nine sections.

72.21 The Sun rises from that Gate, sets in the west, returns to the east, rises in the third Gate for thirty mornings, and sets in the west.

72.22 The Sun rises from that third Gate, sets in the third Gate in the west, and returns to the east. For thirty mornings, it rises in the second Gate in the east and sets in the second Gate in the west of Heaven.

72.24 That day, the night is eleven parts and the day seven.

72.25 On that day, the Sun rises from the second Gate, sets in the west in the second Gate, returns to the east to the first Gate for thirty-one mornings, then sets in the west in the first Gate.

72.26 On that day, the night is twice as long as the day, and the day is six parts.

72.27 After this, the Sun completes its divisions and turns back, coming through that first Gate for thirty-one mornings and setting in the west opposite it.

72.28 On that day, the night is shortened by one part to eleven parts and the day to seven parts.

72.29 The Sun returns to the second Gate in the east and rises and sets for thirty mornings along those divides.

72.30 On that day, the night becomes shorter and the day eight parts and the night ten parts.

72.31 On that day, the Sun rises from the second Gate, sets in the west, returns to the east, rises in the third Gate for thirty-one mornings, and sets in the west.

72.32 On that day, the night becomes shorter and equals the day, and the day becomes nine parts. The year has 364 days.

72.33 The Sun's trip affects day and night length and shortness.

72.34 Its voyage lengthens daily and shortens at night.

72.35 The Sun's voyage and return, sixty times a year, is the vast eternal light, the Sun.

72.36 The great light rises, designated after its appearance as the Lord instructed.

72.37 It rises and sets in its chariot, never stopping. It is seven times brighter than the Moon but the same size.

73.1 I saw another law for the Moon following this one.

73.2 Its disc is like the Sun's, the wind blows its chariot, and it receives fixed light.

73.3 Its rising and setting alter every month, and its days are like the Sun's, and its light is a seventh of the Sun's when uniformly full.

73.4 On the thirtieth morning, it rises eastward. On the thirtieth morning, it appears with the Sun in the Gate through which the Sun rises, becoming the first phase of the Moon for you.

73.5 and a half, with a seventh portion and a fourteenth part of its brightness.

73.6 And on the day that it receives a seventh part and a half of its light, its light amounts to a seventh, and a seventh part and a half.

73.7 The Moon rises with the Sun and receives half its brightness. At the start of the Moon's day, the Moon sets with the Sun and is dark for six and a half hours.

73.8 On one day, it rises exactly a seventh part, goes out, recedes from the Sun, and becomes bright on the other six and seven parts of its days.

74.1 I also noticed its monthly voyage and law.

74.2 Uriel, the Holy Angel in charge, showed me everything, and I noted down their locations.

I recorded their months and light for 15 days.

74.3 It fills its darkness and light in sevenths, east and west.

74.4 It alters its setting and follows its own course in some months.

74.5 In two months, it sets with the Sun in the middle Gates, the third and fourth.

74.6 After seven days, it returns to the Gate where the Sun rises. In that Gate, it fills its light and recedes from the Sun, arriving eight days later at the sixth Gate where the Sun rises.

74.7 When the Sun rises from the fourth Gate, the Moon goes dark for seven days till it rises from the fifth. In seven days, it returns to the fourth Gate, fills its radiance, recedes, and returns to the first Gate in eight days.

74.8 It returns to the fourth Gate where the Sun rises in seven days.

74.9 I watched the Moon and Sun rise and set in those days.

74.10 Five years add thirty days to the Sun. Each year has 364 days.

74.11 The Sun and stars exceed six days. The Moon lags behind the Sun and stars by thirty days in five years with six days each.

74.12 The Moon changes the year in 364 days, never early or late.

74.13 Three years have 1,092 days, five years 1,820, and eight years 2,912 days.

74.14 The Moon has 1,062 days in three years and 50 days in five years.

74.15 The Moon has 2,832 days in eight years since five years have 1,770 days.

74.16 Eight years is eighty days, and the Moon lags behind eighty days.

74.17 They rise from the Gates where the Sun rises and sets for thirty days, completing the year exactly.

75.1 And the leaders of the tens of thousands, who are in charge of the whole creation, all the stars, and the four days that are added, are not separated from their position according to the complete reckoning of the year. These serve on the four non-year-counting days.

75.2 They lead men astray. One light in the first Gate, one in the third Gate, one in the fourth Gate, and one in the sixth Gate serve the world's stations. The 364 global stations complete world harmony.

75.3 The Angel Uriel, who is in command of all the Lights of Heaven, gave me the signs, times, years, and days. The Sun, the Moon, the stars, and all the serving animals who revolve in all the Chariots of Heaven, so they could rule on the Face of Heaven, appear over the earth, and lead day and night.

75.4 Uriel showed me twelve Gate-openings in the disc of the Sun's chariot in the sky, from which the Sun's rays emerge.
When opened at the appointed times, they heat the Earth.

75.5 When they are opened in Heaven, at the ends of the world, the winds and dew spirit have apertures.

75.6 I saw twelve Gates in Heaven at the ends of the earth, from which the Sun, Moon, stars, and all the works of Heaven go out east and west.

75.7 And there are many window openings to the north and south, and each window, at its assigned hour, gives out heat equal to those Gates, from which the stars go out according to His order and set according to their number.

75.8 Heavenly chariots raced above those Gates, where the stars never set.

75.9 One is biggest. It circulates worldwide.

76.1 At the end of the world, I beheld twelve Gates open to all winds, from which the winds blow over the land.

76.2 Three open in front of Heaven, three in back, three on the right, and three on the left.

76.3 The first three are east, followed by north, south, and west.

76.4 Four provide blessings and peace. The other eight send punishing winds that destroy the Earth, its water, its inhabitants, and everything in the water and on the land.

76.5 The east wind exits the first Gate, which faces east. Southern ones bring drought, heat, and disaster.

76.6 Righteousness enters the second Gate in the center. It brings rain, fruitfulness, wealth, and dew. The north-facing third Gate brings cold and drought.

76.7 Three Gates release southerly winds.

First, a scorching breeze blows through the east-facing Gate.

76.8 The middle Gate next to it brings scents, dew, rain, prosperity, and life.

76.9 The west-facing third Gate brings dew, rain, locusts, and destruction.

76.10 After these, winds from the north bring dew, rain, locusts, and devastation from the seventh Gate to the east.

76.11 Rain, dew, life, and wealth come via the middle Gate. Mist, hoarfrost, snow, rain, dew, and locusts enter the west-facing third Gate.

76.12 Then west breezes. Dew, rain, hoarfrost, cold, snow, and frost enter the north-facing first Gate.

76.13 The middle Gate brings dew, rain, prosperity, and blessing.

Drought, desolation, burning, and destruction arrive through the final Gate in the south.

76.14 The twelve Gates of Heaven's four sections are complete.

I showed my son Methuselah all their laws, punishments, and perks.

77.1 Because it was first, they termed it eastern, call the second the south since the Most High descends, especially the blessed forever.

77.2 The western quarter is named waning because all Heaven's lights dim there.

77.3 The north, the fourth quarter, has three components. The first portion is where people live, the second has seas, deeps, woods, rivers, darkness, and mist, and the third is the Garden of Righteousness.

77.4 I saw seven towering mountains, the highest on earth, from which snow falls. Days and years pass.

77.5 I saw seven giant rivers on earth, one of which flows into the Great Sea from the east.

77.6 Two of them dump their water into the east Erythraean Sea from the north.

77.7 The remaining four flow north to their seas—two to the Erythraean Sea and two to the Great Sea—and not into the wilderness, as some believe.

78.1 The first and second names of the Sun are Oryares and Tomases, respectively.

78.2 The Moon has four names: Asonya, Ebla, Benase, and Era'e. Asonya is the first name given to the Moon.

78.3 These are the two great lights of Revelations; their discs are both the same size and resemble the disc of heaven.

78.4 The Sun receives more light than the Moon, and light is sent to the Moon in fixed amounts until a seventh part of the Sun is spent.

78.5 They set, enter the west Gates, circle the north, and rise through the east Gates on Heaven's face.

78.6 When the Moon rises, it has half a seventh of a light, and on the fourteenth day, it becomes fully lit.

78.7 On the fifteenth day, its brightness is full, according to the sign of the year, and fifteen parts.

Half-sevenths create the Moon.

78.8 On the first day, it dims to fourteen parts.

On the second to thirteen parts, on the third to twelve parts, on the fourth to eleven parts, on the fifth to ten parts, on the sixth to nine parts, on the seventh to eight parts, on the eighth to seven parts, on the ninth to six parts, on the tenth to five parts, on the eleventh to four parts, on the twelfth to three, on the thirteenth to two, and on the fourteenth to half of a seventh part.

The complete light disappears on the fifteenth day.

78.9 Sometimes the Moon has twenty-nine days, sometimes twenty-eight.

78.10 Uriel revealed to me another law: when and where light is transported to the Moon from the Sun.

78.11 The Moon's light increases as it becomes opposite the Sun, until it is full in the sky in fourteen days and all ablaze.

78.12 The first day is the New Moon since the sun rises on it.

78.13 Its brightness is full exactly as the Sun sets in the west and rises in the east for the night. The Moon glows all night till the Sun rises and is seen opposite it.

78.14 On the side where the Moon's light appears, it wanes again until all its light departs and its days finish and its disc stays empty without light.

78.15 For three months, at its correct moment, it reaches thirty days and twentynine days, completing its waning in the first period, in the first Gate, 127 days.

78.16 For three months, it rises in thirty-day months. Three months with twenty-nine days each.

78.17 By night, for twenty days each time, it looks like a man, and by day like Heaven, for it is only light.

79.1 My son Methuselah, I have shown you everything and completed the Law of the Stars of Heaven.

79.2 He gave me the full law for these, for every day, time, rule, year, and end thereof, according to its instruction, for every month and week.

79.3 The Moon waned at the sixth Gate, where its light became full, and the month began after that.

79.4 The first Gate's waning, which lasts twenty-five weeks and two days, comes at the right moment.

79.5 And how it lags behind the Sun, according to the stars, by exactly five days in one period of time after completing the course you saw.

79.6 Uriel, the leading Angel, gave me the look and likeness of every light.

80.1 Uriel said, "Behold, I have shown you everything, Oh Enoch.

I have shown all to you so that you can see this Sun, this Moon, those who guide the Stars of Heaven, and all those who turn them, their responsibilities, times, and rising.

80.2 Sinners will have shorter years and late seed on their land and farms. All things on Earth will alter and appear late. Heaven will hold the rain.

80.3 The earth's fruits and the trees' fruits will be late and withheld in those times.

80.4 The Moon will appear late.

80.5 In those days, it will appear in Heaven, ride a big chariot in the west, and shine brighter than usual.

80.6 Many commanding stars will err. These will alter their schedules and not show up.

80.7 The entire law of the stars will be closed to sinners, and the thoughts of people who dwell on Earth will go astray over them, and they will turn from all their ways and deem them gods.

80.8 Many ills will befall them and punishment will destroy them all."

81.1 He said, "Oh Enoch, look at the book of the Tablets of Heaven and read what is written upon it."each detail."

81.2 I noted everything written.

I read the book and everything in it—all the acts of men and all the flesh-born who will live on Earth for eternity.

81.3 I then commended the Lord, the Eternal King of Glory, for making all the world's works, for his patience, and for the sons of Adam.

81.4 I said, "Blessed is the man who dies righteous and good, concerning whom no book of iniquity has been written, and against whom no guilt has been found."

81.5 "Tell everything to your son Methuselah, and show all your children that no flesh is righteous before the Lord, for He created them," these three Holy ones said to me.

81.6 We will leave you with your children for a year until you regain your strength so you can teach them, write these things down, and witness to all your children. We'll choose you in year two.

81.7 Have faith, for the righteous will rejoice with the righteous and wish each other well.

81.8 The apostate will sink and the sinner will die.

81.9 The virtuous will perish because of men's acts and be gathered in because of the impious.

81.10 After they completed speaking, I blessed the Lord of Ages and went to my family.

82.1 Now, my son Methuselah, I tell you and write down these things. I've told you everything and given you books. Keep the books from your father, Methuselah, to pass them on to forever.

82.2 I have given wisdom to you, your children, and those who will be your children, so they can pass it on to future generations.

82.3 Those who comprehend it will not sleep but will bend their ears to learn this wisdom, which will be better for them than good food.

82.4 Blessed are the virtuous and those who do not sin like sinners.

For thirty days, they count the Sun's trip through Heaven's Gates.

With the leaders of the thousands, this order of stars, and the four added and divided between the four seasons, who lead them and appear with them on four days.

82.5 Since of them, men go wrong and don't count them in the whole year since they don't know them.

82.6 They are counted in the year and recorded eternally, one in the first Gate, one in the third, one in the fourth, and one in the sixth. 364 days complete the year.

82.7 For the lights, months, feasts, years, and days, it is true and accurate.

Uriel showed me and inspired me, and the Lord of the whole created world gave me Host of Heaven commandments.

82.8 He has control over night and day to shine light on men from the Sun, Moon, stars, and all the Powers of Heaven, which spin in their orbits.

82.9 The Law of the Stars sets them in their places, times, feasts, and months.

82.10 These are the names of those who lead them and keep watch so they appear at their times, orders, months, periods of rule, and places.

82.11 Their four leaders, who split the four seasons, come first, followed by the twelve leaders of the orders, who divide the months and years into 364 days, and the heads over thousands, who divide the days. Leaders divide the four seasons for the four days added to them.

82.12 These heads over thousands are separated by one, but their leaders do it.

82.14 Melkiel, Helemmelek, Meleyal, and Narel lead the four assigned seasons.

82.14 They lead Adnarel, Iyasusael, and Iylumiel. All others follow the three order leaders, who follow the four position leaders who divide the year.

82.15 Melkiel, the southern Sun, rises first and controls the year for ninety-one days.

82.16 Sweat, heat, and stillness are the signs of his authority on earth. All trees produce fruit, leaves, wheat, and roses.

Winter trees wither as field flowers blossom.

82.17 Their leaders are Berkeel,

Zelebsael, and Heloyaseph, a thousand-headed commander. This rule is over.

82.18 After him, Helemmelec, the Shining Sun, leads for ninety-one days.

82.19 Earthly indications are heat and drought. Trees ripen and dry their fruit. Sheep reproduce.

Men gather all the earth's fruits, fields, and wine vats. These occur during his rule.

82.20 Gedaeyal, Keel, and Heel lead these heads over thousands. Asfael is their head-over-a thousand. His rule ends.

Section IV. Chapters LXXXIIIXC. The Dream-Visions.

83.1 My son Methuselah, I shall now tell all my visions.

83.2 Two visions I had before marrying were different. First when I learned to write, then before I took your mother. I prayed about a dreadful vision.

83.3 As I lay in my grandfather Malalel's house, I saw Heaven fall on Earth.

83.4 When it landed on Earth, I saw how the earth was swallowed up in a great abyss, mountains were hung on mountains, hills slid down upon hills, and tall trees were torn up by their roots, flung down, and plunged into the abyss.

83.5 I said, "The earth is destroyed!"

83.6 Since I laid close to him, my grandfather, Malalel, awakened me and asked, "Why did you cry out so, my son, and why do you moan so?"

83.7 I told him the complete vision, and he responded, "A terrible thing you have seen, my son! Your dream depicts the Earth's sins sinking into the abyss and being destroyed.

83.8 Now, my son, rise and pray to the Lord of Glory, for you are faithful, that a

remnant may remain on Earth and that he may not destroy it.

83.9 My son, all this will come from Heaven and destroy the Earth."

83.10 Then I awoke and prayed, made supplication, and wrote my prayer down for the generations of eternity, and I will show you everything my son Methuselah.

83.11 When I went outside, I saw the sky, the Sun rising in the east, the Moon setting in the west, some stars, the whole Earth, and everything as He knew it from the beginning. I blessed the Lord of Judgment and gave him Majesty because he makes the Sun rise from the east's windows and follow the road shown to it.

84.1 I blessed the Holy and Great One with righteous hands. I spoke using my mouth's breath and my tongue of flesh, which God made for men born of flesh to communicate with. He gave them breath, a tongue, and a mouth to speak with.

84.2 "Blessed are you, Oh Lord King, great and powerful in your majesty, Lord of the whole Creation of Heaven, King of Kings, and God of the world! Your kingly authority, Sovereignty, Majesty, and strength will endure for all time. The Heavens are your throne and the Earth your footstool forever.

84.3 You made and ruled everything, and nothing is too hard for you, and no wisdom escapes you; it does not turn away from your seat or your presence. You see, hear, and know everything.

84.4 Your Heavenly Angels are wrong, and your fury rests on men's flesh until the great judgment.

84.5 Now, Oh God, Lord, and Great King, I beg you to grant my request to leave me a posterity on Earth and not to destroy all flesh and empty the earth forever.

84.6 Now, my Lord, wipe out from the earth the flesh that caused your anger, but establish the flesh of righteousness and uprightness as a seed-bearing plant forever. Oh Lord, don't ignore my petition."

85.1 Then I had another dream, which I'll show you, son.

85.2 Enoch shouted to Methuselah, "To you, my son." Listen to me and your father's dream.

85.3 Before I took your mother, Edna, I saw a vision on my bed: a white bull emerged from the soil.

A heifer and two bullocks—one black and one red—followed.

85.4 The black bullock struck the red one and chased it across the earth, and I never saw it again.

85.5 But that black bullock grew, and a heifer went with it, and I saw numerous bulls like it come out of it and follow it.

85.6 The first cow left the first bull's presence to find the red bullock but failed. It wailed and kept searching.

85.7 I watched until the first bull calmed it, and it stopped crying.

85.8 She had another white bull, then many black bulls and cows.

85.9 In my sleep, I saw that white bull grow and become big. It produced many white bulls like it.

85.10 They had several white bulls like them, one after another.

86.1 Again, as I slept, I saw Heaven above, and a star dropped from Heaven, arose, and ate and pastured among those bulls.

After this, I observed the enormous and black bulls, and they all moved their pens, pastures, and heifers. They started moaning.

86.3 Again, I saw in the vision and looked up at Heaven, and behold, numerous stars came down and were flung down to that first star and fell among those heifers and bulls. They grazed with them.

86.4 I saw them all let out their private parts like horses and mount the bulls'

cows. They all had elephants, camels, and asses.

86.5 They terrified all the bulls. They bit, devoured, and gored with their horns.

86.6 They devoured those bulls, and all the sons of Earth trembled and fled.

87.1 Again, I witnessed them gore and eat each other, and the Earth began to shake, to cry.

87.2 I looked up again and saw white men from Heaven. Four arrived from there, with three others.

87.3 The last three seized my hand and lifted me from the generations of the Earth, pulled me up into a high spot, and showed me a tower high above the earth, and all the hills were lower.

87.4 One told me, "Remain here until you have seen everything that is coming upon these elephants, camels, asses, stars, and all the bulls."

88.1 I saw one of the four who came out first grab the first star that had fallen from Heaven, bind it by its hands and feet, and throw it into an abyss.

That chasm was small, deep, awful, and dark.

88.2 One of them drew his sword and gave it to those elephants, camels, and asses, who started fighting and shook the Earth.

88.3 As I looked in the vision, one of those four who had come out cast a line from Heaven and gathered and took all the large stars, those whose private parts were like horses, and bound them all by their hands and feet and threw them into a chasm of the Earth.

89.1 One of the four tremblingly taught a white bull a riddle. Born a bull, but became a man, built a magnificent vessel, and lived on it with three bulls, who were covered.

89.2 I looked up again and saw a high roof with seven water channels that poured water into an enclosure.

89.3 I looked again, and springs opened on the bottom of that vast cage, and water bubbled up and rose above it. I watched till its floor was flooded.

89.4 Water, darkness, and mist increased on it, and I gazed at the height of that water, which had climbed above that enclosure and was pouring out over it. It remained on the land.

89.5 All the bulls in that enclosure were collected until I witnessed how they sank, were swallowed, and annihilated in that river.

89.6 That vessel floated on the water, but all the bulls, elephants, camels, and asses sank, along with all the animals, so I couldn't see them. They were trapped, destroyed, and sank.

89.7 Again, I watched that vision until those water channels were removed from that lofty roof, the Earth's chasms were leveled, and additional abysses opened.

89.8 The water ran down into them till the earth became visible, that vessel settled on the earth, the darkness disappeared, and light appeared.

89.9 That white bull, now a man, and the three bulls left that vessel. One bull was white like that bull, one was red as blood, and one was black. That white bull died.

89.10 They had lions, tigers, wolves, dogs, hyenas, wildboars, foxes, badgers, pigs, falcons, vultures, kites, eagles, and ravens. A white bull was born.

89.11 They started biting each other, but that white bull, born among them, begat a wild ass and a white bull with it, and the wild asses increased.

89.12 But that bull, which was born from it, begat a black wild boar and a white sheep, which in turn begat numerous boars and twelve sheep.

89.13 When those twelve sheep grew, they gave one to the asses, who gave it to the wolves, where it grew up.

89.14 The Lord brought the eleven sheep to live with it and pasture with it amid the wolves, and they multiplied and became numerous flocks.

89.15 The wolves made them scared and harassed them until they stole their young and flung them into a river with considerable water. The sheep cried out and complained to their Lord.

89.16 A sheep freed from the wolves fled to the wild asses. I saw the sheep sighing and crying out, petitioning the Lord with all their might, until that Lord of the sheep came down at their call from a high room and gazed at them.

89.17 He called the sheep that had fled the wolves and warned it not to touch the sheep.

89.18 The sheep went to the wolves as the Lord commanded, and another sheep joined it. The two of them entered the wolf pack and warned them not to touch the sheep.

89.19 After this, I saw the wolves attack the sheep with all their power, and the sheep cried out.

89.20 Their Lord came to the sheep and beat those wolves. The wolves began to moan, but the sheep became silent and did not cry out.

89.21 I watched the sheep until they escaped, but the wolves were blinded and pursued the animals with all their might.

89.22 The Lord of the sheep led them, and all his sheep followed him. His face was brilliant and his aspect terrifying and wonderful.

89.23 The wolves pursued those sheep until they reached a waterway.

89.24 The water was separated and stood on both sides before them. Their Lord shielded them from the wolves.

89.25 The sheep went into the center of that stretch of water while the wolves hadn't noticed them, but the wolves chased them into the water.

89.26 But when they saw the Lord of the sheep, they turned to run in front of him, but that stretch of water came together again and immediately recovered its natural form, surged up, and covered those wolves.

89.27 I watched until all the wolves who pursued those lambs were drowned.

89.28 The sheep fled that water and went to a desert without water or grass. They opened their eyes and saw the Lord of the sheep pasturing them, feeding them, and leading them.

89.29 The Lord of the sheep sent that sheep up a steep cliff.

89.30 After this, I saw the Lord of the sheep standing before them. He was dreadful and majestic, and all those sheep were scared of him.

89.31 They all shook and called out to that sheep and those in their midst, "We cannot stand before our Lord nor look at him."

89.32 That sheep, which led them, again walked up to the peak of that rock, and the sheep began to be blinded and deviate from the way provided to them, but that sheep did not know.

89.33 The sheep understood the Lord of the sheep was furious and descended off the hill. Summit of the rock and discovered most of the sheep blinded and wandering off his course.

89.34 They shuddered and sought to return to their enclosure when they saw it.

89.35 That sheep brought some other sheep with it and went to the lost sheep, killing them. The sheep were scared of it. That sheep returned the lost sheep to their cages.

89.36 I watched the vision until that sheep became a man, constructed a house for the Lord of the sheep, and made all the sheep stand in it.

89.37 I watched until that sheep, which had met the leading sheep, fell asleep. I watched until all the large sheep were killed and young ones replaced them, and they came to a field near a river.

89.38 The sheep that led them, which had become a man, departed from them and fell asleep, and all the sheep sought it and cried out terribly.

89.39 I watched till they stopped grieving for the sheep and crossed that river. They led instead of the sleeping sheep.

89.40 I looked till the sheep reached a good, pleasant, and lovely land and were satisfied. That lovely and pleasant property has that mansion in the middle of them.

89.41 Sometimes their eyes were opened, sometimes blindfolded, till another sheep led them back. They saw.

89.42 Dogs, foxes, and wild boars devoured those sheep until the Lord of the sheep produced a ram from among them to lead them.

89.43 That ram butted those dogs, foxes, and wild boars on both sides till it killed them all.

89.44 That sheep opened its eyes and saw that ram in the center of the herd, how it relinquished its glory, butted those sheep, and stomped on them.

89.45 The Lord of the sheep sent the sheep to another sheep, and brought it up to be a ram and lead the sheep, instead of that sheep that had forsaken its glory.

89.46 It went to it, spoke with it alone, and elevated that ram to be the sheep's prince and leader. Those dogs oppressed the sheep.

89.47 The first ram pursued the second and it escaped. I watched the hounds kill the first ram.

89.48 The second ram led the tiny sheep, begat many sheep, and fell asleep. A tiny sheep became a ram and led those sheep.

89.49 The sheep grew, but the dogs, foxes, and wild boars were scared and fled. That ram butted and killed all the creatures, and those animals never again prevailed among the sheep or stole anything.

89.50 That house became large and broad, and the Lord of the sheep erected a tower on it. The tower was lofty while the home was modest. That tower held the Lord of the flock and a full table.

89.51 I saw those sheep again, how they went astray, walked in many ways, and left their house; and the Lord of the sheep called some of the sheep, and sent them to the sheep, but the sheep began to murder them.

89.52 One of them escaped and shouted out against the sheep. They wanted to kill it, but the Lord of the sheep saved it from the sheep, brought it to me, and made it stay.

89.53 He sent numerous sheep to those sheep to testify and grieve.

89.54 After this, I observed how they went astray in everything and were blinded when they left the Lord of the sheep's house and tower.
I saw how the Lord of the sheep slaughtered them in their pastures until they invited it and betrayed him.

89.55 He gave them to the lions, tigers, wolves, hyenas, foxes, and all creatures. Wild creatures tore those sheep apart.

89.56 I saw how he abandoned their house and tower to the lions to tear them apart and devour them, and to all the animals.

89.57 I shouted to call the Lord of the livestock and tell him that all the wild creatures were consuming the sheep.

89.58 He saw but remained motionless, rejoicing that they were consumed, swallowed, and carried away.
He fed the animals.

89.59 He called seventy shepherds and let those sheep to pasture them. He told the shepherds and their colleagues, "Each of you, from now on, is to pasture the sheep and do whatever I command you.

89.60 I will give them to you, numbered, and tell you which ones to destroy. He gave them the sheep.

89.61 He called another and said, "Observe and see everything these shepherds do against these sheep for they will destroy from among them more than I have commanded them.

89.62 Record the shepherds' excess and ruin, both at my command and on their own. List each shepherd's destruction.

89.63 And read out in front of me exactly how many they destroy on their own and how many are handed over for destruction to testify against them. So I can judge the herders. I will watch if they follow my command.

89.64 But they must not know this, and you must not show this to them. Only write down against each individual in his time all that the shepherds destroy, and bring it all up to me."

89.65 I watched till those shepherds pastured at their times and started killing and destroying more than they were instructed, giving those sheep to the lions.

89.66 The lions, tigers, and wild boars consumed most of those sheep and burned down that tower and dwelling.

89.67 I was quite sad about that tower since the sheep's house had been demolished, and afterwards I couldn't see if they went in.

89.68 The shepherds and their friends gave those sheep to the animals to eat. Each one had a number, and in a book, it was noted how many were destroyed.

89.69 Each one slaughtered and destroyed more than prescribed, and I wept and cried over those sheep.

89.70 In the vision, the writer wrote down each shepherd's victim each day. He gave the full book to the Lord of the sheep, detailing everything they had done, stolen, and destroyed.

89.71 The book was read to the Lord of the sheep, who took it, read it, sealed it, and put it down.

89.72 After this, the shepherds pastured for twelve hours, and three of those sheep returned, arrived, and began to rebuild all that had fallen from that house, but the wild boars prevented them.

89.73 They built anew and built the great tower. They placed a table before the tower again, but the bread was unclean.

89.74 In addition, the shepherds and livestock were blindfolded. They trampled the sheep and consumed more of them.

89.75 The Lord of the sheep stood motionless until all the sheep were scattered and mixed with them, and they did not save them from the animals.

89.76 The book's author displayed and read it at the Lord of the sheep's house. He begged Him on their behalf and testified against their shepherds, showing Him all their actions.

89.77 He put the book by Him and left.

90.1 I looked until the shepherds had pastured the sheep the same way, and each one finished their time like the first. Others pastured them at their convenience.

90.2 After this, I saw in the vision all the skybirds: eagles, vultures, kites, and ravens. However, the eagles led the birds in devouring those sheep, pecking out their eyes and eating their flesh.

90.3 The sheep screamed aloud because the birds ate them. That shepherd who pastured the sheep made me cry in my sleep.

90.4 I watched as those dogs, eagles, and kites devoured the sheep, leaving only their bones.
Their bones fell and the sheep decreased.

90.5 I watched till twenty-three shepherds pastured fifty-eight times each.

90.6 White sheep had lambs that opened their eyes, saw, and cried to the animals.

90.7 The sheep were incredibly deaf and blind, so they did not cry out or listen to them.

90.8 In the vision, ravens flew upon the lambs, seized one, and dashed the sheep in pieces and devoured them.

90.9 I looked till those lambs had horns, but the ravens lowered theirs. I watched till one sheep got a large horn and opened its eyes.

90.10 It opened their eyes. The sheep saw it and ran to it.

90.11 Eagles, vultures, ravens, and kites continued to tear the sheep apart and soar on them and eat them. Rams howled while sheep were silent.

90.12 The ravens tried to steal its horn, but they failed.

90.13 I watched until the shepherds, eagles, vultures, and kites called to the ravens to break the ram's horn. It fought them and called out for aid.

90.14 I looked until that man, who took down the names of the shepherds and brought them before the Lord of the sheep, came and aided that ram and showed it everything; its help was coming down.

90.15 I watched until that Lord of the sheep came to them in anger, and those who saw him fled and fell into the shadow in front of Him.

90.16 The eagles, vultures, ravens, and kites joined with all the wild sheep and helped each other break the ram's horn.

90.17 I watched that guy, who penned the book at the Lord's order, read that book of the harm those last twelve shepherds had inflicted. He showed the Lord of the sheep that they had destroyed even more.

90.18 I watched until the Lord of the livestock came to them and smote the Earth with His Anger Staff. Earth divides. All the animals and skybirds descended from those sheep and sank into the soil, which closed above them.

90.19 I watched till the sheep got a large sword. Sheep hunted down all the wild creatures. They drove away all the animals and birds.

90.20 I watched until the Lord of the sheep sat on a throne in a pleasant region. They opened all the sealed books before the Lord of the sheep.

90.21 The Lord called the seven first white ones and ordered them to bring the first star, which preceded those stars with horse-like private parts, to Him.

90.22 He said to that man who wrote in front of Him, one of the seven white ones: "Take those seventy shepherds, to whom I handed over the sheep, and who, on their own authority, took and killed more than I commanded them."

90.23 I saw them chained and standing before Him.

90.24 The stars were judged first, and they were found guilty and sent to hell, where they were thrown into a deep pit full of fire and pillars of fire.

90.25 Seventy shepherds were found guilty and thrown into the flames.

90.26 I saw how a similar pit was opened in the centre of the Earth, full of fire, and they brought those blind sheep and judged, found guilty, and thrown into the fire. That house's south abyss.

90.27 I saw the sheep's bones burning.

90.28 I stood up to watch as he folded up the old house, removing all the pillars, beams, and ornamentation. They shifted it south.

90.29 I watched until the Lord of the sheep brought a new house, greater and higher than the original, and built it up in place of the folded-up one. It had new pillars and greater ornamentation than the old one that had been removed. It involved the Lord of the sheep.

90.30 I saw all the remaining sheep, animals, and birds kneel down and worship those sheep, beseeching them and obeying them.

90.31 Then, the three white-clad men who had raised me took my hand again. They lifted me with that ram's hand and placed me in the middle of those sheep before the judgment.

90.32 White sheep with rich, pure wool.

90.33 The Lord of the sheep delighted greatly because they were all good and had returned to His dwelling.

90.34 I watched until they set down that sword, which had been given to the sheep, and carried it back inside his house and sealed it before the Lord. The home held no sheep.

90.35 All of them saw clearly, and none of them did not see.

90.36 That mansion was huge and full.

90.37 I saw a white bull born with large horns, and all the wild animals and sky birds were scared of it and begged it.

90.38 I watched till all their species became white bulls. Wild-oxen were first. That wild-ox was enormous with black horns. The sheeplord rejoiced over them and all the bulls.

90.39 I woke up and saw everything.

90.40 I woke up, blessed the Lord of Righteousness, and praised him after seeing this vision.

90.41 After this, I cried until I couldn't anymore. When I gazed, they ran down because I saw that everything will happen and be completed, and all the deeds of men were shown to me in sequence.

90.42 That night, I remembered my first dream and cried and was worried.

Section V. XCI-CIV A Book of Exhortation and Promised Blessing for the Righteous and of Malediction and Woe for the Sinners.

91.1 Methuselah, call your brothers and your mother's children to me.
For a voice summons me, and a spirit has been poured over me to show you everything that will come upon you forever.

91.2 Methuselah then summoned his brothers and relatives.

91.3 He spoke about righteousness to all his sons, saying, "Hear, my children, all the words of your father, and listen properly to the voice of my mouth, for I will testify and speak to you, my beloved. Live uprightly!

91.4 Walk in justice, my children, and it will guide you in excellent ways and be your companion.

91.5 I know that wrongdoing will continue on Earth, but a tremendous penalty will end all iniquity. It will be uprooted and die.

91.6 "All the deeds of iniquity, wrong, and wickedness will prevail again on Earth."

91.7 When iniquity, sin, blasphemy, injustice, and all kinds of evil deeds increase, and when apostasy, wickedness, and uncleanness expand, a heavy punishment will come from Heaven. The Holy Lord will judge Earth in rage and wrath.

91.8 In those days, dishonesty, iniquity, and wrongdoing will be eradicated.

91.9 They will give up all countries' idols, burn their towers, and remove them from the Earth. They will be cast into the Judgment of Fire and annihilated in rage and eternal judgment.

91.10 The righteous will awaken and get wisdom.

91.11 After this, sinners will be slain by the sword. The sword will chop off blasphemers everywhere.

91.12 After this, the eighth week of righteousness will be given a sword to execute the Righteous Judgment on wrongdoers and deliver sinners to the righteous.

91.13 At its completion, they will get Houses for their righteousness and build a House for the Great King in Glory forever.

91.14 In the ninth week, the world will see the Righteous Judgment. Impious deeds will disappear from Earth. All mankind will follow the Path of Uprightness as the world is destroyed.

91.15 After this, in the tenth week, in the seventh section, the Watchers and the Great Eternal Heaven that shall issue from the Angels will be judged eternally.

91.16 The First Heaven will disappear, a New Heaven will appear, and all the Powers of Heaven will shine eternally with sevenfold light.

91.17 After this, there will be endless nice and righteous weeks. Sin is never addressed again.

91.18 I now show you, my children, the paths of righteousness and wrongdoing. I'll show you again to prepare you.

91.19 Listen, my children: walk in righteousness and not in iniquity, because those who walk in iniquity will be destroyed forever.

92.1 Enoch-the-Scribe wrote this full wisdom and teaching, praised by all men and a judge of the Earth.

My Earthly sons.

For justice and peace's final generations.

92.2 The Holy and Great One has set times for everything.

92.3 The upright man will awaken and walk in righteousness, and all his ways and trips will be in eternal goodness and mercy.

92.4 The righteous shall get mercy, eternal uprightness, and power.

He shall live in righteousness and eternal light.

92.5 Sin will vanish eternally in darkness.

93.1 After then, Enoch began reading:

93.2 "Regarding the sons of righteousness, the chosen of the world, and the plant of righteousness and uprightness, I will tell you, my children.

I, Enoch, according to the Heavenly vision, the Holy Angels' words, and the Tablets of Heaven."

93.3 Enoch then spoke from the books: "I was born the seventh, in the first week, while justice and righteousness still lasted.

93.4 In the second week following me, much injustice and dishonesty will arise. In it, the First End will save a guy. Iniquity will grow afterward, and He will devise a law for sinners.

93.5 At the end of the third week, a man will be chosen as the Plant of Righteous Judgment, followed by the Plant of Righteousness forever.

93.6 Visions of the righteous and holy, a Law for All Generations, and an enclosure will follow in the fourth week.

93.7 At the end of the fifth week, a House of Glory and Sovereignty will be erected forever.

93.8 The sixth week will blind everyone in it.

Without insight, they will fall into impiety. It will climb a man and burn the House of Sovereignty. It will scatter the specified root race.

93.9 The seventh week will bring an apostate generation.

Its deeds will be many but all apostasy.

93.10 At its finish, the picked Righteous from the Eternal Plant of Righteousness will be picked and taught sevenfold about his entire creation.

93.11 Can anyone hear the Holy One's speech without being disturbed? Who thinks his thoughts? Who can see Heaven's works?

93.12 How could anyone understand the works of Heaven, see a soul or spirit, tell about it, climb and see all their ends and comprehend them, or make anything like them?

93.13 Can anyone measure the Earth? Who saw all its measurements?

93.14 Does anyone know the length of Heaven, its height, its foundation, the number of stars, and where all the lights are?

94.1 My children, embrace righteousness and walk in it, for the paths of righteousness are worthy of acceptance, but the paths of wickedness will shortly be destroyed and perish.

94.2 Some future men will see the roads of wickedness and death and avoid them.

94.3 Righteous ones, do not walk on the wicked road, in wrongdoing, or in the paths of death, or you will be destroyed.

94.4 Instead, choose justice, a good life, and peace to live and prosper.

94.5 Keep my words in your heart and do not let them go, for I know that sinners will tempt mankind to debase wisdom, and no place will be found for it, and temptation will never lessen.

94.6 Woe to those who create iniquity and deceit—they will fall fast and have no peace.

94.7 Woe to those who build their houses with evil, for from their foundation they will be thrown down and fall by the sword, and those who gain riches and silver will rapidly be destroyed in judgment.

94.8 Woe to you, affluent people, because you trusted in your riches, but you will leave them because you forgot the Most High.

94.9 You have committed blasphemy and iniquity and are ready for bloodshed, darkness, and the Great Judgment.

94.10 I say and tell you that your creator will throw you down, and there will be no mercy for your fall.

94.11 Your righteousness in those days will shame sinners and the impious.

95.1 Would that my eyes were a rain-cloud so I could grieve over you and pour out my tears like rain to find relief from my anguish!

95.2 Who let you be evil? Sinners, be judged!

95.3 Righteous, do not fear sinners, for the Lord will again bring them to you so you can judge them.

95.4 Woe to you who proclaim unremovable anathema. Sin prevents healing.

95.5 Woe to you who wrong your neighbors; you shall be repaid.

95.6 Woe to you, dishonest witnesses, and those who weigh iniquity, because you will soon be annihilated.

95.7 Woe to you, sinners, for persecuting the righteous, for you will be delivered over and persecuted, you men of wickedness, and their yoke will be hard.

96.1 Be hopeful, righteous, for the sinners will shortly be eliminated before you and you will rule over them.

96.2 When sinners are in difficulty, your young will rise up like eagles and your nest will be higher than vultures. You will go up and enter the earth's cracks and rock's clefts forever, before the lawless, who will groan and wail like satyrs.

96.3 You who have suffered will be healed, a bright light will shine upon you, and Heaven's Voice of Rest will be heard.

96.4 Woe to you, sinners, for your riches make you look righteous yet your hearts are evil.

This word will be a reminder of your wrongdoings.

96.5 Woe to you who eat the best wheat and water and crush the humble with your power.

96.6 Woe to you who drink water constantly—you will soon be repaid and become weary and dry because you have abandoned the source of life.

96.7 Iniquity, deception, and blasphemy will remind you of wickedness.

96.8 You great oppressors of the righteous will be destroyed.

The upright will have many excellent days in your judgment.

97.1 Believe, righteous, that sinners will be shamed and annihilated on Judgment Day.

97.2 Sinners, the Most High recalls and the Angels exult over your doom.

97.3 What will you do, sinners, and whither will you escape on the day of judgment when you hear the righteous pray?

97.4 "You have been associated with the sinners" will not apply to you.

97.5 In those days, the Holy will pray before the Lord, and your judgment will arrive.

97.6 The Great and Holy One will read your iniquity, and your faces will blush with shame. Every deed based on iniquity will be rejected.

97.7 Sinners in the sea or on land, their remembrance will damage you.

97.8 Woe to you who obtain silver and gold, but not in righteousness, and say: "We have become very rich and have possessions, and have acquired everything we desire.

97.9 Now let us do what we intended, for we have accumulated silver and filled our storehouses, and as many as water are our house servants."

97.10 Your life will drain away like water because you got everything in iniquity and will be cursed.

98.1 I swear, wise and foolish, that you will see many things on earth.

98.2 You men will dress in sovereignty, majesty, power, silver, gold, purple, and honors, and food will be poured out like water.

98.3 Thus, they will lack understanding and insight. This will destroy them, their belongings, and their honor.

Their spirits will be cast into the flaming furnace in shame, slaughter, and destitution.

98.4 I swear to you, sinners, that as a mountain has not, and will not, become a slave, nor a hill a woman's maid, so sin was not sent on Earth but formed by man. Its perpetrators will suffer a terrible curse.

98.5 A woman dies childless due to her own actions.

98.6 I swear to you, sinners, by the Holy

and Great One that Heaven sees all your evil acts.

98.7 Do not think in your spirit or declare in your heart that you do not know or see, every transgression is written down every day in Heaven before the Most High.

98.8 From now on, your misbehavior will be recorded daily until your judgment.

Fools, your folly will destroy you. You won't succeed if you ignore the smart.

98.10 You are ready for annihilation. You sinners will perish because you know no ransom. You're ready for the Day of the Great Judgment and your spirits' disgrace and suffering.

98.11 Woe to you, stubborn heart who do evil and consume blood, from where do you get excellent things to eat and drink and be satisfied? From all the blessings our Lord the Most High has bestowed on earth. You won't have peace.

98.12 Evildoers, beware. Why wish yourself well? Know that the righteous will slay and slash your throats.

98.13 You who exult in the righteous' suffering will not be buried.

98.14 You who mock the godly shall die.

98.15 Woe to you who compose lies and impious words so that men may hear and continue their folly. They will perish violently.

99.1 You who conduct impious activities and laud and honor deceptive words will be destroyed and have a bad existence.

99.2 Woe to those who violate the everlasting law and count themselves as sinless; they will be trodden underfoot.

99.3 In such days, righteous, raise your prayers as a reminder and lay them as a testament before the Angels so they can remind the Most High of sinners' sins.

99.4 Nations will be confused and their races will rise on the Day of Destruction.

99.5 In those days, the needy will take their children and cast them out. They will lose their children and cast them out while they are still sucklings, never returning to them or showing mercy.

99.6 Again, sinners, I swear that sin is ready for the Day of Unceasing Bloodshed.

99.7 Some worship stone and create gold, silver, wood, and clay images. Some ignorantly worship demons and filthy spirits.

They won't help.

99.8 Their folly will lead them to impiety, and their fear and ambitions will blind them.

99.9 They will become impious and terrified because they worship stones and lie in all their deeds, and they will be destroyed immediately.

99.10 In those days, blessed are those who receive the words of wisdom, understand them, follow the paths of the Most High, live in justice, and do not act impiously with the impious, for they will be preserved.

99.11 Evildoers shall die in Sheol.

99.12 Woe to you who create foundations of iniquity and dishonesty and cause bitterness on Earth—they will perish.

99.13 Woe to you who build your dwellings with others' labor and sin's sticks and stones—you will not enjoy peace.

99.14 Woe to those who reject the measure and the eternal heritage of their fathers and lead their spirits astray—they will not rest.

99.15 Woe to those who commit wickedness, help injustice, and slay their neighbors until the Day of the Great Judgment—he will throw down your splendor.

99.16 You put evil in your hearts and arouse his rage to kill you all with the sword.

The holy and upright will remember your sin.

100.1 Fathers and sons will fight in one location, and brothers will die

together until their blood runs like a torrent.

100.2 A merciful man will not kill his sons or their sons. The sinner will slaughter his brother from dawn to dusk.

100.3 The horse and chariot will sink in sinners' blood.

100.4 In those days, the Angels will descend into the hidden regions and assemble all those who have helped sin, and the Most High will rise to execute the Great Judgment on all sinners.

100.5 The Holy Angels will guard the righteous and holy like the apple of an eye until all evil and sin are eliminated. The righteous need not worry about long sleeps.

100.6 The wise men will perceive the truth, and the sons of Earth will understand all the teachings of this book, and they will know that their riches cannot save them or overthrow their sin.

100.7 Woe to you, sinners, when you afflict the upright in times of need and burn them with fire.

100.8 Woe to you, twisted heart, who watch to scheme evil; terror will come upon you and no one will aid you.

100.9 You sinners shall burn in hellfire for your impious words and acts.

100.10 Know that the Angels will investigate your offenses from the Sun, Moon, and Stars in Heaven, since you judge the virtuous on earth.

100.11 The clouds, mist, dew, and rain will testify against you because they will not fall on you and will ponder about your transgressions.

100.12 Now offer gifts to the rain and dew, if they have accepted gold and silver from you, so that they may fall on you.

100.13 When hoarfrost, snow, and snow-winds plague you. You cannot face them then.

101.1 Contemplate Heaven, all you sons of Heaven, and all the handiwork of the Most High, and dread him and do not do evil before Him.

101.2 What will you do if He seals the Windows of Heaven and withholds rain and dew from falling on earth because of you?

101.3 Will you not beseech him if he wraths you and your deeds? You speak proudly against his righteousness. You will receive no peace.

101.4 Do you not observe the ship commanders' ships being thrown by seas and battered by winds and in distress?

101.5 For all their fine possessions that go out on the sea with them, they are fearful, thinking nothing positive in their hearts, only that the sea will swallow them up and destroy them.

101.6 Did not the Most High seal and tie all the sea's doings with sand?

101.7 At his reprimand, it dries up and becomes scared, and its fish and everything in it die, but you sinners on Earth do not fear him.

101.8 Did he not create Heaven, Earth, and everything in them? Who taught all living things on land and sea?

101.9 Do ship captains not fear the sea? Sinners don't fear God.

102.1 If he brings a terrible fire upon you in those days, where will you go and be safe?
Will you be afraid when he speaks against you?

102.2 All the Lights will shake with fear, and the Earth will tremble and quail.

102.3 And all the Angels will obey their commands and hide from the Great in Glory, and the children of Earth will fear and shudder, and you sinners will be cursed forever and will not have rest.

102.4 Be brave, virtuous souls, and optimistic, righteous dead.

102.5 Do not be upset that your souls have gone down into Sheol in despair and that your bodies did not receive a reward for your goodness.

102.6 Sinners will say, "As we die, the righteous have also died, and of what use were their deeds?"

102.7 "Behold, like us they died in sadness and darkness. What advantage do they have over us? We're equal now."

102.8 "What will they get and see forever? They have died and will never see the light again."

102.9 "You sinners are content to eat and drink, strip men naked, steal, sin, acquire possessions, and see good days.

102.10 But you saw the righteous, how their end was peace, for they did no wrong until their death."

102.11 "But they were destroyed and became like nothing and their souls went down to Sheol in distress."

103.1 I swear to you, the righteous, by His Great Glory, His Honour, His Magnificent Sovereignty, and His Majesty that I understand this riddle.

103.2 I perused the Tablets of Heaven and saw the Holy Ones' writing. I found inscribed and carved on it that all good, pleasure, and honor have been prepared for the spirits of those who died in righteousness.

103.3 You will be rewarded for your hard work and have a better life than the living.

103.4 Your spirits who died in righteousness will live, rejoice, and be glad, and the Great One will remember them for all eternity. Don't fear their abuse.

103.5 Woe to you, sinners, when you die in your sin and your peers remark, "Blessed were the sinners they saw their days."

103.6 "They died in prosperity and wealth, distress and slaughter they did not see during their life, but they died in glory, and judgment was not executed on them in their life."

103.7 Their souls will be cast into Sheol, wretched, and in severe pain.

103.8 Your spirits shall face the Great Judgment in darkness, chains, and fire. It will last forever. You will suffer forever.

103.9 The righteous and excellent who lived should not declare, "In the days of our affliction we toiled laboriously, saw every affliction, and met many evils. We were exhausted and small-minded.

103.10 We were destroyed without any support. We found nothing. We were tortured and thought we would die.

103.11 We became the tail. We worked hard, but sinners ate us, and the lawless enslaved us.

103.12 Our tormentors ruled us. We bowed to our enemies yet they did not show mercy.

103.13 We fled them to rest. We couldn't hide from them.

103.14 In our anguish, we complained to the rulers and cried out against those who devoured us, but they ignored us and refused to listen.

103.15 They supported those who robbed, devoured, and scattered us, while they disguised their wickedness. They hid our slaughter and forgot that they raised their hands against us."

104.1 I vow to you, righteous, that the Angels in Heaven remember you for good before the Lord.

Glory of the Great One, and that your names are recorded before it.

104.2 Hope! You were shamed by evils and afflictions, but now you will shine like the Lights of Heaven, be noticed, and enter Heaven.

104.3 Persist in your cry for justice, and justice will be exacted from the rulers for all your suffering and from all those who helped those who looted you.

104.4 Be positive and don't give up— you'll be happy like the angels.

104.5 What must you do? On the Great Judgment, you will not be sinners or have to hide. You shall face the Eternal Judgment forever.

104.6 You righteous, do not be terrified when you see the sinners getting strong and thriving in their wants. Do not associate with them and stay away from their wickedness, because you will be associates of the Host of Heaven.

104.7 Sinners say, "None of our sins will be inquired into and written down!" They'll record your sins daily.

104.8 Light and darkness see all your crimes, day and night.

104.9 Do not lie, do not change the truth, do not call the Holy and Great One a liar, and do not laud your idols. Your lies and impiety lead to tremendous sin.

104.10 Now I know this mystery: many sinners will modify and distort the truth, say wicked words, lie, fabricate enormous fabrications, and compose volumes in their own words.

104.11 But when they write my words exactly in their languages, without changing or omitting anything, then I know another mystery:

104.12 That books will give the upright and wise delight, truth, and wisdom.

104.13 They will receive books and believe in them, and all the upright who have learned from them will rejoice.

105.1 In those days, says the Lord, they will call and testify to the sons of Earth about their wisdom. Show them since you are their leaders and the rewards will be worldwide.

105.2 My son and I shall always walk with them in righteousness.

Peace awaits.

Joyful upright sons!

Amen

Noah fragment

106.1 After that, my son Methuselah found a woman for Lamech, who became pregnant and had a son.

106.2 His physique was white like snow, scarlet like a rose, and his hair white as wool. His lovely eyes made the home brilliant like the Sun when he opened them.

106.3 He spoke to the Lord of Righteousness after being taken from the midwife's hand.

106.4 His father Lamech fled to Methuselah, fearful of him.

106.5 He told him, "I have produced a weird son; he is not like a man but like the children of the Angels of Heaven, of a different type and not like us. His face and eyes are radiant.

106.6 He looks to be from the Angels, and I fear that something exceptional may happen on Earth in his days.

106.7 Now, my father, I implore you to go see our father Enoch and learn the truth from him, for he dwells among the angels."

106.8 When Methuselah heard his son's words, he came to me at the extremities of the Earth, knowing I was there. He screamed, and I hurried to him. "Behold, my son, you have come to me," I exclaimed.

106.9 "Because of a great matter and a disturbing vision, I have come near," he replied.

106.10 My father, my son Lamech, has had a child whose form and kind are not like a man. His hair is whiter than white wool and his skin redder than a rose. He opened his eyes and illuminated the house.

106.11 The midwife took him, and he opened his mouth and thanked God.

106.12 Lamech fled to me. He thinks he's from Heaven's Angels, not him.

I came to you to learn the truth."

106.13 "The Lord will do new things on Earth," I, Enoch, said. Some from Heaven disobeyed the Lord in my father Jared's generation.

106.14 They have been promiscuous with women, sinned with them, married some of them, and had children with them.

106.15 There will be a flood and worldwide catastrophe for one year.

106.16 Your child will stay on Earth with his three sons. He and his sons will survive when all men on Earth die.

106.17 They will beget flesh-giants on Earth, causing great anger and cleansing the Earth of corruption.

106.18 Tell Lamech that his son has been born. Call him Noah, for he will be a remnant for you and he and his sons will be saved from the disaster that is coming on the earth due to all the evil and iniquity that will be done in his days.

106.19 After this, there will be greater iniquity on earth. The Lord showed me the mysteries of the Holy Ones, and I read them in the Tablets of Heaven.

107

107.1 I saw written on them that generation after generation would do wrong until a generation of righteousness arises, then wrongdoing shall be eradicated, sin shall leave from the earth, and everything good shall come upon it.

107.2 Now, my son, tell your son Lamech that this child is his son and this is true.

107.3 Methuselah returned, having seen him, and named that infant Noah, for he would soothe the Earth after the disaster.

108

108.1 Enoch authored another book for his son Methuselah and the latter-day lawkeepers.

108.2 You who have observed and are waiting in these days until evildoers and their authority are destroyed.

108.3 Wait until sin passes away, for their names will be removed from the Books of the Holy Ones and their offspring perished forever. Their spirits will die, and they will wail and lament in a chaotic desert and burn in fire since there is no Earth there.

108.4 I observed a cloud-like entity that I couldn't see due to its depth. I saw bright fire flames, and bright mountains rotated and shook.

108.5 I questioned one of the Holy Angels with me, "What is this bright place? There is no sky, only a searing fire and the noises of crying, weeping, moaning, and tremendous pain."

108.6 "This place which you see; here will throw the spirits of the sinners, blasphemers, and evildoers," he stated. And those who change everything the Lord has declared via the prophets regarding the future.

108.7 Angels can peruse their books and records in Heaven to know what's coming to sinners. And upon the lowly, those who suffered and were repaid by God, and those who were abused by bad men.

108.8 God-lovers who sacrificed their bodies to agony.

108.9 Those who never wanted earthly nourishment and considered themselves a breath that passes away. The Lord tried them severely, and their spirits were pure so they may glorify His Name."

108.10 I recorded all their blessings in the books, and he gave them their prize because they valued Heaven more than the earth. Despite being crushed by evil men, reviled, and abused, they blessed their Lord.

108.11 The Lord continued, "And now I will call the spirits of the good, who are of the Generation of Light, and I will transform those who were born in darkness, who in the flesh were not recompensed with honour as was fitting to their faith.

108.12 "I will bring out into the shining light those who love my Holy Name and set each one on the throne of his honour."

108.13 They will shine forever because God's judgment is righteous and He will keep trust in the habitation of upright paths with the faithful.

108.14 The wicked will be cast into darkness while the righteous shine. As they shine, sinners will cry out, but they will go where their days and times are written.

The Book of the Secrets of Enoch A.I.

1.1 There was a wise man, a great artificer, and the Lord conceived love for him and received him, that he might behold the uppermost dwellings and be an eye-witness of the wise and great and inconceivable and immutable realm of God Almighty, of the very wonderful and glorious and bright and many-eyed station of the Lord's servants, and of the Lord's inaccessible throne, and of the degrees and manifestations of the incorporeal hosts, and of the ineffable

2 After my one hundred and sixty-fifth year, I had Mathusal (Methuselah).

3 I lived two hundred years after this and three hundred and sixty-five years total.

4 I slept on my bed alone on the first of the month.

5 When I fell asleep, great distress sprang up into my heart, and I was weeping in my dream, not understanding what was happening or why.

6 And there appeared to me two men, exceeding big, so that I never saw such on earth; their faces were shining like the sun, their eyes too (were) like a burning light, and from their lips was fire coming forth with clothing and singing of various kinds in appearance purple, their wings brighter than gold, their hands whiter than snow.

7 They called my name from the head of my bed.

8 I woke up and saw the two males in front of me.

10 Have courage, Enoch, the eternal God sent us to you, and lo! You shall ascend with us today into heaven, and you shall instruct your sons and all your household all that they shall do without you on earth in your house, and let no one seek you until the Lord returns you to them.

11 I quickly obeyed them and left my house, walked to the doors, and summoned my sons Mathusal (Methuselah), Regim, and Gaidad to tell them about the marvels those guys had told me.

2 1. Listen to me, my children, I know not where I go or what will happen to me; now therefore, my children, I tell you: turn not from God before the face of the vain, who made not Heaven and earth, for these shall perish and those who worship them, and may the Lord make confident your hearts in the fear of him. My children do not look for me until the Lord returns me.

3.1 After Enoch told his sons, the angels lifted him to the first heaven and put him on the clouds. I looked again and saw the ether, and they placed me on the first heaven and showed me a very large sea, larger than the earthly sea.

4.1 They showed me two hundred angels who rule the stars and the heavens and fly around all the sailors.

5.1 I gazed down and saw the treasure-houses of the snow, the angels who guard their awful storehouses, and the clouds from which they come and depart.

6.1 They showed me the treasure-house of the dew, like olive oil, and its form, as well as all the flowers of the earth; numerous angels guarding these treasure-houses; and how they are constructed to shut and open.

7.1 And those men took me and led me up to the second heaven, where I saw darkness, greater than earthly darkness, and prisoners hanging, watching, awaiting the great and boundless judgment, and these angels (spirits) were dark-looking, more than earthly darkness, and weeping all day.

2 I asked my companions: Why are they tortured?

They replied: These are God's apostates, who disobeyed God's commands, took counsel with their own will, and turned away with their lord, who is also fixed on the fifth heaven.

3 I felt sorry for them, and they greeted me and said, "Man of God, pray for us to the Lord." I replied, "Who am I, a mortal man, to pray for angels (spirits)?" Who knows my destination or fate? Who will intercede?

8.1 Then those men took me there and carried me up to the third heaven, where I gazed down and saw the product of these realms, which has never been known for goodness.

2 I noticed all the sweet-flowering trees and their fragrant fruits and snacks.

3 And in the midst of the trees that of life, in that place whereon the Lord rests, when he goes up into paradise; and this tree is of ineffable goodness and fragrance, and adorned more than every existing thing; and on all sides (it is) in form gold-looking and vermilion and fire-like and covers all, and it has produce from all fruits.

4 The earth's end garden is its root.

Paradise lies between incorruptibility and corruption.

6 Two springs come out that send honey and milk, and their springs send oil and wine, and they separate into four sections, go round quietly, and fall down into the PARADISE OF EDEN, between corruption and incorruptibility.

7 They travel the planet and rotate like other elements.

8 Everywhere is blessed, and no tree is unfruitful.

9 Three hundred beautiful angels tend the garden and serve the Lord 24/7 with pleasant singing and voices. I said, "How sweet this place is," and those folks replied:

9.1 This location, O Enoch, is for the virtuous, who tolerate all kinds of offense from those who exasperate their souls, who avert their eyes from iniquity, make righteous judgment, feed the hungry, clothe the naked, raise the fallen, help injured orphans, walk without fault before the Lord, and serve him alone, and for them is prepared this place for eternal inheritance.

10.1 And those two men led me up on the Northern side, and showed me there a very terrible place, and (there were) all manner of tortures in that place: cruel darkness and unillumined gloom, and there is no light there, but murky fire constantly flaming aloft, and a fiery river coming forth, and that whole place is everywhere fire, and everywhere frost and ice, thirst and shivering, while the bonds are very cruel, and the angels (spirits) flitting about. said:

2 This place is awful.

3 And those men told me: This place, O Enoch, is prepared for those who dishonor God, who on earth practice sin against nature, which is child-corruption after the sodomitic fashion, magic-making, enchantments, and devilish witchcrafts, and who boast of their wicked deeds, stealing, lies, calumnies, envy, rancour, fornication, murder, and who, accursed, steal the souls of men, who, seeing the poor take away their goods and themselves wax rich, harming them for other people's possessions; who, able to quench the emptiness, caused the hungering to

In order to prepare this place among these for eternal inheritance, those who die, possess the ability to clothe, strip the naked, and who were unaware of their creator and bowed to soulless (and lifeless) gods, who are unable to see or hear, vain gods.

11.1 Those men took me to the fourth heaven and showed me all the successive goings and sun and moon rays.

2 I measured their goings and compared their light, and the sun was brighter than the moon.

3 Its circle and wheels move like the wind and never stop, day and night.

4 Its transit and return are accompanied by four huge stars, each with a thousand stars to the right of the sun's wheel, and four to the left, each with a thousand stars, altogether eight thousand, emerging with the sun continuously.

5 Fifteen countless angels guard it by day and a thousand by night.

6 Six-winged ones fly with the angels before the sun's wheel into the burning flames, and a hundred angels light the sun.

12.1 And I looked and saw other flying elements of the sun, whose names (are) Phoenixes and Chalkydri, marvelous and wonderful, with feet and tails in the form of a lion, and a crocodile's head, their appearance (is) empurpled, like the rainbow; their size (is) nine hundred measures, their wings (are like) those of angels, each (has) twelve, and they attend and accompany the sun, bearing heat and dew, as God ordered them.

2 Thus, the sun circles, rises, and descends under the earth, shining its rays continuously.

13.1 Those soldiers carried me east to the sun's gates, where the sun rises and sets according to the seasons, months, and hours of the day and night.

2 And I saw six gates open, each gate having sixty-one stadia and a quarter of one stadium, and I measured (them) truly and understood their size (to be) so much, through which the sun goes forth, goes to the west, is made even, rises throughout all the months, and turns back

again from the six gates according to the succession of the seasons; thus (the period) of the whole year is finished after the four seasons return.

14.1 Again, those men led me to the west and showed me six big gates open corresponding to the eastern gates, opposite where the sun sets, according to the days three hundred and sixty-five and a quarter.

2 Thus again it goes down to the western gates, (and) draws away its light, the greatness of its brightness, under the earth; for since the crown of its shining is in heaven with the Lord, and guarded by four hundred angels, while the sun goes round on wheel under the earth, stands seven great hours in night, and spends half (its course) under the earth, when it comes to the eastern approach in the eighth hour of the night, it brings its lights, and the cro

15.1 Then the sun's elements, Phoenixes and Chalkydri, sing, and every bird flutters its wings, joyful at the giver of light. They sang at the Lord's command.

2 The giver of light arrives to give brightness to the whole globe, and the morning guard takes shape, which is the sun's rays, and the sun of the earth goes out and receives its brilliance to light up the whole earth. They showed me this estimate of the sun's going.

3 For this reason, the sun is a vast creation, whose circuit (lasts) twenty-eight years and starts again from the beginning.

16.1 Those guys showed me the moon's course—twelve enormous gates, topped from west to east, through which the moon enters and leaves the regular times.

2 It enters at the first gate to the western places of the sun, by the first gates with (thirty)-one (days) exactly, by the second gates with thirty-one days exactly, by the

third, fourth, fifth, sixth, seventh, eighth, ninth, and tenth gates with thirty-one days exactly.

3 The solar year has three hundred and sixty five and a quarter days, while the lunar year has three hundred fifty four, and it lacks twelve days of the solar circle, which are the lunar epacts of the whole year.

4 The great circle has 532 years.

5 Three years without a quarter, the fourth with it.

6 Because they shift the period of the years to two new months toward completion and two toward reduction, they are taken outside of heaven for three years and not added to the 64 days.

7 When the western gates are built, it returns and goes to the eastern lights, and goes thus day and night about the heavenly circles, lower than all circles, swifter than the heavenly winds, and spirits, elements, and angels flying; each angel having six wings.

8 Its nineteen-year course is sevenfold.

17.1 In the heavens, I saw armed soldiers serving the Lord, with tympana and organs, with incessant voice, sweet voice, and various singing, which is impossible to describe and astonishes every mind, so wonderful and marvelous is the singing of those angels, and I was delighted listening to it.

18.1 The men took me to the fifth heaven and placed me, and there I saw many and countless soldiers, called Grigori, of human appearance, and their size (was) greater than that of great giants and their faces withered, and the silence of their mouths perpetual, and there was no service on the fifth heaven, and I said to the men who were with me:

2 Wherefore are these very withered and their faces melancholy, and their mouths silent, and (wherefore) is there

3 And they said to me: These are the Grigori, who with their prince Satanail (Satan) rejected the Lord of light, and after them are those who are held in great darkness on the second heaven, and three of them went down on earth from the Lord's throne, to the place Ermon, and broke through their vows on the shoulder of the hill Ermon and saw the daughters of men how good they are, and took wives, and befouled the earth with their deeds, who in al-

4 God condemned them harshly, and they cry for their brethren and will be punished on the Lord's great day.

5 I told the Grigori: I saw your brethren, their actions, and their tremendous torments, and I prayed for them, but the Lord has doomed them (to stay) under earth till (the existing) heaven and earth will terminate for ever.

6 I asked: Why do you wait, brethren, and not serve before the Lord's face, lest you anger your Lord?

7 They heeded my advice and addressed the four heavens, and lo! As I stood with those two men, four trumpets blared, and the Grigori sang with one voice, pitifully and movingly, before the Lord.

19.1 And those men took me and bore me up to the sixth heaven, and there I saw seven bands of angels, very bright and very glorious, and their faces shining more than the sun's shining, glistening, and there is no difference in their faces, behavior, or dress; and these make the orders, and learn the goings of the stars, and the alteration of the moon, or revolution of the sun, and the good government of the world.

2 When they observe wrongdoing, they give orders, sing loudly, and praise.

3 These are the archangels who are above angels, measure all life in heaven and on earth, and the angels who are (appointed) over seasons and years, 65 over rivers and sea, and over the fruits of

the earth, and over every grass, giving food to all, to every living thing, and the angels who write all men's souls, deeds, and lives before the Lord's face; in their midst are six Phoenixes and six

20.1 And those two men lifted me up thence on to the seventh heaven, and I saw there a very great light, and fiery troops of great archangels, incorporeal forces, dominions, orders, and governments, Cherubim and seraphim, thrones and many-eyed ones, nine regiments, the Ioanit stations of light, and I became afraid and began to tremble with great terror, and those men took me, and led me after them, and said to me:

2 Have confidence, Enoch, and showed me the Lord sitting on His high throne. Since God lives in the tenth heaven, what is there?

3 God—Aravat in Hebrew—is in the tenth heaven.

4 All the heavenly troops would stand on the ten steps according to their rank, bow to the Lord, and return to their positions in joy and happiness, singing songs in the infinite light with small and soft voices, gloriously serving him.

21.1 The six-winged and many-eyed Cherubim and seraphim around the throne do not leave, standing before the Lord's face doing his will and covering his whole throne, singing with gentle voices: Holy, holy, holy, Lord Ruler of Sabaoth, heavens and earth are full of Your glory.

2 When I saw all these things, those men said to me, "Enoch, thus far is it commanded us to journey with you," and they left me and I never saw them again.

3 I was alone at the end of the seventh heaven, scared, and fell on my face, saying, "Woe is me, what has befallen me?"

4 The archangel Gabriel came and said, "Have courage, Enoch, do not fear, arise

before the Lord's face into eternity, arise, come with me."

5 I answered him and said to myself: My Lord, my spirit is flown from me, from fright and anxiety, and I summoned to the men who carried me up to this spot, on whom I relied, and (it is) with them I go before the Lord's face.

6 Gabriel snatched me like a leaf in the wind and brought me before the Lord.

7 I saw the eighth heaven, called Muzaloth in Hebrew, which changes seasons, drought, and rain, and the twelve constellations of the firmament above the seventh heaven.

8 I saw Kuchavim, the ninth sky, where the twelve constellations of the firmament live.

22.1 On the tenth heaven, Aravoth, I saw the Lord's face, like iron made to light in fire, drawn out, emitting sparks, and burning.

2 In a moment of eternity, I beheld the Lord's face, which is wonderful, marvelous, terrifying, and terrible.

3 Who am I to talk of the Lord's inconceivable being and lovely face? I cannot tell the quantity of his many instructions, and various voices, the Lord's throne (is) very great and not made with hands, nor the quantity of those standing around him, troops of Cherubim and seraphim, nor their incessant singing, nor his immutable beauty, nor who shall tell of the ineffable greatness of his glory.

4 I fell prone and knelt down to the Lord, and the Lord spoke to me:

5 Have courage, Enoch, do not fear, arise and stand before my face forever.

6 The archistratege Michael raised me and brought me before the Lord.

7 And the Lord said to his servants tempting them: Let Enoch stand before my face into eternity, and the magnificent ones bowed down and murmured: Let Enoch depart according to Your word.

8 The Lord told Michael to take Enoch from his earthly robes, anoint him with my lovely ointment, and put him in My glory.

Michael obeyed the Lord. He anointed me and dressed me, and the appearance of that ointment is more than the great light, and his ointment is like sweet dew, and its smell pleasant, gleaming like the sun's ray, and I looked at myself, and (I) was like (transfigured) one of his splendid ones.

10 And the Lord summoned one of his archangels by name Pravuil, whose knowledge was quicker in wisdom than the other archangels, who wrote all the deeds of the Lord; and the Lord said to Pravuil: Bring out the books from my store-houses, and a reed of quick-writing, and give (it) to Enoch, and deliver to him the choice and comforting books out of your hand.

23.1 He told me all the works of heaven, earth, and sea, and all the elements, their passages and goings, and the thunderings of the thunders, the sun and moon, the goings and changes of the stars, the seasons, years, days, and hours, the risings of the wind, the numbers of the angels, and the formation of their songs, and all human things, the tongue of every human song and life, the commandments, instructions, and sweet-voiced singings, and all things tis fitting to learn.

2 Pravuil said: We wrote everything I told you. Sit and record all the souls of men, however many are born, and their eternal locations, for all souls were prepared before the world was formed.

3 I authored 366 books in 30 days and 30 nights.

24.1 Enoch, seat on my left with Gabriel, the Lord commanded.

2 and I bowed down to the Lord, and the Lord said, "Enoch, beloved, all (that) you see, all things that are standing finished I tell to you even from the very beginning, all that I created from non-being, and visible (physical) things from invisible (spiritual).

3 Hear, Enoch, and understand my words, for I have not informed My angels my secret, their ascent, my limitless realm, or my making, which I tell you today.

4 Before all things were visible (physical), I alone traveled in the invisible (spiritual) things, like the sun from east to west and west to east.

5 But even the sun has tranquility, whereas I found no peace since I was creating all things and thought of setting foundations and constructing visible (physical) creation.

25.1 I commanded in the lowest portions that visible (physical) things should come down from unseen (spiritual), and Adoil came down very great, and I saw his belly of vast light.

2 I told him: Undo, Adoil, and let the visible (physical) out.

3 He broke, and a vast light appeared. I was in the vast light, and as light comes from light, a great age burst forth and showed all creation, which I had imagined to create.

I found it good.

5 I sat on a throne and told the light to go higher and fix itself high above the throne and establish a foundation for the highest things.

6 I bent up and peered up from my throne, and there is nothing above the light.

26.1 I summoned the lowest again and said, "Let Archas come forth hard," and he did from the unseen (spiritual).

2 Archas emerged, heavy and red.

3 And I said: Be opened, Archas, and let there be born from you, and he came undone, an age came forth, very great and very dark, bearing the creation of all

lower things, and I saw that (it was) good and said to him: 4 Go thence down below, and make yourself firm, and be a foundation for the lower things, and it happened and he went down and fixed himself, and below the darkness there is nothing else.

27
.1 And I commanded that there should be taken from light and darkness, and I said: Be thick, and it became thus, and I spread it out with the light, and it became water, and I spread it out over the darkness, below the light, and then I made firm the waters, that is to say the bottomless, and I made foundation of light around the water, and created seven circles from inside, and imaged (the water) like crystal wet and dry, that is, like glass, (and) the

2 And I separated light and darkness in the midst of the water hither and thither, and I said to the light, "Be the day," and to the darkness, "Be the night," and there was evening and morning the first day.

28
.1 Then I made the heavenly circle strong, made the lower water under heaven gather into one whole, and made the chaos dry.

2 I formed rock hard and big from the seas, and from the rock I piled up the dry, which I called earth, and in the midst of the earth I called the abyss, the bottomless. I collected the sea in one place and tied it with a yoke.

3 I said to the sea: I give you eternal limitations, and you shall not break loose from your component parts.

4 I fixed the sky. I'm Sunday's first creation.

29
.1 For all the heavenly troops, I imaged the image and essence of fire, and my eye looked at the very hard, firm rock, and from the gleam of my eye the lightning received its wonderful nature, (which) is both fire in water and water in fire, and one does not put out the other

nor dry up the other, therefore the lightning is brighter than the sun, softer than water, and firmer than hard rock.

2 From the rock I broke off a large fire, and from the fire I created the orders of the incorporeal ten troops of angels, whose weapons are flaming and their raiment a burning flame. I ordered each one to stand in his order.

3 One angel, having turned away from his command, devised an inconceivable idea to place his throne higher than the clouds above the earth to become equal in rank to my strength.

4 I tossed him with his angels from the height, and he flew above the deep.

30
.1 On the third day, I directed the land to grow vast and fruitful trees, hills, and seed to sow, and I planted Paradise, surrounded it, and put fire angels as armed guardians. Thus, I created regeneration.

2 The fourth day dawned after evening.

3 [Wednesday]. I ordered bright heavenly circles on the fourth day.

4 On the first highest circle I placed Kruno, Aphrodit, Aris, Zoues, Ermis, the moon, and the lesser stars.

5 The sun, moon, and stars illuminated the lower.

6 I ordered the sun to follow each constellation, twelve, and set the months' names, lives, thunderings, and hourmarkings.

7 The fifth day dawned after evening.

8 [Thursday]. On the fifth day, I directed the sea to bring forth fishes, feathered birds of many sorts, and all animals creeping over the soil, walking on four legs, and soaring in the air, male and female, and every soul breathing the spirit of life.

9 The sixth day dawned after evening.

10 [Friday]. On the sixth day, I ordered my wisdom to create man from seven consistencies: flesh from the earth; blood from the dew; eyes from the sun; bones

from stone; intelligence from the swiftness of the angels and from cloud; veins and hair from the grass of the earth; and soul from my breath and from the wind.

11 I gave him seven natures: body hearing, eyes sight, soul fragrance, veins touch, blood taste, bones endurance, to the intelligence sweetness [enjoyment].

12 I conceived a cunning saying to say, I created man from invisible (spiritual) and visible (physical) nature, of both are his death and life and image, he knows speech like some created thing, small in greatness and again great in smallness, and I placed him on earth as a second angel, honorable, great, and glorious, and appointed him as ruler to rule on earth and to have my wisdom, and there was none like him of earth of all my existing creatures.

13 I named him Adam from the four component parts—east, west, south, and north—and gave him four distinct stars. I showed him the light and darkness and informed him:

14 This is excellent and bad—I need to know if he loves me or hates me to know which in his race adores me.

15 I have seen his nature, but he has not seen his own nature, so he will sin harder, and I said After sin (what is there) but death?

16 I instilled sleep into him and he fell asleep. I took a rib from him and fashioned him a wife, so his wife would kill him, and I took his final word and called her mother, Eva (Eve).

31.1 I established a garden in Eden in the east for Adam to keep the testament and command.

2 I opened the heavens so he might see the angels singing victory and the gloomless light.

3 He was always in paradise, and the devil recognized that I intended to build another world because Adam ruled and controlled it.

4 The devil is the evil spirit of the lower places. As a runaway, he made Sotona from the skies as Satanail (Satan), thereby becoming different from the angels, but his intelligence and understanding of right and wrong did not change.

5 He realized his punishment and his past sins, so he thought against Adam and entered and seduced Eva (Eve) without touching Adam.

6 But I cursed stupidity, not man, the land, or other creatures, but man's bad fruit and acts.

32.1 I told him: ground you are, and into the ground from I took you you shalt go, and I will not damage you, but send you.

2 I can receive you again.

3 I blessed my bodily and spiritual creations. Adam spent five-and-a-half hours in paradise.

4 I blessed the Sabbath, when he rested.

33.1 I also appointed the eighth day to be the first created after my work, that (the first seven) revolve in the form of the seventh thousand, and that at the beginning of the eighth thousand there should be a time of not-counting, endless, with neither years nor months nor weeks nor days nor hours.

2 Now, Enoch, all that I have told you, all that you have understood, all that you have seen of heavenly things, all that you have seen on earth, and all that I have written in books by my great wisdom, I have devised and created from the uppermost foundation to the lower and to the end, and there is no counselor or inheritor to my creations.

3 I am everlasting, unmade, and unchanging.

4 My intellect, wisdom, and words are

made, and my eyes see all things trembling with horror.

5 Everything will be destroyed if I hide.

6 Apply your thinking, Enoch, and realize who is speaking to you, and take the books you wrote.

7 I give you Samuil and Raguil, who led you up, and the books. Go down to earth and tell your sons everything I have told you and everything you have seen, from the lower heaven up to my throne and all the troops.

8 I created all the forces and they all submitted to me. For all serve my monarchy.

9 Give them the handwritten books, and they will read them and recognize me as the creator of all things and comprehend that there is no other God but me.

10 Let them distribute your handwritten books to children, generations, and nations.

11 I will grant Enoch, my intercessor, the archistratege Michael for the handwritings of your fathers Adam, Seth, Enos, Cainan, Mahaleleel, and Jared.

34.1 They have rejected my commandments and my yoke, worthless seed has come up, not fearing God, and they would not bow down to me, but have begun to bow down to vain gods, denied my unity, and laden the whole earth with untruths, offenses, abominable lecheries, namely one with another, and all manner of other unclean wickedness, which is disgusting to relate.

2 Therefore, I will hurl down a deluge and destroy all humanity, and the earth will disintegrate into profound darkness.

35.1 Behold, from their seed shall arise another generation, much later, although many will be terribly insatiate.

2 He who raises that generation shall unveil the records of your handwriting, of your fathers, to whom he must point out the guardianship of the world, to the devoted men and laborers of my delight, who do not acknowledge my name in vain.

3 They will inform another generation, and those who read will be praised more than the first.

36.1 Right now, Enoch, I offer you a period of thirty days to spend in your home and tell your sons and everyone else in your household that they may hear from my face what you have told them and that they may read and comprehend how there is no other God but me.

2 and that they learn to read and comprehend the books written in your handwriting so that they may always observe my commandments.

3 And after 30 days, I'll send my angel to get you; he'll bring you to me from Earth and from your boys.

37.1 Then the Lord sent one of the more terrifying and menacing older angels to stand by me; he was white as snow and had ice-like hands that gave the appearance of heavy frost. He froze my face because I was unable to withstand the terror of the Lord, just as it is impossible to withstand a stove's fire, the sun's heat, and the air's frost.

2 Enoch, if your face is not frozen here, no man will be able to see your face, the Lord replied to me.

38.1 Let Enoch go down to earth with you, and wait for him until the appointed day, the Lord said to the ones who initially led me up.

2 And they put me in my bed at night.

3 Mathusal (Methuselah), who was keeping watch at my bed day and night in anticipation of my arrival, was filled with wonder when he heard me arrive. I told him, "Let all my household come together," so that I could tell them everything.

39.1 Oh my children, my cherished ones, pay attention to your father's warning, to the extent that it is in line with the Lord's will.

2 I have been given permission to visit you today and inform you of all that is, was, is, and will be until the day of the judgment—not from my lips, but from the Lord's.

3 Since the Lord permitted my arrival, you are listening to the words of a man who is too large for you, but I am one who has seen the face of the Lord, and like iron heated by fire, it burns and spews sparks.

4 You observe my eyes today, which are those of a man who are enormous and full of significance for you, but I have seen the Lord's eyes, which shine like the sun's beams and fill human eyes with amazement.

5 You now see, my children, the right hand of a man who aids you, but as the Lord assisted me, I saw the Lord's right hand fill heaven.

6 You see the compass of my labor as you view your own, but I have seen the Lord's unbounded, flawless, and unending compass.

7 You hear what I say just as I did when I heard what the Lord said: like rumbling clouds and enormous thunder that never stops.

8 And now, my children, listen to the father of the earth's discourses about how terrifying and awful it is to appear before the ruler of the earth, and how much more terrifying and awful it is to appear before the ruler of heaven, the controller (judge) of the quick and dead, as well as the heavenly forces.

Who could stand that constant suffering?

40.1 And now, my children, I am fully aware of everything since it has been revealed to me by the Lord and has been seen by my eyes from beginning to end.

2 I am aware of everything and have recorded it in books, including the skies and their fullness, end, and marchings of all the armies.

3 The vast, incalculable number of stars that I have measured and described.

4 What guy has witnessed their entrances and revolutions? Even the angels cannot see their number, even though I have recorded all of their names.

5 I also counted the hours, measured the sun's circle, and measured its rays. I also wrote down everything that happens on the planet, including how the clouds live, what they are made of, how they spread their wings, and how they carry raindrops. I have also recorded how the earth is nourished, as well as all the plants, animals, and seeds that are produced there.

6 I looked into everything, wrote down the path taken by thunder and lightning, and was shown the guardians, keys, and places where they rise and go. It is released (gently) in measure by a chain so as not to violently hurl down the angry clouds and destroy everything on earth.

7 I noted the snow's treasure homes, as well as the cold and frosty airs' stores, and I noticed how their season's key-holder fills the clouds with them while not depleting the stores.

8 And I noted the resting places of the winds and observed and saw how their key holders carried scales and measures; first, they placed the weights in one scale, then in the other, and cleverly released them according to measure over the entire earth, so as not to cause the earth to tremble with their loud breathing.

9 Then I took measurements of the entire planet, including all of its mountains, hills, fields, trees, stones, and rivers. I also noted their heights relative to the seventh heaven and the lowest hell, as well as the judgment hall and the extremely large, open, and weeping hell.

10 I also observed the suffering of the captives while they awaited the final, final judgment.

11 I also recorded all of the people the judge was judging, along with all of their verdicts, sentencing, and works.

41.1 And when I saw Adam and Eva (Eve), I wept and sighed, saying, "Woe is me for my infirmity and (for that of) my forefathers." I then thought in my heart, "Blessed (is) the man who has not been born or who has been born and shall not sin before the Lord's face, that he come not into this place, nor bring the yoke of this place."

42.1 I witnessed the key-holders and gatekeepers of hell standing like enormous serpents, with faces like burning lamps, eyes of fire, and sharp teeth. I also observed all of the Lord's works and how they are righteous, in contrast to the mixed nature of human endeavors, some of which are good and others which are bad, and which reveal those who tell lies.

43.1 My children and I measured and recorded each work, each measure, and each just judgment.

2 As (one) year is more honorable than another, so (one) man is more honorable than another. Some are more honorable for great possessions, some are more honorable for wisdom of heart, some are more honorable for particular intellect, some are more honorable for cunning, some are more honorable for silence of the lips, others are more honorable for cleanliness, others are more honorable for strength, others are more honorable for comeliness, some are more honorable for youth, others are more honorable for

44.1 After making man with his own hands in the image of his own face, the Lord made him both little and large.

2 Whoever despises the face of the ruler and loathes the face of the Lord has scorned the Lord's face; he who vents his wrath on a man without harm will be cut down by the Lord's great wrath; and he who spits reproachfully on a man will be brought low by the Lord's great judgment.

3 Because on the day of the great judgment every weight, every measure, and every makeweight (will be) as in the market, that is, (they will be) hung on scales and stand in the market, (and each one) shall learn his own measure, and according to his measure shall take his reward), blessed is the man who does not direct his heart with malice against any man, and helps the injured and condemned, and raises the broken down, and shall do charity to the needy.

45.1 Whoever rushes to bring offerings before the Lord's face will, in turn, have the Lord speed up that offering by allowing him to complete his task.

2 However, if a person lights more candles in front of the Lord but does not use accurate discernment, the Lord will not enhance his wealth in the highest world.

3 When the Lord asks for bread, candles, animal meat, or any other sacrifice, it is meaningless; instead, God wants pure hearts, and all of that does is try a person's character.

46.1 Listen to what I have to say, my people, and take it all in.

2 Will an earthly ruler not be enraged with someone who brings gifts to him while harboring disloyal thoughts in his heart, refuse his gifts, and subject him to judgment?

3 Or if a person uses their tongue to deceive another while harboring bad intentions, will the other person not recognize his heart's betrayal and condemn him because it was obvious that he was lying?

4 And when the Lord sends a great light, there will be judgment for the righteous and the unrighteous, and no one will be able to hide.

47.1 And now, my children, give it some thought and pay close attention to what your father has said to you because it has all come from the Lord's mouth.

2 Read these books written in your father's handwriting.

3 From there are several books, you can learn about all of the works of the Lord—both those that have existed from the beginning of time and those that will do so until the end—in them.

4 Because there is no one else save the Lord, not in heaven, not on earth, not in the very lowest (places), not in the (one) foundation, you will not trespass against the Lord if you pay attention to what I write.

5 Who has counted the water and the foundation of the unfixed, or the dust of the earth, or the sand of the sea, or the drops of the rain, or the morning dew, or the wind's breathings? The Lord has laid the foundations in the unknown and has spread forth heavens visible (physical) and invisible (spiritual); he fixed the earth on the waters, and created countless creatures. Who has populated the land, the sea, and the eternal winter?

6 I created heaven, adorned it, and placed it in their midst after cutting the stars from fire.

48.1 He has two thrones on which he rests, rotating back and forth above the thrones of the months, from the seventeenth day of the month Tsivan to the month Thevan, from the seventeenth of Thevan it goes up. The sun travels along the seven heavenly circles, which are the appointment of one hundred and eighty-two thrones, that it goes down on a short day, and again one hundred and eighty-two, that it goes down on a big day.

2 As a result, when it gets close to the earth, it makes the earth happy and encourages the growth of its fruits. Conversely, when it gets far away, the earth is depressed, and all trees and fruits lack florescence.

3 He accurately timed the hours and fixed a measurement for both the visible (physical) and invisible (spiritual) elements. While remaining invisible (spiritual), he created everything that is seen (physical) from the invisible (spiritual).

5 In this way, I reveal to you, my children, and distribute the books to your offspring throughout all of your generations and to the nations who will have the wisdom to fear God. May these people accept the books and grow to love them more than food or earthly sweets, read them, and put them to use.

A severe punishment awaits those who do not comprehend the Lord, do not fear God, do not accept but reject, and do not accept the (books).

7 The one who drags them along while bearing their yoke is blessed because he will be set free on the day of the final judgment.

49.1 I make a promise to you, my children, but not in the presence of the heavens, the earth, or any other creature that God created.

2 The Lord declared, "There is no injustice or oath in me, only truth."

3 Let people swear with the words Yea, yea or Nay, nay if they are not truthful.

4 And I swear to you, yes, yes, that there has never been a man in his mother's womb; rather, there has always been a space prepared for the repose of that soul and a measure established as to how much a man is to be tested in this life.

5 Yes, kids, don't fool yourselves; every human soul has a location that has already been prepared for it.

50.1 I have documented every human being's contributions, so neither their identities nor their works can be kept secret.

Therefore, my children, spend the remaining days of your life with patience and humility so that you may receive eternal life.

4 Put up with every pain, damage, insult, and assault for the Lord's sake.

5 If bad things happen to you, don't take them out on your neighbors or your enemies because the Lord will take them out on you and be your vindicator on the day of great judgment, so there won't be any human vengeance in this world.

6 Whoever among you spends wealth or silver for the benefit of his brother will earn a plentiful reward in the hereafter.

7 Do not harm widows, orphans, or foreigners lest God's wrath befall you.

51.1 According to your abilities, extend your hands to the underprivileged.

2 Don't bury your silver in the ground.

3 Assist the faithful person who is suffering, and trouble will not come your way.

4 And bear all of the painful and severe yokes that are placed upon you for the glory of the Lord; in doing so, you will receive your reward on the day of judgment.

5 It is beneficial to visit the Lord's house in the morning, lunchtime, and evening for the honor of your creator.

6 Because everything that breathes glorifies him, and every living thing—both physical and spiritual—returns the favor.

52.1 The one who praises the Lord with his heart and opens his mouth to the God of Sabaoth is blessed.

2 Cursed is every man who opens his mouth to disparage and discredit his neighbor because by doing so, he discredits God.

3 He who opens his mouth in thanksgiving and praise to God is blessed.

4 Whoever opens his mouth to curse and abuse is cursed before the Lord all of his days.

5 He that blesses all the works of the Lord is blessed.

6 Whoever despises the Lord's creation will be cursed.

7 He who looks down and helps the downtrodden is blessed.

8 Cursed is the one who longs for the destruction of that which is not his.

9 He who maintains the steadfast foundations laid by his forefathers is blessed.

10 Cursed is the man who twists his ancestors' laws.

11 He who spreads peace and love is blessed.

12 He who disturbs those who love their neighbors is cursed.

13 He who addresses everyone with a humble heart and mouth is blessed.

14 He who speaks of peace with his words but has only a sword in his heart is cursed.

15 For on the day of the great judgment, all of these things will be made manifest in the books and the weighing scales.

53.1 And now, my children, do not pretend that your father is appealing to God for forgiveness of our sins because no one who has sinned has a helper.

2 You can see how I recorded every action taken by every man before he was created, as well as everything that has been done by all men throughout history. No one can read my writing, however, because the Lord is aware of how vain every thought is and where it is hidden in the heart's treasures.

3 And now, my children, pay close attention to everything I tell you about

your father lest you later ask yourself, "Why didn't our father tell us?"

54.1 At that point, if you didn't grasp this, let these books I've given you be an inheritance for your tranquility.

2 Give them to everyone who requests them, and instruct them so they can witness the Lord's extraordinarily vast and marvelous acts.

55.1 My children, see, the time and day of my term are drawing near.

2 Because they are waiting to hear what has been told to them while standing here on earth, the angels who will be traveling with me urge me to leave you.

3 Because I'm going to ascend to heaven tomorrow and go to the highest Jerusalem to claim my eternal inheritance.

4 As a result, I command you to carry out all of the Lord's good pleasure before his face.

56.1 After responding to his father Enoch, Mathosalam asked: "What is pleasing in your sight, father, that I may make before your face, that you may bless our homes, and your sons, and that your people may be made glorious through you, and then (that) you may depart thus, as the Lord said?"

2 Enoch replied to his son Mathosalam and said, "Listen, child, (there has been) no food in me from the time the Lord anointed me with the ointment of his glory, (and) my soul remembers no earthly enjoyment, neither do I desire anything earthly."

57.1 My child Methosalam, gather your family, friends, and elders so that I can speak with them and leave as it is intended for me to do.

2 Before the face of his father Enoch, Methosalam hurriedly gathered his brothers Regim, Riman, Uchan, Chermion, Gaidad, and all the elders of the community. He blessed them and said to them,

58.1"Listen to me today, my children."

2 After creating all of his creatures, including all reptiles and birds of the air, the Lord visited all of them in those days when he descended to earth for Adam's benefit. At that time, the Lord summoned all of the earth's animals and brought them before our ancestor Adam.

3 And Adam gave all living things on earth names.

4 Then the Lord made him the supreme ruler over everything, submitted everything to his control, and rendered everything deaf and dull so that it would do all he commanded.

5 In the same manner, the Lord made each man the lord of all his property.

6 Because men have a special place in the universe, the Lord will not judge a single animal soul for the sake of a man, but will instead evaluate human souls in relation to their animal counterparts.

7 And just as every human soul is assigned a specific number, so too will all of the animal souls that the Lord created survive until the final judgment, at which point they will accuse man of wrongdoing if they were mistreated.

59.1 Anyone who pollutes the soul of a beast also pollutes his own soul.

Because of this, man sacrifices clean creatures as atonement for sin in order to heal his soul.

3 And if they offer clean animals and birds as sacrifices, man is healed; his soul is healed.

4 Everything that has been given to you for food should be bound by its four feet in order to make good the cure and heal the soul.

5 But anyone who kills a beast without inflicting any wounds also murders and defiles his or her own soul.

6 And whoever secretly harms a beast in any way is engaging in bad deeds and pollutes his own soul.

60.1 There is no permanent remedy for the one who works the death of a man's soul; he also destroys his own soul and body.

2 Whoever places a guy in a trap will fall into it himself, and there will never be a way to get him out.

3 At the final, grand judgment, no one who puts a man in any vessel will escape punishment.

4 A person who acts dishonestly or speaks evil of another soul won't be able to obtain justice for themselves forever.

61.1 And now, my children, guard against any injustice in your hearts since the Lord detests it. I am aware of all things, and I know that in the great time to come there is much inheritance prepared for men, good for the good and bad for the bad, beyond number. Just as a man seeks something for his own soul from God, so let he do to every living soul.

2 Blessed are those who enter the excellent households, for there is neither peace nor release from them in the wicked houses.

3 Listen, my little and big ones! When a person has a good intention and offers the Lord presents from his labors that were not made by his hands, the Lord will turn away from the work of his hand and the man will be unable to locate the work of his hands.

4 Furthermore, if his hands succeeded but his heart continued to pound unabatedly, he would not benefit.

62.1 The one who patiently presents his gifts before the Lord's face in trust is blessed because he will get sins forgiveness.

2 But if he retracts his statements before the appointed time, there is no hope for him; similarly, if the appointed time has passed and he does not fulfill the pledge of his own free choice, there is no hope for him in the afterlife.

3 Because anything a man does before the time is an act of dishonesty in the eyes of other people and sin in the eyes of God.

63.1 Man shall receive reward from God when he covers the naked and feeds the hungry.

2 But if his heart quavers, he commits a double evil, ruining both himself and what he offers, and as a result, there will be no recompense for him.

3 He commits contempt, forfeits his ability to endure poverty, and will not receive compensation for his good works if his heart is full with his own food, flesh, and clothing.

4 Every arrogant and eloquent person is repulsive to the Lord, and every lie wrapped in a lie will be severed with the edge of the sword of death and sent into the fire where it will burn forever.

64.1 Everyone heard how the Lord was summoning Enoch when he had just finished speaking these things to his sons. They conferred together:

2 Let us go and kiss Enoch, and 2,000 men gathered and went to the location of Achuzan, where Enoch and his sons were.

3 Then all of the elders of the nation came, bent before Enoch, kissed him, and said: 4 "Our father Enoch, (may) you (be) blessed of the Lord, the eternal ruler, and now bless your sons and all the people, that we may be glorified today before your face."

5 Because the Lord picked you over all other men on earth and designated you as the writer of all of his creation—both visible and invisible—and as the redeemed one from human crimes as well as the helper of your household, you

will be exalted before the Lord's face forever.

65.1 Then Enoch addressed his entire audience, saying, "Listen, my children, before the Lord created all living things, He first created the visible (physical) and invisible (spiritual) things."

2 And as much time as there has been and has passed, realize that after all of that, he made man in his image, giving him eyes to see, ears to hear, a heart to reflect, and a mind to reason.

3 The Lord then saw all of humankind's creative endeavors, split time into its component parts, fixed the years, assigned the months, assigned the days, and assigned the number seven to the days.

4 For man to reflect on time and count years, months, and hours, (their) alternation, beginning, and end, and that he might count his own life, from the beginning until death, and consider his sin and write his work good and bad; because no work is hidden from the Lord, that every man might know his works and never break all his commandments, and that he might keep my handwriting from generation to generation.

5 Every person goes to the great judgment when all visible (physical) and invisible (spiritual) creation, as the Lord created it, comes to an end. At that point, time will have passed, including the years, and there will no longer be any months, days, or hours; they will be bound together and not be counted.

6 There will be one aeon, and all the righteous who will escape the Lord's great judgment will be gathered in it. For the righteous, the great aeon will begin, and they will live eternally; additionally, there won't be any work, illness, humiliation, anxiety, need, brutality, night, or darkness among them. Instead, there will be great light.

7 And they will have a huge impenetrable wall as well as a paradise that is eternal and bright. This is because all corruptible (mortal) things will perish and there will be eternal life.

66.1 Now guard your hearts from all forms of injustice, which the Lord detests.

2 Serve him alone while you tremble and run from fear in front of his face.

3 Bring all right offerings before the Lord's face, bowing down to the true God rather than to foolish idols. The Lord abhors injustice.

4 For the Lord sees all things; when a person thinks, they counsel their intellects, and every thought is constantly brought before the Lord, who founded the earth and placed all living things on it.

5 If you think about the sea's depths and all of the underworld, the Lord is there. If you look to heaven, the Lord is there.

6 For all things were created by the Lord. Do not worship man-made objects and turn away from the Creator of all things, for nothing can be concealed from the Lord's sight.

7 Walk, my children, in patience, meekness, honesty, provocation, grief, faith, and truth; rely on promises; endure illness, abuse, wounds, temptation, bareness, and privation; and show one another love until you pass from this age of ills and are heirs to all time.

8 Blessed are the righteous who escape the great judgment, for they will shine more brightly than the sun seven times, for in this world everything is taken away from the seventh part, including light, darkness, food, enjoyment, sorrow, paradise, torture, fire, and other things. He wrote everything down so that you could read it and understand it.

67.1 When Enoch finished speaking to the people, the Lord sent darkness upon the earth. This darkness covered the men who were standing next to Enoch, and they carried him up to the highest heaven, where the Lord (is). The Lord accepted Enoch and placed him before his face, and the darkness vanished from the earth, and light once more appeared.

2 Then, while not understanding how Enoch had been kidnapped, the people witnessed what had happened and worshiped God. They also discovered a roll on which The Invisible (spiritual) God was written, and everyone returned to their homes.

68.1 Enoch, who lived for 365 years, was born on the sixth day of the month of Tsivan.

He was raised to heaven on the first day of the month of Tsivan and stayed there for sixty days.

2 He recorded all these signs of the Lord's created universe, wrote 366 books, gave them to his sons, and spent 30 days on earth before being raised to heaven once more on the sixth day of the month Tsivan, at the exact time and date of his birth.

3 After calling everyone together, they prepared the sacrifice and offered it in front of the Lord.

4 Every man's nature in this life is dark, and that includes how he is conceived, born, and leaves this existence.

5 Everyone who attended the feast, including the community's elders and the entire congregation, brought gifts to give to the sons of Enoch.

6 He was born at the same hour he was conceived, and he passed away at the same time.

7 And they celebrated for three days, giving thanks to God for sending Enoch, who had won his favor, to give them this sign, and for telling them to pass it on to their sons from generation to generation, from age to age.

8 All the sons of Enoch, including Methosalam, hurriedly built an altar at the location known as Achuzan, from which and where Enoch had been transported to heaven.

9 Amen.

ENOCH 3
THE BOOK OF ENOCH A.I.

CHAPTER I
R. Ishmael ascends to heaven to view the vision of the Merkaba and is entrusted to Metatron.
And Enoch walked with God, but he was no longer there because God had taken him (Gen. v. 24).
The following are the words of Rabbi Ishmael:

(1) When I ascended on high to see the Merkaba and had entered the six Halls, one within the other:

(2) As soon as I arrived at the door of the seventh Hall, I stood still in prayer before the Holy One, blessed be He, and, lifting up my eyes on high (i.e. towards the Divine Majesty), I said:

(3) "Lord of the Universe, I pray that the merit of Aaron, the son of

(4) The Holy One, blessed be He, then despatched Metatron, his Servant ('Ebed) the angel, the Prince of the Presence, to me. He came to meet me, spreading his wings in great delight, to deliver me from their grasp.

(5) Then, in their presence, he grabbed hold of me and said, "Enter in peace before the high and exalted King3 and see the picture of the Merkaba."

(6) After entering the seventh Hall, he took me to the Shekina camp(s) and brought me before the Holy One, blessed be He, so I might see the Merkaba.

(7) The flame-breathing Seraphim and the princes of the Merkaba immediately focused their attention on me. The Holy One, blessed be He, scolded them, saying:

(8) "My servants, my Seraphim, my Kerubim, and my 'Ophanniml," and I immediately shook and fell to the ground,

benumbed by the bright image of their eyes and the glorious aspect of their faces. To prevent Ishmael from trembling or shuddering, please cover your eyes in front of him. He is my son, friend, cherished, and my glory.

(9) Metatron, the Prince of the Presence, then arrived and lifted my spirits and helped me up.

(10) After that (moment), I lacked the power to speak before the wonderful King—the mightiest of all monarchs and the most excellent of all princes—on the Throne of Glory until after the hour had passed.

(11) The Holy One, blessed be He, opened to me the gates of Shekina, peace, wisdom, strength, and power after an hour had passed. He also opened the gates of speech (dibbur), song, and qedushsha, as well as the gates of chant.

(12) He also used terms of psalm, song, praise, exaltation, gratitude, extolment, glorification, hymn, and eulogy to illuminate my eyes and my heart. The Holy Chayyoth beneath and above the Throne of Glory responded and said, "HOLY" and "BLESSED BE THE GLORY OF YHWH FROM HIS PLACE!" as I opened my mouth to sing before the Holy One, blessed be He.

(That is, recited the Qedushsha).

CHAPTER II

Metatron responds to questions from the highest grades of angels regarding R. Ishmael. R. Ishmael stated:

(1) At that time, the fiery 'Ophannim, consuming fire Seraphim, and Merkabah eagles addressed Metatron as

(2) "Youth! Why do you permit a lady to enter and view the Merkabah?

Which country or tribe does this one belong to? What is his personality?

(3) "From the nation of Israel, whom the Holy One, blessed be He, chose for his people from among seventy tongues (nations), from the tribe of Levi, whom he

set aside as a contribution to his name, and from the seed of Aaron, whom the Holy One, blessed be He, did choose for his servant and bestow upon him the crown of priesthood on Sinai," Metatron responded.

(4) They then said, "In fact, this one is worthy to see the Merkaba."

"Happy is the people that are in such a case!" they exclaimed.

Chapter III

Metatron has 70 names, yet God refers to him as "Youth".

(1) I enquired of Metatron, the angel and Prince of the Presence, "What is thy name," at that hour, R. Ishmael answered.

(2) In response, he said, "I have seventy names, corresponding to the seventy tongues of the world, and all of them are based upon the name Metatron, angel of the Presence; but my King calls me 'Youth' (Na'ar)."

CHAPTER IV

R. Ishmael stated: That Metatron is similar to Enoch, who was taken to heaven during the Deluge.

(1) I asked Metatron, "Why art thou named by the name of thy Creator, by seventy names? Why do they refer to you as "Youth" in the high heavens when you are greater than all princes, angels, and servants, and honored beyond all the powerful ones in kingship, magnificence, and glory?

(2) In response, I heard him say: "Since I am Enoch, Jared's son.

(3) Because the Holy One, blessed be He, removed me from their midst to serve as a witness against them in the high heavens to all peoples of the world so they would not say: "The Merciful One is cruel," when the generation of the flood sinned and were perplexed in their deeds, saying to God: "Depart from us,

for we desire not the knowledge of thy ways" (Job xxi. 14).

(4) What sin did those countless numbers of people commit that led to the destruction of the world along with them in the flood waters, together with their wives, children, cattle, horses, mules, and other livestock, as well as all of the world's birds?

(5) As a result, the Holy One, blessed be He, exalted me in front of their eyes throughout their lifetime to serve as a witness against them in the afterlife. Blessed be He, the Holy One chose me to be a prince and a ruler among the ministering angels.

(6) At that time, three ministering angels named 'UZZA, 'AZZA, and 'AZZAEL appeared and submitted accusations against me before the Holy One, blessed be He, saying:

"The Ancient Ones (First Ones) did not say to Thee rightly: 'Do not create man.'" Blessed be He who said, "I have made and I will bear, yea, I will carry and I will deliver," the Holy One said to them. (Is. xlviii.4)

(7) As soon as they noticed me, they bowed down to Him and said, "Lord of the Universe! What is this one that he is supposed to reach the heights of? Is he not one of the descendants of those who died during the time of the Flood?
What does he do in the region?

(8) The Holy One, blessed be He, responded once more and questioned them, asking: "What are ye, that ye enter and talk in my presence? Because I love this person more than I love any of you, he will be your prince and head of state in the high heavens.

(9) Everyone then got up, came out to greet me, knelt down in front of me, and exclaimed, "Happy art thou and happy is thy father for thy Creator doth favor thee."

(10) They refer to me as "Youth" (Na'ar) since I am small and a youth among them in terms of days, months, and years.

CHAPTER V
God removes the idols because of the generation of Enosh's idolatry.

Shekina, a human. The worship that 'Azza, 'Uzza, and 'Azziel inspired

R. Ishmael stated: "Metatron, the Prince of the Presence, said to me: (1) Shekina was residing on a Kerub under the Tree of Life from the day the Holy One, blessed be He, drove the first Adam out of the Garden of Eden (and onward)."

(2) In order to carry out His will across the entire universe, the ministering angels gathered and descended from the skies in groups, from the Raqia in organizations, and from the heavens in camps.

(3) The first man and his generation were waiting outside the Garden's entrance to see the Shekina's magnificent presence.

(4) For the splendor of the Shekina was 365,000 times greater than the splendor of the sun's sphere, and it crossed the globe from end to end. Everyone who took advantage of the Shekina's splendor was free from illness and pain, and neither flies nor gnats were able to rest on them. He was not possessed by any demons, nor were they able to harm him.

(5) When the Holy One, blessed be He, traveled from the Garden to Eden, from Eden to the Garden, from the Garden to Raqia, and from Raqia to the Garden of Eden, everyone saw the beauty of His Shekina and was unharmed;

(6) this continued until the generation of Enosh, who was the leader of all idolaters in the world at the time.

(7) What did the Enosh generation do? They traveled the globe, bringing precious stones, pearls, and silver in heaps the size of mountains and hills, which they used to fashion idols that were worshipped all over the world. They built the idols all throughout the earth, each measuring 1000 parasangs in height.

(8) Then they brought the sun, moon, planets, and constellations down to earth and set them in front of the idols on their right and left sides, as they do with the Holy One, blessed be He, as it is stated in 1 Kings xxii.19: "And all the host of heaven was standing by him on his right hand and on his left."

(9) What ability did they possess that allowed them to bring them down? If not for 'Uzza, 'Azza, and 'Azziel teaching them sorceries that they used to bring them down, they would not have been able to do so.

(10) During that time, the ministering angels accused them in front of the Holy One, blessed be He, saying: "Master of the World! What do the children of men have to do with thee? According to the verse in Psalm viii that reads, "What is man (Enosh) that thou art mindful of him?" 'Mah Adam' is not written here; rather, 'Mah Enosh' is, as he (Enosh) is the leader of the idolaters.

(11) Why have you left the highest of the high heavens, where your majestic 84 Name resides, and the high and exalted Throne in "Araboth Raqia" in the highest, and gone to live among them who worship idols and consider you to be an idol?

(12) Both you and the idols are currently present on earth. What do the people who live on earth and worship idols have to do with thee?

(13) The Holy One, may He be praised, immediately raised His Shekina from the ground, in the midst of them. (14) At that very moment, the army of 'Araboth in ten thousand camps and a thousand hosts, the troops of hosts, and the ministering angels appeared. They fetched trumpets, took the horns in their hands, and surrounded the Shekina with a variety of melodies.As it is said in Psalm xlvii:5 that "God has gone up with a shou" (God has ascended to the lofty sky), He did so.

CHAPTER VI

God banishes the Shekina from earth as a result of the idolatry of the Enosh generation. The worship that 'Azza, 'Uzza, and 'Azziel inspired

R. Ishmael stated: "Metatron, the Prince of the Presence, said to me:

(1) Shekina was residing on a Kerub under the Tree of Life from the day the Holy One, blessed be He, drove the first Adam out of the Garden of Eden (and onward)."

(2) In order to carry out His will across the entire universe, the ministering angels gathered and descended from the skies in groups, from the Raqia in organizations, and from the heavens in camps.

(3) The first man and his generation were waiting outside the Garden's entrance to see the Shekina's magnificent presence.

(4) For the splendor of the Shekina was 365,000 times greater than the splendor of the sun's sphere, and it crossed the globe from end to end. Everyone who took advantage of the Shekina's splendor was free from illness and pain, and neither flies nor gnats were able to rest on them. He was not possessed by any demons, nor were they able to harm him.

(5) When the Holy One, blessed be He, traveled from the Garden to Eden, from Eden to the Garden, from the Garden to Raqia, and from Raqia to the Garden of Eden, everyone saw the beauty of His Shekina and was unharmed; (6) this continued until the generation of Enosh, who was the leader of all idolaters in the world at the time. (7) What did the Enosh generation do? They traveled the globe, bringing precious stones, pearls, and silver in heaps the size of mountains and hills, which they used to fashion idols that were worshiped all over the world. They built the idols all throughout the earth, each measuring 1000 parasangs in height.

(8) Then they brought the sun, moon, planets, and constellations down to earth and set them in front of the idols on their right and left sides, as they do with the Holy One, blessed be He, as it is stated in 1 Kings xxii.19: "And all the host of heaven was standing by him on his right hand and on his left."

(9) What ability did they possess that allowed them to bring them down? If not for 'Uzza, 'Azza, and 'Azziel teaching them sorceries that they used to bring them down, they would not have been able to do so.

(10) During that time, the ministering angels accused them in front of the Holy One, blessed be He, saying: "Master of the World! What do the children of men have to do with thee? According to the verse in Psalm viii that reads, "What is man (Enosh) that thou art mindful of him?" 'Mah Adam' is not written here; rather, 'Mah Enosh' is, as he (Enosh) is the leader of the idolaters.

(11) Why have you left the highest of the high heavens, where your majestic 84 Name resides, and the high and exalted Throne in "Araboth Raqia" in the highest, and gone to live among them who worship idols and consider you to be an idol?

(12) Both you and the idols are currently present on earth. What do the people who live on earth and worship idols have to do with thee?

(13) The Holy One, may He be praised, immediately raised His Shekina from the ground, in the midst of them. (14) At that very moment, the army of 'Araboth in ten thousand camps and a thousand hosts, the troops of hosts, and the ministering angels appeared. They fetched trumpets, took the horns in their hands, and surrounded the Shekina with a variety of melodies.As it is said in Psalm xlvii. 5: "God is gone up with a shout, the Lord with the sound of a trumpet," He then ascension to the high sky.

CHAPTER VI
Enoch and the Shekina were both transported to heaven.

(1) When angels protest, God responds.
R. Ishmael stated: "When the Holy One, blessed be He, desired to lift me up on high, He first sent 'Anaphiel H (H =Tetragrammaton) the Prince, and he took me from their midst in their sight and carried me in great glory upon a flaming chariot with flaming horses, servants of glory." Along with the Shekina, he raised me to the lofty sky.

(2) As soon as I reached the high heavens, the Holy Chayyoth, the 'Ophannim, the Seraphim, the Kerubim, the Wheels of the Merkaba (the Galgallim), and the ministers of the consuming fire, perceiving my smell from a distance of 365,ooo myriads of parasangs, said: "What smell of one born of woman and what taste of a white drop (is this) that ascends on high, and (lo, he is merely) a gnat among those who 'divide flames (of fire)'?"

(3) The Holy One, may He be praised, responded and addressed them, saying, "My slaves, my hosts, my Kerubim, my 'Ophannim, and my Seraphim! Do not let this cause you to be angry! I have withdrawn my Shekina from among them and have hoisted it up on high since all the children of men have rejected me and my vast Kingdom and have gone out to serve other gods. Although he is equal to all of them in terms of faith, righteousness, and perfection of deed, the person I have chosen from among them is an ELECT ONE among (the inhabitants of) the world, and I have chosen him as (as) a tribute from my world beneath all the skies.

CHAPTER VII
Enoch ascended to the location of the Throne, the Merkaba, and the heavenly hosts on the wings of the Shekina.

R. Ishmael stated:

(1) "When the Holy One, blessed be He, took me away from the Flood generation, he lifted me on the wings of the wind of Shekina to the highest heaven and brought me into the great palaces of the "Araboth Raqia" on high, where are the glorious Throne of Shekina, the Merkaba, the troops of wrath, the armies of vehemence, the fiery Shin'anim," the And he appointed me to regularly attend the Throne of Glory.

CHAPTER VIII

Metatron entered through the opened gates of the heavenly treasures.
R. Ishmael reported that Metatron, the Prince of the Presence, spoke to him as follows:

(1) The Holy One, blessed be He, opened to me 300,000 gates of Understanding before He designated me to serve the Throne of Glory. Thirty thousand gates of subtilty
Three Hundred Thousand Doors of Life, Grace, and Loving-Kindness, Three Hundred Thousand Doors of Love, and Three Hundred Thousand Doors of Tora thirty thousand gates of meekness, thirty thousand gates of upkeep, and thirty thousand gates of mercy
thirty thousand gates of heaven's terror
(2) The Holy One, blessed be He, added to me at that time knowledge after knowledge, understanding after understanding, subtlety after subtlety, mercy after mercy, instruction after instruction, love after love, loving-kindness after loving-kindness, goodness after goodness, meekness after meekness, power after power, strength after strength, might after might, brilliance after brilliance, beauty after beauty, and splendor after splendor, and I was honored.

CHAPTER IX

Enoch is blessed by the Most High and adorned with angelic characteristics in chapter nine.
Metatron, the Prince of the Presence, spoke these words to me, according to R. Ishmael:

"(1) The Holy One, blessed be He, put His hand upon me and blessed me with 5360 blessings after all these things."
(2) I was also magnified and grown to be as big as the entire planet.
(3) And He gave me 72 wings—36 on each side—by giving them to me. And every wing was as big as the entire world.
(4) And He set 365 eyes on me, each as bright as a vast luminary.
The splendor, brilliance, radiance, and beauty He left in (all) the lights of the universe were all directed at me.

CHAPTER X

Ishmael said: Metatron, the Prince of the Presence, said to me:

(1) All these things the Holy One, blessed be He, made for me:He made me a Throne, similar to the Throne that the Holy One, blessed be He, made for Himself. Metatron, the Prince of the Presence, said to me:
(2) He made me a Throne, similar to the Throne that the Holy One, blessed be He, made for Himself. And He extended a dazzling, beautiful, gracious, and merciful curtain over me, resembling the one covering the Throne of Glory, with all the lights of the cosmos concentrated on it.
(3) Then He seated me on it and set it at the entrance to the Seventh Hall.
(4) The herald then announced: "This is Metatron, my servant," and he traveled to every heaven.
With the exception of the eight great princes—the honored and adored ones who are known as YHWH—by the name of their King, I have made him a prince and a ruler over all the princes of my kingdoms and over all the children of heaven.

(5) And each angel and each prince who has something to say in my presence (before me) will enter his presence (before him) and speak to him.

(6 And you are to obey and carry out whatever directive he issues to you in my name. I have promised to teach him from the Prince of Wisdom and the Prince of Understanding the wisdom of heavenly and earthly things, the wisdom of this world and the world to come.

(7) In addition, I have placed him in charge of all the palapes of Araboih's coffers and all the life-giving supplies I possess in the upper heavens.

Chapter XI
God discloses to Metatron all of the mysteries and secrets.

(1) The Holy One, blessed be He, has since revealed to me all the mysteries of Tora, all the secrets of wisdom, and all the depths of the Perfect Law; in addition, all living things' innermost thoughts, all the universe's secrets, and all the secrets of Creation have been revealed to me, just as they have been revealed to the Creator of Creation. This is what R. Ishmael said: "Metatron, the angel, the Prince of the Presence, said to me: "

(2) I kept a close eye out to see the fascinating mystery and the depth's hidden secrets. I witnessed it before a man secretly thought about it, and I beheld it before a man created anything.

(3) Furthermore, nothing was hidden from me in the deep or up high.

Chapter XII
Metatron is given a regal crown, a garment of majesty, and the moniker "the Lesser YHWH" by God.
R. Ishmael stated: "Metatron, the Prince of the Presence, spoke to me:

(1) Because the Holy One, blessed be He, loved me with a love greater than all the children of heaven, He created me a garment of glory, and He dressed me in it.

(2) He also created me an honorable robe that was adorned with various forms of beauty, splendor, brilliance, and majesty.

(3) He then created for me a regal crown that was set with 49 pricey stones that resembled the sun's brilliance.

(4) For its splendor permeated the seven heavens, the four corners of the world, the four quadrants of the "Araboth Raqia," and all of them. He then placed it on my head.

(5) In front of His entire heavenly household, He addressed me as THE LESSER YHWH, as it is said in Exodus xxiii. 21: "For my name is in him."

Chapter XIII
Because the Holy One, blessed be He, loved and treasured me more than all the children of heaven, He wrote with His ringer with a flaming style upon the crown on my head the letters by which were created heaven and earth.
R. Ishmael said: "Metatron, the angel, the Prince of the Presence, the Glory of all heavens, said to me: "

(1) Because the Holy One, blessed be He, loved and treasured me more than all the children of

(2) Every single letter also continuously sent out what appeared to be lightning, torches, flames of fire, and (rays) that appeared to represent the rising of the sun, moon, and planets.

Chapter XIV
the foundational angels, all the highest princes, and the

(1) When they see Metatron crowned, planetary and sideric angels experience fear and trembling.

When the Holy One, blessed be He, placed this crown on my head, all the princes of kingdoms who are at the height of 'Araboth Raqiaf and all the hosts of every heaven — even the princes of the 'Elim, the princes of the 'Er'ellim, and the princes of the Tafsarim, who are superior to all the ministering angels who minister before the Throne of 87 G — trembled before

(2) Even Sammael, the Prince of the Accusers, who is superior to all princes of high realms, trembled and frightened before me.

(3) Even the angel of fire, the angel of hail, the angel of the wind, the angel of the lightning, the angel of anger, the angel of the thunder, the angel of the snow, and the angel of the rain; and the angel of the day, the angel of the night, the angel of the sun, the angel of the moon, the angel of the planets, and the angel of the constellations who rule the world under their hands, feared and trembled and were troubled

(4) These are the titles of the world's rulers: Gabriel, the angel of fire, Baradiel, the angel of hail, Ruchiel, appointed over the wind, Baraqiel, appointed over the lightning, Za'amiel, appointed over the vehemence, Ziqiel, appointed over the sparks, appointed over the commotion, Zdaphiel, appointed over the storm-wind, Ra'amiel, appointed over the thunders, Rctashiel, appointed over the earthquake, and Shalgiel

"Ophanniel, who is designated over the moon's surface, Kokbiel, who is designated over the planets, and Rahatiel, who is designated over the constellations.

(5) When they saw me, they all prostrated themselves. And because of the majestic splendor and beauty of the appearance of the brilliant light of the crown of glory upon my head, they were unable to see me.

Chapter XV
Metatron changed into flames.

(1) As soon as the Holy One, blessed be He, took me in (His) service to attend the Throne of Glory and the Wheels (Galgallim) of the Merkaba and the needs of Shekina, immediately my flesh was changed into flames, my sinews into flaming fire, my bones into coals of burning juniper, the light of my eyelids into splendor of lightnings, and my eyeballs into fire-bran. R. Ishma

(2) In addition, there were six divisions of blazing flames on my right, firebrands on my left, stormwinds and a tempest all around me, and thunderclaps and an earthquake in front of and behind me.

ASCENSION OF MOSES FRAGMENT

(1) Metatron, the Prince of the Presence and the Prince over All Princes, is standing in front of Him who is greater than all the Elohim, according to R. Ishmael. He then enters beneath the Throne of Glory. He also has a sizable light tabernacle in the sky.

To prevent the Holy Chayyoth from hearing the voice of the Word (Dibbur) that emanates from the Divine Majesty's mouth, he summons the fire of deafness and pours it into their ears.

(2) After reaching his highest point, Moses fasted for 121 days until the habitations of the chashmal were shown to him. He then saw the lion's heart inside its body and the countless armies of hosts gathered around him. And they wanted to set him on fire. But Moses pleaded for mercy, first for Israel and then for himself. As a result, the One who sits atop the Merkaba opened the windows over the Kerubim's heads.

The Prince of the Presence, Metatron, joined a group of 1800 advocates as they traveled to meet Moses. They then used the prayers of Israel as a crown for the Holy One, may He always be blessed.

(3) And they exclaimed, "Hear, O Israel; the Lord our God is one Lord," in reference to Deuteronomy chapter four, and their faces beamed with joy at Shekina. Subsequently, they asked

Metatron, "What are these? And to whom do they accord all of this glory and honor? "To the Glorious Lord of Israel," they replied. "Hear, O Israel: The Lord, our God, is one Lord," they cried. Who else but You, YHWH, the Divine Majesty, the King, living and eternal, shall be given great honor and majesty?

(4) Akatriel Yah Yehod Sebaoth said to Metatron, the Prince of the Presence, at that same instant, "Let no prayer that he prays before me return (to him) void.

Hear his petition and grant his request, no matter how big or small.

(5) Next, Metatron, the Prince of the Presence, addressed Moses, calling him "Son of Amram! Do not be afraid because God loves you right now. And then make your request to the Glory and Majesty. Because of this, thy face is radiant from one end of the globe to the other. Moses said, "I fear lest I bring guilt upon myself," in response to his question. Receive the letters of the oath, in (by) which there is no breaking the covenant, said Metatron, negating any possible breach of the bond.

CHAPTER XVI 1

As a result of Acher mistaking Metatron for a second Divine Power, he was likely further stripped of his right to rule from a throne of his own. Metatron, the Angel, the Prince of the Presence, and the Glory of all heaven, spoke to me, according to R. Ishmael, and said: "

(1) At first, I was sitting upon a huge Throne at the door of the Seventh Hall, and I was ruling the children of heaven, the household on high, by authority of the Holy One, blessed be He. The princes of kingdoms were standing in front of me, on my right and on my left, under the authority of the Holy One, blessed be He, as I presided in the Celestial Court (Yeshiba), and I distributed Greatness, Kingship, Dignity, Rulership, Honor and Praise, as well as the Diadem and Crown of Glory to all of them.

(2) However, when Acher arrived to see the Merkaba and fixed his eyes on me, he trembled and feared before me, and his soul was so terrified of me that it fled from him because of fear, horror, and dread of me, when he saw me sitting on a throne like a king with all the ministering angels serving me and all the princes of kingdoms surrounding me wearing crowns:

(3) He then said, "In fact, there are two Divine Powers in heaven," as soon as he opened his mouth.

(4) Bath Qol, also known as the Divine Voice, then uttered the following words from heaven before the Shekina: "Return, ye backsliding children (Jer. iii. 22), except Acher!"

(5) Then the Holy One, blessed be He, sent "Aniyel, the Prince, the honored, glorified, beloved, marvelous, revered and scary one, and He gave me sixty blows with lashes of fire and made me stand on my feet.

CHAPTER XVII

The princes of the seven heavens, the sun, the moon, the planets, the stars, and their respective angelic suites
Says R. Ishmael

(1) Seven (are) the princes, the great, beautiful, adored, marvelous and honored ones who are appointed over the seven heavens, said Metatron, the angel, the Prince of the Presence, the splendor of all skies. Those are they, then: BAKARIEL, BADARIEL, PACHRIEL, GABRIEL, SHATQIEL, SHACHAQIEL, and MIKAEL.

(2) Each of them is a prince among the hosts of (one) heaven. And there are 496,000 myriads of ministering angels who surround each of them.

(3) The seventh heaven, the highest one, located in the 'Araboth, is given to

MIKAEL, the mighty prince. The sixth heaven, which is located in Makon, is under the control of GABRIEL, the 89th prince of the host.

The fifth heaven, which is located in Ma'on, is overseen by SHATAQIEL, prince of the host.

SHAHAQi'EL, prince of the host, is given charge of Zebul's fourth heaven.

The third heaven, which is located in Shehaqim, is under the direction of BADARIEL, prince of the host.

BARAKIEL, prince of the host, is given charge of the second heaven, which is located in (Merom) Raqia's height.

PAZRIEL, prince of the host, is given charge of Wilon, the first heaven, which is located in Shamayim.

(4) Under them is GALGALLIEL, the prince designated as in charge of the sun's globe (galgal), and he is accompanied by 96 magnificent and honored angels who move the sun in Raqia'.

'OPHANNIEL, the prince who is seated above the moon's globe ('ophari), is underneath them. When the moon is at its turning point in the East each night, 88 angels work with him to move the moon's globe 354 thousand parasangs.

When does the moon reach its turning point while it is sitting in the East? the fifteenth day of each month, to be exact.

(6) The prince designated to oversee the constellations is RAHATIEL, who is placed under them.

Additionally, he is escorted by 72 powerful and revered angels. And why is RAHATIEL his name? Because he directs 339 thousand parasangs to travel from the East to the West and from the West to the East every night, making the stars run (marhit) in their orbits. Since the sun, moon, planets, and stars all migrate at night from the West to the East, the Holy One, blessed be He, has created a tent for them all.

(7) The prince assigned to rule over all the planets is KOKBIEL, who is under them. Additionally, he is accompanied by 365,000 myriads of ministering angels, mighty and illustrious beings who transport the planets from one city to another and from one province to another in the Raqia' of skies.

(8) And standing tall over them are 72 PRINCES OF KINGDOMS, which correspond to the 72 languages spoken throughout the world. And they are all dressed in royal attire, wearing royal crowns, and swathed in royal cloaks. Additionally, each of them is carrying a royal sceptre while riding on regal horses. The royal servants that accompany each of them when they travel in Raqia' do so in tremendous splendor and majesty, just as they do when they are on earth when they ride in chariots with horses and massive armies and do so in splendor, magnificence, acclaim, song, and honor.

CHAPTER XVIII
The ranking of the angels and the respect shown to the higher ranks by the lower ranks, The angel Metatron, the Prince of the Presence, and the splendor of all heaven, according to R. Ishmael, stated to me: "

(1) THE ANGELS OF THE FIRST HEAVEN, when(ever) they see their prince, they dismount from their horses and fall on their faces."

When THE PRINCE OF THE FIRST HEAVEN spots THE PRINCE OF THE SECOND HEAVEN, he dismounts, takes off his crown of splendor, and falls to the ground.

When THE PRINCE OF THE THIRD HEAVEN appears, THE PRINCE OF THE SECOND HEAVEN takes off his crown of splendor and collapses to the ground.

When THE PRINCE OF THE THIRD HEAVEN meets the prince of the fourth heaven, he takes off his crown of splendor and collapses to the ground.

And when THE PRINCE OF THE FOURTH HEAVEN sees the prince of the fifth heaven, he takes off his crown of splendor and collapses to the ground.

When the prince of the sixth heaven approaches, the prince of the fifth heaven removes his crown of splendor and collapses to the ground.

When THE PRINCE OF THE SIXTH HEAVEN sees the prince of the 90th seventh heaven, he takes off his crown of glory and collapses to the ground.

(2) When THE PRINCE OF THE SEVENTH HEAVEN sees THE SEVENTYTWO PRINCES OF KINGDOMS, he takes off his crown of glory and collapses to the ground.

(3) The 72 princes of nations take off their regal crowns and collapse to the ground as they witness THE DOOR KEEPERS OF THE FIRST HALL IN THE ARABOTH RAQIA in the highest position.

When THE DOOR KEEPERS OF THE FIRST HALL see THE DOOR KEEPERS OF THE SECOND HALL, they take off their crowns of glory and collapse to the ground.

When THE DOOR KEEPERS OF THE THIRD HALL approach, THE DOOR KEEPERS OF THE SECOND HALL take off their crowns of glory and fall to their knees.

When THE DOOR KEEPERS OF THE THIRD HALL see THE DOOR KEEPERS OF THE FOURTH HALL, they take off their crowns of glory and collapse to the ground.

When THE DOOR KEEPERS OF THE FOURTH HALL see THE DOOR KEEPERS OF THE FIFTH HALL, they take off their crowns of glory and collapse to the ground.

When THE DOOR KEEPERS OF THE FIFTH HALL see THE DOOR KEEPERS OF THE SIXTH HALL, they take off their crowns of glory and collapse to the ground.

When THE DOOR KEEPERS OF THE SIXTH HALL notice THE DOOR KEEPERS OF THE SEVENTH HALL, they take off their crowns of glory and collapse to the ground.

(4) And the doorkeepers of the seventh Hall remove the crown(s) of glory from the heads of THE FOUR GREAT PRINCES, the honored ones, WHO ARE APPOINTED OVER THE FOUR CAMPS OF SHEKINA, and fall on their faces.

(5) The four great princes take off their crowns of glory and collapse to the ground when they see TAG'AS, the prince, standing at the head of all the children of heaven, great and honored with song (and) praise.

(6) And Tag' ael, the illustrious prince, removes the crown of glory from his head and collapses to the ground upon seeing BARATTIEL, the illustrious prince of three fingers, in the height of 'Araboth, the highest heaven.

(7) And when Barattiel, the great prince, sees HAMON, the great prince, the feared and honored, pleasant and terrifying one who causes all the children of heaven to tremble, when the time draws near (that is set) for the saying of the "(Thrice) Holy," as it is written (Isa. xxxiii. 3): "At the noise of the tumult (hamon) the peoples are fled; at the lifting up

(8) And when Hamon, the great prince, sees TUTRESIEL, the great prince, he takes off his crown of glory and collapses to the ground.

(9) When Tutresiel H', the great prince, recognizes ATRUGIEL, the great prince, he takes off his crown of glory and collapses to the ground.

(10) When Atrugiel the Great Prince meets NA'ARIRIEL H', the Great Prince, he takes off his crown of glory and collapses to the ground.

(11) When Na'aririel H', the great prince, meets SASNIGIEL H', the great prince, he takes off his crown of glory and collapses to the ground.

(12) Sasnigiel H' then removes his crown of splendor from his head and collapses to the ground upon seeing ZAZRIEL H', the great prince.

13) When Zazriel H', the prince, recognizes GEBURATIEL H', the prince, he takes off his crown of glory and collapses to the ground.

(14) And when the prince 'ARAPHIEL H' appears, Geburatiel H', the prince, takes off his crown of glory and collapses on the ground.

(15) And "Araphiel H," the prince, takes the crown of glory from his head and collapses to the ground upon seeing "ASHRUYLU," the prince, who preside over all meetings of the children of heaven.

(16) And Ashruylu H, the prince, removes the crown of glory from his head and collapses to the ground when he sees GALLISUR H', THE PRINCE WHO REVEALS ALL THE SECRETS OF THE LAW (Tora).

(17) Gallisur H', the prince, then takes off his crown of glory and collapses to the ground upon seeing ZAKZAKIEL H', the prince chosen to record Israel's merits on the Throne of Glory.

(18) And when Zakzakiel H', the great prince, sees 'ANAPHIEL H', the prince who guards the heavenly Halls' keys, he takes off his crown of glory and collapses to the ground. Why is he referred to as "Anaphiel"? Because all of the chambers of 'Araboth Raqia are covered in (overshadowed by) the branches of his honor, majesty, crown, splendor, and brilliance, just as the Maker of the World does. Similar to how it is stated of the Creator of the World (Hab. iii. 3): "His glory covered the heavens, and the earth was full of his praise," 'Anaphiel's honor

and majesty cover all of 'Araboth the highest splendour.

(19) And when he sees SOTHER "ASHIEL H," the prince, the mighty, revered, and honored one, he takes off his crown of splendor and collapses to the ground.

Why is Sother Ashiel his name? Because every prince who leaves or enters before the Shekina does so solely with his consent and because he is appointed over the four heads of the flaming river opposite the Throne of Glory.

He has been given the keys to the flaming river's seals. Additionally, he stands 7000 myriads of parasangs tall. He then goes out and enters before the Shekina to explain what is written (recorded) about the world's people. He also stirs up the river's fire. The books were opened, as it is said in Daniel vii. 10: "the judgment was set."

(20) Sother 'Ashiel the prince pulls his crown of splendor from his head and collapses to the ground when he sees SHOQED CHOZI, the great prince, the mighty, dreadful, and honored one.

Why is he known as Shoqed Chozi?

Because, in the sight of the Holy One, may God Bless Him, he balances all the merits (of man).

(21) And when he sees ZEHANPURYU H', the mighty and terrifying one who is revered, adored, and dreaded throughout the entire heavenly household, he takes off the crown of glory from his head and collapses to the ground.

Why is Zehanpuryu his name? Because he chastises the raging river and forces it to return to its proper place.

(22) And when he sees 'AZBUGA H', the great prince, glorified, revered, honored, adorned, marvelous, exalted, beloved, and feared among all the great princes who understand the mystery of the Throne of Glory, he takes off the crown of glory from his head and collapses to the ground. Why is he known as "Azbuga"?

Because he will eventually gird (clothe) the upright and devout of the earth in the clothes of life and envelop them in the cloak of life so that they may live an eternal existence in them.

(23) He then takes off his crown of glory and collapses to the ground when he notices the two powerful, glorified princes standing over him. The two princes' names are as follows:

The great prince, the honourable, glorified, blameless, venerable, old, and mighty one SOPHERIEL H' (WHO) KILLETH, (Sopheriel H' the Killer), and SOPHERIEL H' (WHO) MAKETH ALIVE (Sopheriel H' the Lifegiver), the great prince, the blameless, venerable, ancient, and mighty one.

(24) Why is he referred to as Sopheriel H' the Killer (Sopheriel H' the killer)? Because he has been given control over the dead people's records, everyone must enter their names in the books of the dead when their death date approaches.

What does it mean when he is referred to as Sopheriel H' who maketh alive (Sopheriel H' the Lifegiver)? He is in charge of the books of the living (of life) by MAQOM, therefore he records every person the Holy One, blessed be He, will bring into life in the book of the living (of life). Maybe you might say: "They also sit when writing because the Holy One, blessed be He, is sitting on a throne." (Answer): According to the Bible, "And all the host of heaven are standing by him" (1 Kings xxii. 19, 2 Chron. xviii. 18).

According to legend, "the host of heaven" was created to demonstrate to us that even the Great Princes, none of whom exist in the upper heavens, cannot fulfill the Shekina's wishes while seated. But given that they are standing, how is it conceivable that they can write?

It is as follows:

(25) One is standing on the tempest's wheels, and the other is on the storm-wind's wheels.

The one is dressed like a king, while the other is dressed like a king.

Both of them are shrouded in a garment of majesty, one more so than the other.

Both are crowned with royal crowns: the one on the left and the other on the right.

Both the other's and the first person's bodies are covered in eyes.

The appearance of one is comparable to that of lightning, while the appearance of the other is comparable to that of lightning.

The eyes of one are powerful like the sun, while the eyes of the other are powerful like the sun.

The height of one is comparable to the height of the seven heavens, while the height of the other is comparable to the height of the seven heavens.

The wings of one are equal to the number of days in a year, while the wings of the other are equal to the number of days in a year.

Raqia's width is covered by the wings of one, while Raqia's width is covered by the wings of the other.

One's lips are like the East's gates, while the other's lips are like the East's gates.

Both tongues are as high as the waves of the sea, with the tongue of one being higher than the other.

A flame emerges from the mouth of the first, and another flame emerges from the mouth of the second.

Lightning erupts from the mouths of the two individuals, one more powerful than the other.

Fire is ignited from one person's sweat, and from the other person's perspiration.

A torch is burning from the tongue of one, and another torch is burning from the tongue of the other.

A sapphire stone is on the head of the first, and a sapphire stone is on the head of the second.

One has a wheel of a swift cherub on their shoulders, and the other has a wheel of a rapid cherub.

One person has a burning scroll in his hand, while the other also holds a burning scroll.

Both men hold flame styles in their hands, one more than the other.

The scroll is 3000 myriads of parasangs in length, the style is 300 myriads of parasangs in width, and each letter they write is 365 parasangs in height.

CHAPTER XIX
Rikbiel, the ruler of the Merkabah's wheels. the area around the Merkaba. At the time of the Qedushsha, Metatron, the Angel, the Prince of the Presence, spoke to me and described the turmoil among the angelic hosts as follows:

(1) Above 2 these three angels, these great princes, there is one Prince, distinguished, honored, noble, glorified, adorned, fearful, valiant, strong, great, magnified, glorious, crowned, wonderful, exalted, blameless, beloved, lordly, high and lofty, ancient and mighty The magnificent and adored Prince who is by the Merkaba is identified as RIKBIEL H'.

(2) Why is he known as RIKBIEL?

The Merkaba's wheels are under his control because he has been given authority over them.

(3) How many wheels are there in total? Eight; two going each way. Additionally, four winds surround them on all sides. "The Storm-Wind," "The Tempest," "The Strong Wind," and "The Wind of Earthquake" are their names.

(4) And beneath them, one scorching river flows on each side of four continuously flowing rivers. Four clouds are planted (put) around them, between the rivers. They are "clouds of fire," "clouds of lamps," "clouds of coal," and "clouds of brimstone," and they are leaning up against [their] wheels.

(5) The Chayyoth's feet are also resting on the wheels. Additionally, an earthquake is roaring and thunder is storming between each wheel.

(6) And when the time for the recital of the Song is drawing near, (then) the multitudes of wheels are moved, the multitude of clouds tremble, all the chieftains (shallishim) are made afraid, all the horsemen (parashim) do rage, all the mighty ones (gibborim) are excited, all the hosts (seba'im), all the troops (gedudim), all the appointed ones (memunnim), and all the

(7) And each wheel emits a sound that may be heard by the others, with each Kerub, Chayya, and Seraph (speaking) (Ps. lxviii. 5) "Extol to him who rides in 'Araboth, by his name Jah and rejoice before him!"

Metatron, the angel and Prince of the Presence, told me: "

CHAPTER XX

(1) Above these, there is one great and mighty prince," according to CHAYYLIEL, the prince of the Chayyoth R. Ishmael. His name is CHAYYLIEL H, and he is a great and revered prince, a splendid and mighty prince, a great and revered prince, one who all the children of heaven fear before, and one who is capable of swallowing the entire planet in one go (at a mouthful).

(2) Why is he referred to as Chayyli El H? Because he is designated to be in charge of the Holy Chayyoth, smite them with fire lashes, and glorify them when they give praise, glory, and joy. He also prompts them to hasten to say "Holy" and "Blessed be the Glory of H' from his place!"

in this case, the Qedushshd.

CHAPTER XXI
According to the Chayyoth R. Ishmael, Metatron is an angel and I was told by the Prince of the Presence: "

(1) Four (are) the Chayyoth, which correspond to the four winds." Every Chayya resembles the size of the entire world. Each one has four faces, each of which resembles the face of the East.

(2) Each one has four wings, each of which resembles the universe's cover or roof.

(3) Each of them also has wings in the midst of wings and faces in the center of faces. Both the faces and the wings are the equivalent size of 248 faces and 365 wings, respectively.

(4) And 2000 crowns are placed on the heads of each person. Each crown is comparable to the cloud-based bow. And its splendor is comparable to that of the sun's globe. And the sparks that emanate from each person are comparable to the splendor of Venus, the morning star in the east.

CHAPTER XXII 1
KERUBIEL, the Kerubim's Prince.
An explanation of the Kerubim
Says R. Ishmael

(1) Above these la there is one prince, noble, wonderful, strong, and praised with all kinds of praise, the angel Metatron, the Prince of the Presence, remarked to me. KERUBIEL H' is his name; he is a strong prince, full of might and strength; a prince of Highness, and Highness (is) with him; a prince of righteousness, and righteousness (is) with him; a prince of holiness, and holiness (is) with him; a prince glorified in (by) thousand hosts, exalted by ten thousand armies.

(2) When he is angry, the earth trembles, the camps are moved, people cower in dread, and the 'Araboth quake when he is rebuked.

(3) He is as tall as flaming coals. His height is comparable to that of the seven heavens. His stature is as wide as the seven heavens in breadth, and as thick as the seven heavens in thickness.

(4) His mouth is like a light of fire when it opens. His mouth is a devouring fire. His eyebrows have the same brilliance as lightning. His eyes are like brilliant sparks. His expression is like a raging fire.

(5) Additionally, a crown of holiness with the Explicit Name engraved on it is placed on his head, and lightning flashes from it. And between his shoulders is the Shekina bow.

(6) In addition, his sword is like lightning, his loins are covered in arrows that are like flames, his armor and shield are covered in a consuming fire, coals of burning juniper are on his neck, and there are coals of burning juniper all around him.

(7) And Shekina's splendor is on his face, along with grandeur horns on his wheels and a crown perched on his head.

(8) His body is covered in eyes. And wings encompass the entirety of his tall stature (literally, all of his height is covered by wings).

(9) Coals are burning from a fire on his left hand and a flame is burning on his right hand. And his body is emitting firebrands. And from his visage, lightning is released. Always thunder upon thunder is with him, and always earthquake upon earthquake is by his side.

(10) He is also joined by the two Merkabah princes.

(11) Justification for the title "Prince," KERUBIEL H. because he has been given control of the Kerubim chariot. And he is given command over the powerful Kerubim. He also polishes the diadem on their skulls and adorns the crowns on their heads.

(12) He highlights their beauty in look. And he exalts the splendor of their majesty. And he makes their honor greater still. He directs the singing of the hymn of their adoration. He amplifies their stunning power. He makes their glory shine with all its brilliance. He makes their

gracious mercy and loving kindness more beautiful. He encircles their fairness with brightness. He enhances the attractiveness of their merciful beauty. He exalts their moral magnificence.

To secure the residence of him "who dwelleth on the Kerubim," he extols the order of their adoration.

(13) And the Kerubim are standing by the Holy Chayyoth, and Shekina is (resting) upon them, and the brilliance of the Glory is upon their faces, and song and praise are in their mouths. Their hands are under their wings, and their feet are covered by their wings, and the horns of glory are upon their heads, and the splendor of Shekina is upon their face, and Shekina is (resting) upon them an anointing of praise

(14) There is a sapphire on one side and a second sapphire on the other, and beneath the sapphires are juniper-burning embers.

(15) There is one Keruvi standing in each direction, but they spread their wings to sing with the skies' inhabitants and to extol the dread majesty of the king of kings. Their wings encircle one another above their skulls in splendour.

(16) Additionally, KERUBIEL H', the prince in charge of them, dresses them in attractive, lovely, and enjoyable arrangements and exalts them in many ways with majesty and grandeur. In order to fulfill their Creator's desire at every time, he hastens them in majesty and power. Because of this, the splendour of the high king "who dwelleth on the Kerubim" abides constantly above their lofty heads.

CHAPTER XXII, part (b):

In addition, there is a court in front of the Throne of Glory that

(1) neither a seraph nor an angel can enter, (2) and it is 36,000 myriads of parasangs large, as it is said in Isaiah chapter five verse two: "and the Seraphim are standing above him" (Lamech-Vav, which has the numeric value of 36 as its final letter).

(3) The number of bridges there is represented by the number Lamech-Vav (36).

(4) There are 24 myriads of fire wheels. And there are 12,000 myriads of ministering angels. In addition, there are 12,000 snow treasuries and 12,000 rivers of hail.

Additionally, there are chariots of fire and flames in the seven Halls that are unbounded by time, space, or purpose.

Metatron, the angel and Prince of the Presence, spoke to me as R. Ishmael said:

"(1) How are the angels standing on high?" Similar to how a bridge is built over a river so that everyone can cross it, Pie stated, a bridge is built from the entrance's beginning to its conclusion.

(2) Three ministering angels encircle it and sing to YHWH, the God of Israel, as they do so. A thousand times a thousand and ten thousand times a ten thousand lords of dread and captains of fear are positioned in front of it, and they are singing praise and songs to YHWH, the God of Israel.

(3) There are several bridges, including many bridges made of hail and fire. In addition, there were many snow treasuries, hail rivers, and fire wheels.

(4) How many ministering angels are there? 12,000 myriads, divided into two groups of six (thousand myriads each) above and below. The snow treasuries total 12,000; there are six above and six below. Additionally, there are 24 myriads of fire wheels, with 12 myriads above and below. They also encircle the rivers of hail and fire as well as the bridges. Numerous ministering angels are building entrances for all the creatures that are

present in the area, matching to (against) Raqia Shamayim's routes.

YHWH, the God of Israel and the King of Glory, does what? The visage of the powerful and imposing Great and Fearful God is hidden.

(6) In Araboth, there are 660,000 countless glories angels defending the throne of glory and the divisions of blazing fire. And the King of Glory covers His face because, absent His covering, the Araboth Raqia would be torn in two by the majesty, splendor, beauty, radiance, attractiveness, brightness, and excellency of (the Holy One), blessed be He.

(7) There are many ministering angels carrying out his will, many kings, many princes in the "Araboth of his delight, angels who are revered among the rulers in heaven, distinguished, adorned with song and reminding people of love: (who) are frightened by the splendor of the Shekina, and their eyes are dazzled by the shining beauty of their King, their faces turn black, and their strength doth fail.

(8) There go forth rivers ofjoy, streams of gladness, rivers of rejoicing, streams of triumph, rivers of love, streams of friendship (another reading:) of commotion and they flow over and go forth before the Throne of Glory and wax great and go through the gates of the paths of 'Araboth Raqia at the voice of the shouting and musick of the CHAYYOTH, at the voice of the rejoicing of the timbrels of his 'OPHANNIM and at the melody of the cymbals of His Kerubim.

"HOLY, HOLY, HOLY, IS THE LORD OF HOSTS; THE WHOLE EARTH IS FULL OF HIS GLORY," they chant as they grow large and move about in a flurry.

CHAPTER XXII c

R. Ishmael stated in "Metatron, the Prince of the Presence, said to me:

(1) How far apart are the bridges from one another? 12 many parasangs. There are 12 myriads of parasangs in their rise and 12 myriads of parasangs in their descent.

(2) The distance between the rivers of fear and the rivers of fear is 22 myriads of parasangs; the distance between the rivers of hail and the rivers of darkness is 36 myriads of parasangs; the distance between the lightning chambers and the clouds of compassion is 42 myriads of parasangs; the distance between the clouds of compassion and the Merkaba is 84 myriads of parasangs; the distance between the Merkaba and the Kerubim is 148 myriads of para

(3) And there are 40,000 myriads of parasangs from the foot of the Throne to the seat.

And may the name of the One who occupies it be hallowed!

(4) The Bow's arches are positioned above the 'Araboth and are 1,000,000,000 and 10,000,000,000 times 10,000,000,000 (of parasangs) high. They are measured in accordance with the Watchers' and Holy Ones' (Irin and Qaddishin) standards. According to the verse in Genesis ix.13, "My bow I have set in the cloud." Not "I will set" but "I have set," (i.e., already), is written here in reference to the clouds that envelop the Throne of Glory. The hail angels (change into) burning coal as His clouds pass by.

(5) And from the Holy Chayyoth, a voice-fire descends. In response to that voice's breath, people "run" (Ezek. i. 14) to a different location out of dread that it will tell them to leave, and they "return" out of fear that it will hurt them from the opposite direction. As a result, "they run and come back" (Ezek. i. 14).

(6) Furthermore, the splendor and beauty of the Bow's arches surpass those of the sun at the summer solstice. They are enormous and magnificent, and they are whiter than a blazing fire.

(7) The wheels of the 'Ophannim are located above the Bow's arcs. Following the measurements of the Seraphim and the Troops (Gedudim), their height is 1,000,000 and 10,000,000 times 10,000 units.

CHAPTER XXIII

The kerubim's wings are being blown by the winds.

(1) There are countless winds blowing under the wings of the Kerubim, according to R. Ishmael's revelation from Metatron, the Angel and Prince of the Presence.

As it is said in Genesis 1:2: "and the wind of God was brooding upon the face of the waters," there is "the Brooding Wind" blowing.

(2) As it is stated in Exodus xiv. 21: "And the Lord caused the sea to go back by a strong east wind all that night," there is "the Strong Wind" blowing.

(3) As stated in Exodus x.13, "the east wind brought the locusts," there is "the East Wind" blowing.

(4) As it is stated in Number xi. 31: "And there went forth a wind from the Lord and brought quails," there is "the Wind of Quails" blowing.

(5) As stated in Numbers 14: "And the wind of jealousy came upon him," there is "the Wind of Jealousy" blowing.

(6) As stated in i Kings.xix. 1: "and after that, the wind of the earthquake; but the Lord was not in the earthquake," there is the "Wind of Earthquake" blowing.

(7) As stated in Ex. xxxvii. i., "and he carried me out by the wind of H' and set me down," the "Wind of H'" is blowing there.

(8) The "Evil Wind" is present, as stated in I Samuel xvi. 23: "and the evil wind departed from him."

(9) The "Wind of Wisdom," "Wind of Understanding," "Wind of Knowledge," and "Wind of the Fear of H'" are present, as it is stated in Isaiah (chapter xii, verse 2): "And the wind of H shall rest upon him; the wind of wisdom and understanding, the wind of counsel and might, the wind of knowledge and of the fear.

(10) The "Wind of Rain" is blowing, as it is said in Proverbs xxv. 23: "The north wind bringeth forth rain."

(11) According to Jeremiah 13:16, "he makes 97 lightnings for the rain and brings forth the wind out of his treasuries," there is the "Wind of Lightnings" blowing.

(12) According to I Kings xix. n., "the Lord passed by and a great and strong wind (rented the mountains and broke in pieces the rocks before the Lord)," there is the "Wind, Breaking the Rocks" blowing.

(13) As stated in Genesis viii. 1: "And God made a wind to pass over the earth, and the waters assuaged," there is the "Wind of Assuagement of the Sea."

(14) As stated in Job i.19, "and behold there came a great wind from the wilderness and smote the four corners of the house and it fell," there is the "Wind of Wrath" blowing.

(15) The "Storm-Wind" is blowing, as it is stated in Psalm cxlviii:8: "Storm-wind, fulfilling his word."

(16) Additionally, Satan is present among these winds since "Satan" is nothing more than "storm-wind," and all of these winds only blow when they are covered by the wings of the Kerubim, in accordance with what is stated in Psalm xviii. n: "And he rode upon a cherub and did fly, yea, and he flew swiftly upon the wings of the wind."

(17) Where do all of these breezes go? As it is stated in Eccl. i. 6: "The wind goeth toward the south and turneth about unto the north; it turneth continually in its course and the wind 14 returneth again to its circuits," the Bible tells us that they emerge from under the wings of the Kerubim and descend on the surface of

the sun. As it is stated in the Bible (Amor iv.13): "For lo, he that formeth the mountains and createth the wind," they also return to the sun's sphere and descend upon the rivers and seas, the mountains, and the hills.

(18) And from the mountains and hills, they turn back and descend to the seas and rivers; from the seas and rivers, they turn back and descend upon (the) cities and provinces; from the cities and provinces, they turn back and descend into the Garden; and from the Garden, they turn back and descend to Eden, as it is written in Genesis chapter iii: "walking in the Garden in the wind of day." And in the middle of the Garden they come together and blow from one side to the other and are perfumed with the pure spices of the Garden even from its farthest parts, until they separate from one another and bring the fragrance from the farthest reaches of Eden and the spices of the Garden to the righteous and godly who in the future shall inherit the Garden of Eden and the Tree of Life, as it is written (Cant. iv. (19) Let my beloved enter his garden and consume his priceless produce.

CHAPTER XXIV

The various chariots of the Holy One, praise be to Him He Says R. Ishmael.

(1) The Holy One, blessed be He, has many chariots. He has the "Chariots of (the) Kerubim," as it is recorded (Ps. xviii.11, 2 Sam. xxii.11): "And he rode upon a cherub and did fly." Metatron, the Angel, the Prince of the Presence, the glory of all heaven, said to me.

(2) As it is stated (ib.): "and he flew swiftly upon the wings of the wind," he possesses the "Chariots of Wind."

(3) As it is stated in Isaiah xix. i: "Behold, the Lord rideth upon a swift cloud," he has the "Chariots of (the) Swift Cloud."

(4) As it is stated in Exodus xix. 9: "Lo, I come unto thee in a cloud," he has "the Chariots of Clouds."

(5) According to the verse "I saw the Lord standing upon the Altar" in Am. ix. i, He has the "Chariots of the Altar."

(6) According to Ps.lxviii.18, "The chariots of God are Ribbotaim; thousands of angels," He has the "Chariots of Ribbotaim".

(7) As stated in Deut. xxxi. 15: "And the Lord appeared in the Tent in a pillar of cloud," he has the "Chariots of the Tent."

(8) As it is said in Leviticus 1: "And the Lord spoke unto him out of the tabernacle," he possesses the "Chariots of the Tabernacle."

(9) As it is said in Numbers VII:89, "then he heard the Voice speaking unto him from upon the mercy-seat," he possesses the "Chariots of the Mercy-Seat."

(10) As it is said in Exodus xxiv. 10: "and there was under his feet as it were a paved work of sapphire stone," he possesses "Chariots of Sapphire Stone."

(11) He possesses the "Chariots of Eagles," in accordance with Exodus xix. 4's declaration that "I bore you on eagles' wings." Here, "they that fly swiftly as eagles" is meant instead of genuine eagles.

(12) According to the verse in Psalm xlvii that states "God is gone up with a shout," he possesses "chariots of shout."

(13) As it is stated in Psalm lxviii:5: "Extol Him who rideth upon the 'Araboth," He hath the "Chariots of 'Araboth."

(14) According to Psalm civ. 3: "who makes the thick clouds His chariot," He possesses the "Chariots of Thick Clouds."

(15) He possesses the "Chariots of the Chayyoth," as it is said in Ezekiel chapter one verse fourteen: "And the Chayyoth ran and returned." Shekina is over their heads, therefore they must run with permission and return with permission.

(16) According to Ezekiel x. 2: "And he said: Go in between the whirling wheels," he has the "Chariots of Wheels (Galgallim)".

(17) According to Ps. xviii.10 and Is. xix.1, "riding on a swift cherub," lying has the "Chariots of a Swift Kerub."

And when He mounts a quick kerub, He glances through eighteen thousand planets in a single glimpse as He places one foot on the animal before placing the other foot on its back. Then, as it is stated in Ezekiel (Ezek. xlviii. 35): "Roughly eighteen thousand," he sets down the other foot upon him after discerning and seeing into each of them and understanding what is within each of them.

Where do we get the information that He examines each one of them daily? He gazed down from heaven on the human race to see if any were intelligent and actively sought after God, as it is said in Psalm xiv. 2.

(i8) According to Ezekiel XII:12, "and the 'Ophannim were full of eyes roundabout," he possesses the "Chariots of the 'Ophannim." As it is said in Psalm xlvii:8 that "God sitteth upon his holy throne," 12

(19) He has the "Chariots of His Holy Throne."

(20) As it is stated in Exodus xvii. 16: "Because a hand is lifted up upon the Throne of Jah," he possesses the "chariots of the Throne of Yah."

(21) As it says in Isaiah 16: "but the Lord of hosts shall be exalted in judgment," he possesses the "Chariots of the Throne of Judgement."

(22) As it is said in Jeremiah xvii. 12: "The Throne of Glory, set on high from the beginning, is the place of our sanctuary," he has the "Chariots of the Throne of Glory."

(23) As it is said in Isaiah chapter five verse one, "I saw the Lord sitting upon the high and exalted throne," he has the "Chariots of the High and Exalted Throne."

CHAPTER XXV
'Ophphanniel, the prince of the 'Ophannim, appears in. Information about the "Ophannim"

(1) Above these there is one great prince, venerated, high, lordly, terrible, old and strong. His name is OPHPHANNIEL H., stated R. Ishmael: "Metatron, the Angel, the Prince of the Presence."

(2) He has 100 wings on each side in addition to sixteen faces with four faces on each side. Additionally, he has 8466 eyes, one for each day of the year. [2190 on either side, however some sources indicate 2116.] (16 on each side, 2191/2196 total).

(3) And those two eyes on his face are flashing with lightning, and firebrands are blazing from each of them; nothing can see them because everyone who glances at them is instantaneously burned.

(4) His height is equivalent to a voyage of 2500 years. Only the King of kings, the Holy One, blessed be He, alone can see and speak of the overwhelming majesty of his strength.

(5) Why is OPHPHANNIEL his name?
He has been given authority over the "Ophannim" and is responsible for them. Every day, he stands, attends to them, and makes them beautiful. And he exalts and orders their residence, polishes their place of standing, makes their homes bright, straightens out their corners, and cleans their seats. And he waits on them both early in the morning and late at night, day and night, to heighten their beauty, elevate their dignity, and inspire them to be "diligent in praising their Creator."

(6) All of the "Ophannim" have a lot of eyes, and they all have a lot of brilliance; 72 sapphire stones are sewn onto their clothing, with 72 of them on their left side and 72 of them on their right.

(7) And on the crown of every single one are four carbuncle stones, whose splendor extends in the four directions of 'Araboth just as the splendor of the sun's globe extends in all parts of the cosmos. Why is it known as the Carbuncle (Bareqet)? Because of the way lightning appears in all its splendor (Baraq). And because of the brilliant appearance of their eyes, tents of splendor, tents of brilliance, and tents of brightness as of sapphire and carbuncle surround them.

CHAPTER XXVI
The Prince of the Seraphim is SERAPHIEL.
The Seraphim's description
R. Ishmael stated:

(1) Above these there is one prince, marvelous, noble, great, honorable, mighty, terrible, a chief and leader 1 and a quick scribe, glorified, honored and liked.

(2) He is completely full of brilliance, light, and beauty, and his entire being is brimming with goodness and magnificence. He is also completely full of praise and gleaming.

(3) His body is like an eagle's, but his countenance is entirely like (that of) angels.

(4) His splendor is comparable to lightning, his appearance to firebrands, his beauty to sparks, his honor to burning coals, his majesty to chashmals (amber), and his brilliance to Venus's light.
His likeness resembles the Greater Light. He stands as tall as the seven skies.
His brows emit a light that is similar to a sevenfold light.

(5) The sapphire stone on his head is the same size as the entire cosmos and brilliance equal to that of the heavens themselves.

(6) His body is covered in countless, uncountable eyeballs that like the stars in the night sky.

Every eye is comparable to Venus. However, some of them resemble the lesser light, while others resemble the greater light. From his ankles to his knees, from his thighs to his loins, from his loins to his neck, from his neck to his skull, from his neck to his loins, (they are) like stars of lightning, from his neck to his head, like the Light Imperishable. Zeph iii. 5 (Cf.

(7) His headdress resembles the splendor of the Throne of Glory. The distance of 502 years' travel equals the size of the crown. No splendor, brilliance, radiance, or light exists anywhere in the universe but what is fixed on that crown.

(8) The prince's name is SERAPHIEL H. "The Prince of Peace" is the name of the crown on his head. And why is he referred to as "SERAPHIEL"? owing to his appointment as Seraphim's leader. And he is handed control of the blazing Seraphim.
In order for them to proclaim the beauty of their King in all manners of Praise and Sanctification (Qedushsha), he rules over them day and night and teaches them singing, praise, and proclamations of beauty.

(9). How many Seraphim exist? The four winds of the planet are represented by the number four. And how many wings do each of them have? Six, representing the number of creational days. How many faces do they have? They all have four faces.

(10) The Seraphim's dimensions and individual heights are equal to those of the seven heavens. Each wing's size corresponds to the total length of Raqia.
Each face is the same size as the face of the East.

(11) And each of them emits light comparable to the splendor of the Throne of Glory, making it impossible for even the Holy Chayyoth, the esteemed 'Ophannim, and the majestic KeruUm to

see it. Every person who sees it has their eyes clouded by its immense splendor.

(12) Why do they go by the name Seraphim?

Because they destroy (saraph) Satan's writing tables: Every day, Satan sits down with SAMMAEL, the Prince of Rome, and DUBBIEL, the Prince of Persia, and they write down Israel's transgressions on writing tables that they give to the Seraphim so they can present them to the Holy One, blessed be He, so He can exterminate Israel from the face of the earth.

However, the Seraphim are aware of the Holy One's secrets, blessed be He, and are aware that he does not wish for this people of Israel to perish.

How does the Seraphim behave? In order to prevent them from coming before the Holy One, blessed be He, when he is sitting upon the Throne of Judgement and truly judging the entire world, they receive (accept) them from the hand of Satan every day and burn them in the burning fire opposite the high and exalted Throne.

CHAPTER XXVII
The keeper of the Book of Records is RADWERIEL.

(1) beyond the Seraphim there is one prince, elevated beyond all the princes, more wonderful than all the servants, Metatron, the Angel of H', the Prince of the Presence, stated to me. He is RADWERIEL H, and he is in charge of the books' treasury.

(2) He presents the Case of Writings—which contains the Book of Records—before the Holy One, blessed be He. He then unseals the case, opens it, pulls out the volumes, and presents them to the Holy One, may He be blessed. In order for the Scribes to read them in the Great Beth Din (The court of justice) at the height of "Araboth Raqia," in front of the celestial household, the Holy One,

blessed be He, accepts them from his hand and gives them in his sight.

(3) Why is RADWERIEL the name given to him?

Because every time he speaks, an angel is born; additionally, he sings before the Holy One, blessed be He, as the time for the recitation of the (Thrice) Holy comes near. He stands in the songs (of the singing company) of the ministering angels.

CHAPTER XXVIII
"Irin" and "Qaddishin"
Metatron, the Angel, the Prince of the Presence, said to me:

(1) There are four great princes above all of these, named Lin and Qaddishin, who are high, honored, adored, cherished, lovely, and glorious ones, greater than all of the children of heaven. None of the celestial princes are comparable to them, and none of the Servants are on par with them. Because they are all equal, each one stands alone.

(2) Furthermore, their residence is situated opposite the Throne of Glory, and they are positioned opposite the Holy One, praised be He, so that their residence reflects the Throne of Glory's splendor. And the splendor of Shekina is reflected in the splendor of their visage.

(3) And they are exalted by (through) Shekina's exaltation and praised by (through) the splendour of the Divine Majesty (Gebura).

(4) In addition, the Holy One, blessed be He, never acts in his domain without first consulting them. Only then does he act. "The sentence is by the decree of the 'Irin and the demand by the word of the Qaddishin," it says in Dan. iv. 17 (translated).

(5) There are two LIrin and two Qaddishin. And how do they appear before the Holy One, may He be blessed? It should be clear that one 'Ir and the other 'Ir are standing on opposite

sides, just as one Qaddish is standing on one side and the other on the other.

(6) And they constantly elevate the humble, degrade the arrogant, and lift the humbling to the highest positions.

(7) And while the Holy One, blessed be He, sits on the Throne of Judgement and rules over the entire universe, the Books of the Living and the Books of the Dead are opened in front of Him, and all of the children of heaven are standing before him in awe, terror, and trepidation. When the Holy One, blessed be He, is sitting on the Throne of Judgement at that time to administer justice, his clothing is white as snow, his hair is pure wool, and his entire cloak is like the brilliant light. And virtue has wrapped itself around him like a coat of mail.

(8) Those "Irm" and "Qaddishin" are standing in front of him as judicial assistants before the judge. As it is said in Dan. iv. 17: "The sentence is by the decree of the 'Irm and the demand by the word of the Qaddishin," they present, defend, and conclude every case that is brought before the Holy One, blessed be He, for judgment.

(9) In the Great Beth Din in 'Araboth, some of them argue while others pass judgment.

Some of them bring requests to the Divine Majesty, while others bring instances to the Most High. Others conclude by descending and (confirming) carrying out the sentences on the ground below. As it is said in the Bible (Dan. iv. 13–14): "Behold, a 'Ir and a Qaddish came down from heaven, cried out, and said, "Hew down the tree, and cut off his branches, shake off his leaves, and scatter his fruit: let the beasts get away from under it, and the fowls from his branches."

(10), What does "Irin and Qaddishint" mean? Because, as it is said in Hos. vi. 2: "After two days will he revive us: on the third he will raise us up, and we shall live

before him," they sanctify the body and the spirit with fire on the third day of judgment.

CHAPTER XXIX
An explanation of a group of angels
Says R. Ishmael

(1) Each of them has seventy names that correspond to the seventy tongues of the globe, said Metatron, the Angel and Prince of the Presence. And each one of them is founded on the name of the Holy One, may He be blessed. Additionally, each individual name is inscribed in a fiery manner on the Fearful Crown (Keiher Nora), which is placed on the high and exalted King's head.

(2) Sparks and lightning also emanate from each of them. Each of them is surrounded by horns of splendor on all sides. Even the Seraphim and the Chayyoth, who are greater than all the children of heaven, are unable to see them because each one is encircled by tents of brilliance and radiating lights.

CHAPTER XXX
The 72 princes of Kingdoms and the Prince of the World preside over the Great Sanhedrin in heaven R. Ishmael stated: "

(1) When the Great Beth Din is seated in the 'Araboth Raqia' on high, there is no opening of the mouth for anyone in the world except those great princes who are called H' by the name of the Holy One, blessed be He.

(2) How many princes are there? There are 72 princes of the world's kingdoms in addition to the Prince of the World who, in accordance with what is stated in (Daniel 7:10), "The judgment was set and the books were opened," speaks (pleading) on behalf of the world before the Holy One, blessed be He, every day at the hour when the book is opened, in which all the deeds of the world are recorded.

CHAPTER XXXI

"The Characteristics of," Truth, Justice, and Mercy by the Throne of Judgment

R. Ishmael stated:

(1) When the Holy One, blessed be He, is seated on the Throne of Judgement, (then) Justice is standing on His right and Mercy is standing on His left, and Truth is standing in front of His face.

(2) And when a person comes before Him for judgment, the splendor of the Mercy extends toward him like a staff and stands in front of him.

As it is said in verse five of Isaiah chapter xvi, "And with mercy shall the throne be established, and he shall sit upon it in truth," the human being immediately falls to the ground, (and) all the angels of destruction fear and tremble before him.

CHAPTER XXXII

The execution of judgment on the wicked is covered in. God's saber

(1) When the Holy One, blessed be He, opens the Book, half of which is fire and half flame, (then) they go out from before Him at every moment to execute judgment on the wicked with His sword, which is drawn out of its sheath and whose splendor shines like a lightning and permeates the world from one end to the other, as it is written (Is. lxvi. 16): "For by fire will they make an atonement for iniquity.

(2) And when they see His sharpened sword like a lightning bolt from one end of the world to the other, and sparks and flashes the size of the stars of Raqia' coming out from it, all the inhabitants of the world (literally, those who enter the world) fear and tremble before Him, as it is written (Deut. xxxii. 41): "If I whet the lightning of my sword."

CHAPTER XXXIII

Angels of Mercy, Peace, and Destruction at the Judgment Throne.

The angels by the Throne of Glory and the flaming rivers underneath it, the scribes, (vv. 1, 2), and the rivers of fire. (vss. 3-5)

(1) When the Holy One, blessed be He, is seated on the Throne of Judgement, (then) the angels of Mercy are standing on His right, the angels of Peace are standing on His left, and the angels of Destruction are standing in front of Him. This is what Metatron, the Angel, the Prince of the Presence, said to me.

(2) A scribe is standing underneath Him, and another is standing in front of Him.

(3) The majestic Seraphim surround the Throne of Glory with walls of lightning on all four sides, and the Ophannim encircle them with firebrands. They are encircled by clouds of fire and clouds of flames, and the Holy Chayyoth carry the Throne of Glory from below, each with three fingers. Each person's fingers measure 800,000,000, 700,000,000, 66,000 parasangs, and more.

(4) And beneath Chayyoth's feet, seven scorching rivers are flowing and gushing. Additionally, each river has a 365 thousand parasang width and a 248 thousand countless parasang depth. Its length cannot be measured or searched for.

As it is stated in Jeremiah (Jeremiah xxiii. 19): "Behold, a whirlwind of the Lord, even his fury, is gone; yea, a whirling tempest; it shall burst upon the head of the wicked," each river turns around in a bow in the four directions of "Araboth Raqict," and (from there) it falls down to Ma'on and is stayed, and.

CHAPTER XXXIV

The several concentric circles surrounding the Chayyoth, which are made up of angels chanting the Qedushsha responsorium (chant or anthem) and fire, water, hailstones, etc.

Metatron, the Angel, the Prince of the Presence, spoke to me: "

(1) The Chayyoth's hoofs are encircled by seven clouds of blazing coals," R. Ishmael remarked. Seven walls of flame (or flames) encircle the burning coal clouds on the outside. The seven walls of hailstones (stones of 'Et-gabish, Ezek. xiii. 11, 13, xxviii. 22) encircle the seven walls of flame (or walls of flame). X hailstones (stone of Barad) encircle the hailstones on all sides. The stones of "the wings of the tempest" encircle the hailstones on the exterior.

Fire flames envelop the stones of "the wings of the tempest" on all sides.

The chambers of the whirlwind encircle the flames of fire. Fire and water encircle the whirlwind's interior chambers on all sides.

(2) Those who utter "Holy" are gathered around the fire and the water. The people who utter "Blessed" are positioned close to those who utter "Holy." Bright clouds are all around those who utter the blessing. Coals of burning juniper surround the bright clouds on all sides, and thousands of fire camps and tens of thousands of hosts of flames surround the coals of burning juniper. In order to prevent them from being burned by the fire, there is a cloud between each multiple camp and each multiple host.

CHAPTER XXXV

The angels reciting the Qedushsha in Araboth Raqia's angel encampment

1 R. Metatron, the Angel and Prince of the Presence, spoke to Ishmael and said:

(1) The Holy One, blessed be He, has 506 thousand myriads of camps in the height of 'Araboth Raqia." And there are 496 thousand angels in each camp.

(2) Each angel has a height equal to that of a large body of water, the appearance of his countenance to that of lightning, the appearance of his eyes to that of lamps of fire, the color of his arms and feet to that of polished brass, and the roaring voice of his words to that of a great multitude.

(3) And they are all arranged in four rows in front of the Throne of Glory. At the front of each row, the army's princes are positioned.

In accordance with what is stated in (Daniel 7:10), "Thousand thousands ministered unto him, and ten thousand times ten thousand stood before him: the judgment was set, and the books were opened," some of them utter "Holy" and others utter "Blessed," some of them run as messengers, and others are standing in attendance.

(4) And in the hour, as the time for saying the "Holy" draws near, (then) first a whirlwind from before the Holy One, blessed be He, bursts upon the camp of Shekina, and there arises a great commotion among them, as it is written (Jer. xxx. 23): "Behold, the whirlwind of the Lord goeth forth with fury, a continuing commotion."

(5) Immediately after that, 4,000,000 of them are transformed into sparks, a million of them into firebrands, a million of them into flashes, a million of them into flames, a million of them into men, a million of them into women, a million of them into winds, a million of them in burning fires, a million of them in flames, a million of them in sparks, a million of them in chashmals of light, until they They are then transformed back into their original forms, and now they are and have the fear of their King before them constantly, just as it is stated in Isaiah chapter five verse three: "And one cried unto another and said (Holy, Holy, Holy, etc.)".

CHAPTER XXXVI

Before reciting the "Song," the angels take a dip in the blazing river says R. Ishmael.

(1) Nehar di-Nur (the fiery stream) rises with many thousand thousands and myriads of myriads" (of angels) of power and strength of fire and it runs and passes under the Throne of Glory, between the camps of the ministering angels and the troops of 'Araboth. This happens when the ministering angels desire to say (the) Song.

(2) All of the ministering angels first descend into Nehar di-Nur, where they immerse their bodies in fire and dip their tongues and mouths seven times. Then, they ascend and don the "Machaqe Samal" garment and chashmal cloaks, and they stand in four rows in front of the Throne of Glory across all of the heavens.

CHAPTER XXXVII

The four Shekina camps and the area around them Metatron, the Angel, the Prince of the Presence, spoke to me and said: "

(1) In the seven Halls there are standing four Shekina chariots, and before each of them are standing the four Shekina camps."

A river of fire is continuously pouring in between each camp.

(2) Each river is surrounded by dazzling clouds, and between each cloud, pillars of brimstone have been erected. Standing flame wheels are positioned around them, between each pillar. Additionally, there are flames of fire all around between each wheel. Treasures of lightning are located between one flame and another, and the wings of the stormwind are located behind the treasures of lightning. The chambers of the tempest are located behind the stormwind's wings; these rooms are filled with winds, voices, thunder, sparks on sparks, and earthquakes on earthquakes.

CHAPTER XXXVIII

The dread that descends upon all of heaven at the sound of the "Holy?" specially the celestial bodies.
These were appeased by R. Ishmael, Prince of the World, who said:

(1) At the time, when the ministering angels utter (the Thrice) Holy, then all the pillars of the heavens and their sockets do tremble, and the gates of the Halls of Araboth Raqia' are shaken, and the foundations of Shechaqim and the Universe (Tebel) are moved, and the orders of Ma'on and the

(2) Until the world's prince summons them and orders them to "Be ye silent in your place! Do not be afraid because the ministering angels before the Holy One, blessed be He, sing the Song. "When the morning stars sang together and all the children of heaven shouted for joy," it says in Job.xxxviii.7.

CHAPTER XXXIX

At the time of the Qedushsha, all the various angelic forces bow before the throne as the explicit names fly off from it. According to R. Ishmael, Metatron, the Angel and Prince of the Presence, told him:

"(1) When the ministering angels utter the "Holy," all the specific names inscribed on the Throne of Glory in a fiery manner take flight like eagles with sixteen wings.

And on the four sides of the location of His Shekina1, they encompass and surround the Holy One, blessed be He.

(2) And the hosts of angels, the flaming Servants, the mighty 'Ophannim, the Kerubim of the Shekina, the Holy Chayyoth, the Seraphim, the 'Er'ellim, the Taphsarim, and the troops of consuming fire, and the fiery armies, and the flaming hosts, and the holy princes, girt with loftiness, fall upon their faces three times, saying: "Blessed

CHAPTER XL

When the word "Holy" is uttered in the correct order, ministering angels are rewarded with crowns; otherwise, they are punished by consuming fire. The consumed angels were replaced by new ones, R. Ishmael stated:

(1) "When the ministering angels properly say "Holy" before the Holy One, blessed be He, the attendants of His Glory, the servants of His Throne, go forth with great mirth from under the Throne of Glory," said Metatron, the Angel, the Prince of the Presence.

(2) They then put these crowns of stars, which resemble Venus in appearance and are carried by each of them in their hands by thousands of thousands and ten thousand times ten thousand, on the great princes and ministering angels who cry the word "Holy".

Every single one of them received three crowns: one for saying "Holy," another for saying "Holy, Holy," and a third for saying "Holy, Holy, Holy, is the Lord of Hosts."

(3) When they pronounce the word "Holy" out of order, a consuming fire, as described in Psalm xcvii. 3: "A fire goeth before him and burneth up his adversaries round about," shoots forth from the little finger of the Holy One, blessed be He, and descends in the middle of their ranks. It is then divided into 496 thousand parts, which correspond to the four camps of the ministering angels, and consumes them in an instant.

(4) The Holy One, blessed be He, then opens His mouth, speaks, and creates new ones just like them in their place. And each one says the "Holy" as it is written in Lam. iii. 23: "They are new every morning; great is thy faithfulness" as they stand before His Throne of Glory.

CHAPTER XLI
R. Ishmael says that Metatron, the Angel, the Prince of the Presence, said to him:

(1) Come and behold the letters by which heaven and the earth were created, the letters by which the mountains and hills, the seas and rivers, the trees and herbs, the letters by which were created the seas and rivers, the letters by which were created the mountains and hills.

(2) the letters by which the Throne of Glory and the Wheels of the Merkaba were created, the letters by which the necessities of the worlds were created, and

(3) the letters by which wisdom, understanding, knowledge, prudence, meekness, and righteousness were created, virtues that support the entire world.

(4) As I walked by his side, he took hold of me, lifted me onto his wings, and revealed to me all of the letters that are inscribed on the Throne of Glory in a fiery manner. Sparks shoot from these letters and fill all of Araboth's chambers.

CHAPTER XLII
Polar opposites that have been balanced by a number of Divine Names and other such wonders R. Ishmael stated:

(1) Come and I will show you where the waters are suspended in the highest, where fire is burning in the middle of hail, where lightnings lighten out of the middle of snowy mountains, where thunders are roaring in the celestial heights, where a flame is burning in the middle of the burning fire, and where voices make themselves heard in the middle of thunder and earthquake.

(2) After that, I followed by his side and he got hold of me, hoisted me on his wings, and revealed all of those things to me. As stated in Psalm civ.13, "(He watereth the mountains from his chambers) the earth is satisfied with the fruit of thy work," I saw the waters suspended above Araboth Raqia by the (force of) name YAH 'EHYE 'ASHER

'EHYE (Jah, I am that I am), and their fruits coming down from heaven and watering the face of the world.

(3) And I observed fire, snow, and hailstone mixed together yet unharmed by the word 'ESH 'OKELA (consuming fire), as it is stated in Deuteronomy iv. 24: "For the Lord, thy God, is a consuming fire."

(4) And I witnessed lightnings that struck snow-covered mountains but were unaffected (quenched) by the name YAH SUR 'OLAMIM (Jah, the everlasting rock), in accordance with what is stated in Isaiah (Isa. xxvi. 4): "For in Jah, YHWH, the everlasting rock."

(5) The term 'EL-SHADDAI RABBA (the Great God Almighty) as it is stated in Genesis xvii. 1: "I am God Almighty" caused thunders and voices to resound in the midst of fierce flames without being destroyed or muted.

(6) And I saw a flame (and) a glow (glowing flames) that were flaming and glowing amid burning fire but were not damaged (devoured) by (force of) the name YAD 'AL KES YAH (the hand upon the Throne of the Lord) as it is written (Ex. xvii. 16): "And he said: For the hand is upon the Throne of the Lord."

(7) Then I saw rivers of fire flowing alongside rivers of water, and I noticed that they were unaffected by the term 'OSE SHALOM (Maker of Peace), as it is said in Job xxv. 2: "He maketh peace in his high places." Because of this, he brings harmony between the fire and the water, the hail and the fire, the wind and the cloud, and the earthquake and the sparks.

CHAPTER XLIII
The home of the unborn souls and the spirits of the virtuous dead is shown to R. Ishmael by Metatron.

(1) Metatron told me, "Come and I will show you where the spirits of the righteous who have been created and have returned, and the spirits of the righteous who have not yet been created are," according to R. Ishmael.

(2) He then pulled me close to the Throne of Glory by the Shekina and lifted me there. He then revealed the Throne of Glory to me and showed me the spirits that had been created and had come back. They were flying above the Throne of Glory before the Holy One, blessed be He.

(3) After that, I went to interpret the following verse of Scripture (Isa. lvii. 16), and I discovered that the phrase "for the spirit clothed itself before me, and the souls I have made" (or "for the spirit was clothed before me") refers to the spirits of the righteous that have been created in the chamber of creation of the holy and have returned before the Holy One, blessed be He.

CHAPTER XLIV
R. Ishmael is shown by Metatron the middle and wicked's dwelling places in Sheol. The Patriarchs pray for Israel's deliverance (vss. 1-6); (vss. 7–10)

(1) Metatron, the Angel and Prince of the Presence, said to me, "Come and I will show you the spirits of the wicked and the spirits of the intermediate where they are standing and the spirits of the intermediate, whither they go down, and the spirits of the wicked, where they go down," according to R. Ishmael.

(2) Then he informed me that two destructor angels, ZA'APHIEL and SIMKIEL, are responsible for sending the wicked's spirits to She'ol.

(3) Because of the tremendous benevolence of the Prince of the Place (Maqom), SIMKIEL is assigned over the intermediate to help them and purify them. ZA'APHIEL is given charge of the evil spirits in order to drive them from the presence of the Holy One, blessed be He, and from the splendor of the Shekina

to She'ol, where they will be tormented in Gehenna's fire with burning coal staves.

(4) As I followed him, he took hold of my hand and used his fingers to display them to me all.

(5) Then I noticed that their bodies resembled eagles and that their faces resembled the children of men, which, lo, it was. In addition, because of their actions, the intermediate's face was a faint grey color. This is because they still bear the stains of their transgressions until they are purified by the fire.

(6) Due to the evil of their deeds, the wicked had a color similar to the bottom of a pot.

(7) Then I beheld the ghosts of the patriarchs Abraham, Isaac, and Jacob, as well as the rest of the righteous who have been raised from the dead and have risen to heaven (Raqirf). They prayed, "Lord of the Universe! ", as they bowed before the Holy One, blessed be He. How much longer will you continue to sit on (your) Throne with your right hand behind you, like a mourner in his days of grief, without delivering your offspring or making the revelation of your Kingdom to the world? And how much longer will you show no compassion for your children who are sold into slavery by other countries? Not to mention on your right hand, which is behind you, with which you stretched out the heavens, the earth, and the skies of heavens. When do you intend to feel compassion?

(8) Then the Holy One, blessed be He, addressed each of them, saying, "How could I surrender my great Right Hand in the fall by their hands (caused by them), because these wicked do sin thus and so, and transgress with such and such offenses against me.

(9) Metatron called me at that same moment and said, "My servant! Take the books, and read their horrible doings!" I then opened the books and began to read about their deeds. For each immoral person, there were 36 offenses (written down), and in addition, they had broken every letter of the Tora, as it is stated in Daniel ix. u: "Yea, all Israel have broken thy Law." Since they broke 40 laws for each letter from 'Aleph to Taw, it is not written 'al torateka but 'et (JIN) torateka instead.

(10) Abraham, Isaac, and Jacob then started crying. The Holy One then addressed them, "Jacob, my firstborn! Abraham, my beloved, Isaac, my Elect one!"

How can I now rescue them from among the world's nations? As soon as this happened, MIKAEL, the Prince of Israel, began to sob and ask the Lord, "Why are you so far away?" (Ps. x. i).

CHAPTER XLV
R. Ishmael is shown by Metatron past and future events depicted on the Curtain of the Throne.

(1) "Come, and I will show you the Curtain of MAQOM (the Divine Majesty), which is spread before the Holy One, blessed be He, and (on which) are inscribed all the generations of the world and all their deeds, both what they have done and what they will do until the end of all generations," said R. Ishmael.

(2) I went, and Mike—a father who teaches his kids the letters of Tora—showed it to me while pointing it out with his fingers.

And I saw every generation—every generation's heads, every generation's rulers, every generation's oppressors (drivers), every generation's keepers, every generation's scorers, every generation's overseers, every generation's judges, every generation's court officials, every generation's educators, every generation's backers, every generation's supporters, every generation's chiefs, and every generation's presidents of ac

(3) And I saw Adam, his generation, their deeds and thoughts, Noah, his generation, their deeds and thoughts, the flood generation, their deeds and thoughts, Shem, his generation, Nimrod, and the generation of the confusion of tongues, and his generation, their deeds and thoughts, Abraham, his generation, their deeds and thoughts, and Isaac, his generation, their deeds and thoughts.

(4) Aaron and Mirjam their works and their doings, the princes and the elders, their works and doings, Joshua and his generation, their works and doings, the judges and their generation, their works and doings, Eli and his generation, their works and doings, "Phinehas, their works and doings, Elkanah and his generation, their works and their doings, Samuel and his generation, their works and doings, the kings of Judah with their generations, their works and their doings, the kings of Israel and their generations, their works and their doings, the princes of Israel, their works and their doings; the princes of the nations of the world, their works and their doings, the heads of the councils of Israel, their works and their doings ; the heads of (the councils in) the nations of the world, their generations, their works and their doings; the rulers of Israel and their generation, their works and their doings ; the nobles of Israel and their generation, their works and their doings ; the nobles of the nations of the world and their generation(s), their works and their doings; the men of reputation in Israel, their generation, their works and their doings; the judges of Israel, their generation, their works and their doings ; the judges of the nations of the world and their generation, their works and their doings ; the teachers of children in Israel, their generations, their works and their doings ; the teachers of children in the nations of the world, their generations, their works and their doings; the counsellors (interpreters) of Israel, their generation, their works and their doings ; the counsellors (interpreters) of the nations of the world, their generation, their works and their doings ; all the prophets of Israel, their generation, their works and their doings; all the prophets of the nations of the world, their generation, their works and their doings;

(2) I saw Messiah, son of Joseph, and his generation "and their" works and their doings that they will perform against the countries of the world, as well as all the battles and wars that the nations of the globe waged against the people of Israel during the time of their rule. And I witnessed the coming of the Messiah, the son of David, along with his generation, all the battles and conflicts, as well as all the good and bad things they would do to Israel. And (3) I witnessed every battle and war that Gog and Magog will engage in throughout the reign of the Messiah, as well as all that the Holy One, blessed be He, will do to them in the future.

(4) And the rest of the leaders of the generations and all of their works—both those that have already been done and those that will be done in the future for all generations until the end of time—were inscribed on the Curtain of MAQOM. This applies to both Israel and the other countries of the world. And after I had seen it all with my own eyes, I began to extol MAQOM (the Divine Majesty), saying, "For the King's word hath power (and who may say unto him: What doest thou?)" Ecclesiastes viii. 4, 5.

Whoever keeps the commandments will not know evil. And I cried out, "O Lord, how numerous are thy works!" (Ps. civ. 24).

CHAPTER XLVI
The location of the stars as revealed to R. Ishmael

(1) (Come and I will show thee) the space of the stars that are standing in Raqia' night after night in awe of the Almighty

(MAQOM), and (I will show thee) where they go and where they stand, Metatron said to me, according to R. Ishmael.

(2) As I followed him, he grabbed my hand and used his fingers to show me everything. And they were circling the Merkabah of the Almighty (MAQOM) while standing on flaming sparks. What action took Metatron? He then clapped his hands and shooed them away from their position. They immediately took off on fiery wings, rose, and fled from the four corners of the Throne of the Merkaba. As they flew, he gave me the names of each and every one of them. The Holy One, blessed be He, has given each star a name, as it is written (Ps. cxlvii. 4): "He telleth the number of the stars; he giveth them all their names.

(3) And they all arrive in numbered order to Raqia' ha-shSHamayim to serve the earth under the direction of (lit. through, by the hands of) RAHATIEL. According to Psalm xix. i, "The heavens declare the glory of God," they leave in numbered order to sing and chant praises to the Holy One, blessed be He.

(4) However, the Holy One, blessed be He, will recreate them in the future, as it is said in the verse "They are new every morning" (Lam. iii. 23). They then open their mouths and sing.

Which tune are they singing? When I think of your heavens (Ps. viii. 3).

CHAPTER XLVII
R. Ishmael is shown the spirits of the persecuted angels by Metatron.

(1) Come, and I will show thee the souls of the angels and the spirits of the ministering servants whose bodies have been consumed in the fire of MAQOM (the Almighty) that emanates from his little finger. This is what Metatron said to me, according to R. Ishmael. And in the middle of the flaming river (Nehar di-Nur), they have been reduced to scorching coals. However, the Shekina is standing behind their spirits and souls.

(2) The places (chambers) of the whirlwind are where the ministering angels are burned and consumed by the fire of their Creator and by a flame from their Maker. The whirlwind blows upon them and drives them into the Nehar di-Nur, where they are transformed into numerous mountains of burning coal. But they all stand behind their Master, their spirit and soul returning to their Creator.

(3) As I followed him, he grabbed hold of my hand and began to show me the souls of the angels and the spirits of the serving ministers who were standing behind the Shekina with walls of fire enclosing them.

(4) At that point, Metatron unlocked the walls' gates for me, revealing their position behind the Shekina. And when I lifted up my eyes to look at them, I saw that they were all formed in the image of angels, with wings made of flaming fire that resembled those of birds. How marvelous are thy works, O Lord, I cried out in praise of MAQOM at that same instant (Ps. xcii. 5).

CHAPTER XLVIII (A)
The Right Hand of the Most High, now inert behind Him but later destined to work Israel's redemption, is revealed to R. Ishmael by Metatron.
In response to R. Ishmael's question, Metatron said to him:

(1) "Come, and I will show thee the Right Hand of MAQOM, laid behind (Him) because of the destruction of the Holy Temple; from which all manner of splendor and light shine forth; by which the 955 heavens were created; and whom not even the Seraphim and the "Ophannim are permitted (to behold), until the day of salvation shall come.

(2) When I followed him, he took me by the hand and showed me (the Right Hand of MAQOM), accompanied by every kind of adoration, joy, and singing; no word

can express its acclaim, and no eye can behold it due to its magnificence, dignity, majesty, glory, and beauty.

(3) In addition, every righteous soul deserving of seeing Jerusalem's joy is prostrating and praying in front of it three times daily, saying (Is. li. 9) "Awake, awake, put on strength, O arm of the Lord," as it is written (Is. xiii. 12): "He caused his glorious arm to go at the right hand of Moses."

(4) The Right Hand of MAQOM was crying at that same moment. Five times, which correspond to the fingers of his Great Right Hand, there came forth from its five fingers five rivers of tears that flowed into the great sea and shook the entire world, as it is written (Is. xxiv. 19, 20): "The earth is utterly broken (1), the earth is clean dissolved (2), the earth is moved exceedingly (3), the earth shall stagger like a drunken man (4) and shall be moved to and fro like a hut (5)."

(5) But when the Holy One, blessed be He, observes that there is no pious man (Chasid) on earth, no righteous man in the generation, and no justice in the hands of men; and (that there is) no Moses-like figure, and no comparable intercessor to Samuel who could pray before MAQOM for the salvation and for the deliverance, and for His Kingdom, that it be revealed in the entirety of the world; and for His great Right Hand, that He place it He wondered why there was no intercessor like Samuel

(6) who approached the Holy One, blessed be He, and called to Him and He answered him and fulfilled his desire, even though it was not fitting (in accordance with the Divine plan), as it is written (Is. lix. 16): "And he saw that there was no man" (that is:) like unto Moses who prayed repeatedly for Israel in the desert and averted the (Divine) decrees from them. I'll pray to the Lord.

(7) In addition, He established fellowship with Moses everywhere, as it is stated in Psalm xxcix.6: "Moses and Aaron among His priests." Additionally, it is said in Jeremiah xv. i: "Though Moses and Samuel stood before me" and in Isaiah ixiii. 5: "My own arm brought salvation unto me."

(8) In that moment, the Holy One, may He be praised, said: "How long should I wait for the human race to bring about salvation via their righteousness for my arm? I will give up my arm and use it to redeem my children from among the peoples of the world for my own sake, for the sake of my merit, and for the sake of my righteousness.

I shall do it for my own sake, as it is stated in Scripture (Is. xlviii. n). How dare you insult my name, after all.

(9) The Holy One, blessed be He, will make known His Great Arm at that time and display it to the peoples of the world; for it is as long as the globe and as wide as the world. And it appears to be as magnificent as the sun when it is at its strongest during the summer solstice.

(10) Israel will soon be delivered from the clutches of the world's countries. And the Messiah will appear to them, bringing them joyfully to Jerusalem.

Additionally, Israel will travel from all four corners of the globe to dine with the Messiah. But as it is said in Isaiah 10:10, "The Lord hath made bare his holy arm in the eyes of all the nations; and all the ends of the earth shall see the salvation of our God," the nations of the world shall not dine with them. The Lord alone led him, and there was no other god with him, according to Deut. xxxii. 12. "And the Lord shall be king over all the earth" (Zech. xiv. 9).

CHAPTER XLVIII (continued) (B)
Angels sing "Holy" and "Blessed" as the Divine Names emanate from the Throne of Glory while being crowned, accompanied by innumerable

heavenly hordes through the skies, and returning to the Throne.

(1) The Holy One, blessed be He, has 72 names inscribed on his or her heart.

SS, SeDeQ (righteousness), SBI, SaDdlQ (righteous), S'Ph, SHN, SeBa'oTh (Lord of Hosts), ShaDdaY (God Almighty), 'eLoHIM (God), YHWH, SH, DGUL, W'DOM, SSS", 'YW, 'F, 'HW, HB, YaH, HW, WWW, SSS, PPP, NN, HH, HaY living, HaY, ROKeB 'aRaBOTh riding upon the 'Araboth', Ps. lxviii. 5, YH, HH, WH, MMM, NNN, HWW, YH, YHH, HP And with them are thousands upon thousands of powerful angels who lead them like a king with fear and awe, reverence and trembling, honor and majesty and terror, greatness and dignity, glory and strength, understanding and knowledge, a pillar of fire, a pillar of flame, lightning, and their light is as lightnings of light, just like the chashmal.

(2) They respond by exclaiming, "Holy, Holy, Holy," before them as they give them glory.

And they transport them (convoy) across every heaven in the form of great, revered princes.

All of the Chayyoth beside the Merkaba then open their mouths in honor of His wonderful name, saying: "Blessed be the name of His glorious kingdom for ever and ever," when they return them all to the location of the Throne of Glory.

CHAPTER XLVIII (FURTHER) (c)
A piece by Enoch-Metatron ALT 1

(1) Enoch, the son of Jared, whose name is Metatron, is referred to as "I seized him, and I took him, and I appointed him," which means that I snatched him from among the offspring of men (5) and gave him a Throne opposite to mine. Which is that Throne's size?

Seventy thousand fire parasangs total.

(9) I gave him responsibility for all of the family above and below and committed to

him 70 angels that represented the nations of the world.

(7) And I gave him more wisdom and intelligence than I did to any of the angels.

And I referred to him as "the Lesser Yah," which has the Gematria of 71. And I organized all of Creation's efforts for him.

And I gave him transcendence (lit. I granted him authority greater than that of all the ministering angels.

ALT 2

(3) He gave all treasuries to Metatron, who is Enoch, the son of Jared. And I gave him control over every store I have in every heaven. And I gave him the key to every celestial storehouse.

(4) I made him the prince over all the princes and a minister of my Throne of Glory to care for and arrange the Holy Chayyoth, wreathe crowns for them (to crown them with crowns), dress them in honor and majesty, and prepare a seat for them when he is sitting on his throne to magnify his glory in the height.

(5) His stature among people who are of lofty stature is seventy thousand parasangs at its highest. And I increased his glory to match my own in grandeur.

(6) and his eyes, which were as brilliant as the Throne of Glory.

(7) His royal crown, which is 500 by 500 parasangs in size, is worn with honor and majesty.

ALT 3

(1) Aleph1 Metatron, my servant who is one (unique) amid all the children of heaven, is the one I created strong, I took, and I appointed. In the first Adam's generation, I strengthened him. However, I went and took my Shekina away from among them when I saw how corrupt the males of the flood generation were.

As it is stated in Psalm xlvii. 6: "God is gone up with a shout, the Lord with the sound of a trumpet," I lifted it up in the air with a trumpet sound and a yell.

(2) "And I took him" refers to Enoch, the Jared-son, who was chosen from among them. To be my witness alongside the Chayyoth by the Merkaba in the future, I hoisted him up to the high heavens with the sound of a trumpet and a tera'a (shout).

(3) I gave him control over all of my treasures and coffers in every heavenly realm. And I gave him the keys to every single one of them.

(And I appointed him over) the Holy Chayyot to wreathe crowns upon their heads; the majestic 'Ophannim, to crown them with strength and glory; the honored Kerubim, to clothe: them in majesty; over the radiant sparks, to make them shine with splendor and brilliancy. (4) I made (of) him the prince over all the princes and a minister of the Throne of Glory, to exalt and arrange it; and As well as to laud and glorify my glory at the height of my might; (and I have entrusted him with 113 the secrets of above and below, of heaven and earth).

(5) I elevated him above everyone. Seventy thousand parasangs were made during the height of his stature, among all those of high stature. I elevated his Throne via the splendor of mine own. And I boosted its brightness by honoring my own grandeur.

(6) I changed all of his bones into blazing coals and his flesh into torches of fire. I also made his eyes look like lightning and his brows' brightness appear to be eternal light. I gave him a face as radiant as the sun, and I gave him eyes that sparkled like the Throne of Glory.

(7) I gave him the attire of honor and majesty, the covering garment of beauty and height, and a royal crown measuring 500 by (times) 500 parasangs as a diadem. And I bestowed upon him my honor, grandeur, and splendor, which are found in my Throne of Glory. I referred to

him as the LESSER YHWH, the Prince of the Presence, and the Knower of Secrets because I revealed every secret to him in the manner of a parent, and I confessed all mysteries to him in honesty.

(8) In order for him to sit and decide on the heavenly household on high, I set up his seat at the entrance to my Hall. And I brought every prince before him to ask for permission to carry out his wishes.

(9) To further his glory, I adopted 70 of (my) names and used them to address him.

I gave him control of 70 princes so that he could give them my instructions and my words in every language. He was to use his words to bring the arrogant to their knees and the humble to their thrones; to strike kings with his speech, to divert kings from their course, and to establish the rulers over their domains as it is written in Daniel chapter two verse 21: "and he changeth the times and the seasons, and to give wisdom unto all the wise of the world Here, "asdh" (he shall accomplish) is written instead of "E'eseh" (I shall accomplish), signifying that Metatron stands and carries out all words and utterances made before the Holy One, blessed be He. The decrees of the Holy One, blessed be He, are also established by him.

CHAPTER XLVIII (D)
the titles Metatron has. On Mount Sinai, the treasures of Wisdom were unlocked for Moses. The angels protest against Metatron for telling Moses the secrets, and God responds and corrects them. The transmission of mysteries through tradition and their ability to treat illnesses

(1) The Holy One, blessed be He, gave Metatron seventy names by borrowing them from his own name. And these they are: YeHOEL, YaH, YeHOEL, YOPHIEL and Yophphiel, and 'APHPHIEL and MaRGeZIEL, GIPpUYEL, Pa'aZIEL,

'A'aH, PeRIEL, TaTRIEL, TaBKIEL,'W, YHWH, DH, WHYH, 'eBeD, DiBbURIEL, 'aPh'aPIEL, SPPIEL, PaSPaSIEL, SeNeGRON, MeTaTRON, SOGDIN, 'ADRIGON, ASUM, SaQPaM, SaQTaM, MIGON MITTON, MOTTRON, ROSPHIM, QINOTh, ChaTaTYaH, DeGaZYaH, PSPYaH, BSKNYH, MZRG, BaRaD.., MKRKK, MSPRD, ChShG, ChShB, MNRTTT, BSYRYM, MITMON, TITMON, PiSQON, SaPhSaPhYaH, ZRCh, ZRChYaH, B', BeYaH, HBH BeYaH, PeLeT, PLTYaH, RaBRaBYaH, ChaS, ChaSYaH, TaPhTaPhYaH, TaMTaMYaH, SeHaSYaH, IRURYaH, 'aL'aLYaH, BaZRIDYaH, SaTSaTKYaH, SaSDYaH, RaZRaZYAH, BaZRaZYaH, 'aRIMYaH, SBHYaH, SBIBKHYH, SiMKaM, YaHSeYaH, SSBIBYaH, SaBKaSBeYaH, QeLILQaLYaH, fKIHHH, HHYH, WH, WHYH, ZaKkIKYaH, TUTRISYaH, SURYaH, ZeH, PeNIRHYaH, Z1Z'H, GaL RaZaYYa, MaMLIKYaH, TTYaH, eMeQ, QaMYaH, MeKaPpeRYaH, PeRISHYaH, SePhaM, GBIR, GiBbORYaH, GOR, GORYaH, ZIW, 'OKBaR, the LESSER YHWH, after the name of his Master, (Ex. xxiii. 21) "for my name is in him", RaBIBIEL, TUMIEL, Segansakkiel ('Sagnezagiel' / 'Neganzegael), the Prince of Wisdom.

(2) Why is he referred to as Sagnesakiel? Because he has all the stores of wisdom in his possession.

(3) All of them were revealed to Moses on Mount Sinai so that he could learn them during the forty days that he was standing there. These included the Torah in all seventy aspects of all seventy tongues, the Prophets in all seventy aspects of all seventy tongues, the Writings in all seventy aspects of all seventy tongues, the Halakas in all seventy aspects of all seventy tongues, the Traditions in all seventy aspects of all seventy

(4) However, as soon as the forty days were through, he instantly forgot all of them. Then, through Yephiphyah, the

Prince of the Law, they were presented to Moses as a gift by the Holy One, blessed be He. According to what is stated in Deuteronomy XIV: "and the Lord gave them unto me." It stayed with him after that. And how can we know that it was still present in his memory?

Considering that it is said in the Bible (Mai. iv. 4) to "Remember the Law of Moses my servant which I commanded unto him in Horeb for all Israel, even my statutes and judgments."

The Tora, the Prophets, and the Writings comprise the Law of Moses. The Halakas and the Toseftas comprise the "statutes" and "judgments," respectively. And Moses received every one of them from above on Mount Sinai.

(5) The explicit name(s) on the Merkaba inscribed upon the Throne of Glory are reflected in these seventy names. The reason for this is that the Holy One, blessed be He, took from His Explicit Name(s) and put upon the name of Metatron: Seventy Names of His by which the ministering angels call the King of the kings of kings, blessed be He, in the high heavens, and twenty-two letters that are on the ring upon his finger with which are sealed the destinies of the princes of kingdoms on high in greatness and power and with which are sealed the lots

(6) "I am Metatron, the Prince of the Presence, the Prince of the Wisdom, the Prince of the Understanding, the Prince of the Kings, the Prince of the Rulers, the Prince of the Glory, the Prince of the High Ones, and the Prince of the High Ones, the exalted, great, and honored ones, in heaven and on earth," said Metatron.

(7) "H, the God of Israel, is my witness in this thing, (that) when I revealed this secret to Moses, then all the hosts in every heaven on high raged against me and said to me: (8) Why dost thou reveal this secret to son of man, born of woman, tainted and unclean, a man of a

putrefying drop, the secret by which were created heaven and earth, the sea and the dry land, the mountains and hills, Why do you expose this to people made of flesh and blood?

I said, "Because the Holy One, blessed be He, has granted me authority. In addition, I have received approval from the high and exalted Throne, from which all the Explicit Names emanate with burning chashmallim.

(9) However, they remained unsatisfied until the Holy One, blessed be He, chastised them and sent them fleeing with a rebuke from in front of him, telling them: "I delight in, and have set my love on, and have entrusted and committed unto Metatron, my Servant, alone, for he is One (unique) among all the children of heaven.

(10) Metatron then took them from his house of treasuries and committed them to Moses, Joshua, the elders, the prophets, the men of the Great Synagogue, Ezra, the Scribe, Hillel the elder, R. Abbahu, R. Abbahu to R. Zera, R. Zera to the men of faith, and the men of faith (committed them) to give warning and to heal.

(Completed and ended. God the World's Creator deserves praise.

Book 1: The Watchers A.I.
Chapter 1: Blessing of Enoch

The words of Enoch's blessing, in which he praised the chosen and upright people who would live throughout the time of affliction when all the evil and godless people would be eliminated. Taking up his parable, Enoch, a righteous man whose eyes had been opened by God, said, "I saw the vision of the Holy One in the heavens, which the angels showed me. From them I heard everything, and from them I understood as I saw, but not for this generation, but for a distant one which is to come." I spoke of the elect and continued my narrative about them by stating: "The Holy Great One will come forth from His habitation, and the Eternal God will tread upon the ground, even on Mount Sinai, and make His presence known in the majesty of His power from the heaven of heavens. And everyone will be overcome with fear, the Watchers will tremble, and this fear and trembling will extend to the ends of the earth. The tall mountains will be shaken, the high hills will be brought down, and they will melt like wax in front of the flame. And the earth will be completely torn apart, everything on it will perish, and everyone will face judgment. But He will make peace with the just. And will guard the chosen, and mercy will be shown to them. They will all be happy, and they will all belong to God. They will all flourish. They will all receive assistance from Him, light will dawn upon them, and He will reconcile them. And lo, He comes with ten thousand of His holy ones to execute judgment upon all, to kill all the wicked, and to convict all flesh of all their ungodly deeds and of all the grievous things that ungodly sinners have spoken about Him.

Chapter 2: The Creation

Pay attention to everything that happens in the sky, how the planets do not alter their orbits, and how the stars rise and arrange themselves in the sky, each in its own time and not out of sequence. Look at the earth and pay attention to what happens there from beginning to end. Notice how stable these events are and how nothing on earth changes, but all of God's handiwork are clearly visible to you. Observe how the earth is completely covered in water during the summer and winter, and how clouds, dew, and rain fall upon it. Except for fourteen trees, which keep their old foliage for two to three years before producing new foliage, all trees appear to have wilted and lost all of their leaves in the winter. Observe once more how the sun is overhead and directly opposite the earth throughout the summer. Because of the sun's heat and the earth's developing heat, you seek cover and protection from the elements. Because of this heat, you are unable to walk on the ground or a rock. Look at how the trees grow green leaves and produce fruit; as a result, pay attention to all of His handiwork and understand how He who lives forever created them. All of His works and the activities that His servants carry out on His behalf never change; rather, everything is carried out exactly as God has planned. And observe how the sea and the rivers carry out their responsibilities in a similar manner and do not deviate from His commands. But you have not remained firm, nor have you carried out the Lord's commands; rather, you have turned away and uttered words of arrogance and harshness. In opposition to His glory with your unclean mouths. Oh, you cold-hearted people, you won't find any peace. As a result, your days will be expiated, your years of life will end, and your years of ruin will be prolonged in endless abomination, and you won't be shown pity. During those times, you will convert the names of all the righteous into an eternal abomination, and everyone who curses will do it because of you. You are to imprecate upon all the sinners and the godless. And a curse will befall you, godless ones. All the virtuous will rejoice, sins will be forgiven, and there will be mercy, peace, and forbearance in abundance. There will be a godly light that will bring them salvation. And there will be no salvation for any of you sinners; rather, the mark of the beast will be upon you all. But for the chosen, there will be light, gladness, and peace, and they will receive the earth as their inheritance.

After that, wisdom will be given to the elect, and they will all live and never commit sin again—either out of ungodliness or pride—but wise people will have humility. And they won't sin or transgress again during their lives, and they won't pass away in a fit of rage or wrath; instead, they will live out the full number of days allotted to them. And the days of their lives will be prolonged in tranquility, and the years of their bliss will be doubled in everlasting joy and tranquility.

Chapter 3: The Fallen Angels

And it happened that they began to have gorgeous and attractive daughters born to them as the number of human beings increased. Then, when the angels, who are the children of heaven, saw them, they lusted for them and said to one another, "Come, let us choose us wives from among the children of men and beget us children." The group's leader, Semjaza, then replied, "I fear ye will not indeed agree to do this deed, and I alone shall have to pay the penalty of a great sin." They all responded to him by saying, "Let us all take an oath, and by mutual imprecations, bind us all to not abandon this plan but to carry it out." After making a collective vow, they each entered into an imprecatory agreement with one another. They totaled 200 people and descended from Mount Hermon's summit during Jared's reign. They gave the mountain its name because they had made mutual imprecations there to swear and bind one another. And these are their leaders' names: Samlazaz, their leader; Araklba; Rameel; Kokablel; Tamlel; Rameel; Danel; Ezeqeel; Baraqijal; Asael; Armaros; Batarel; Ananel; Zaqlel; Samsapeel; Satarel; Turel; Jomjael; Sariel. They have chiefs of tens like this. And all the others joined them in taking wives, each choosing one for themselves, and they started going into them and profaning themselves with them. They also introduced them to plants and taught them charms and enchantments as well as how to cut roots. Then they conceived and gave birth to enormous giants, each of whom stood three thousand ells tall and devoured all the possessions of humanity. And when men were no longer able to support them, the giants turned on them and ate up humanity. And they started committing sins against fish, reptiles, birds, and other animals. They also started eating and drinking each other's blood and flesh. The earth then accused those who broke the law. And Azazel taught men how to craft weapons like swords, knives, shields, and breastplates. He also taught them about earthen metals and the art of working with them, as well as how to make bracelets, jewelry, and eyelid beautifiers using antimony. And a great deal of godlessness developed, leading to adultery, confusion, and corruption in all spheres of life. Semjaza taught root-cuttings and enchantments, Armaros taught how to break enchantments, Baraqijal taught astrology, Kokabel taught constellations, Ezeqeel taught cloud knowledge, Araqiel taught earth signs, Shamsiel taught sun signs, and Sariel taught moon phases. And as men died, they wept, and their weeping reached the heavens.

Chapter 4: Intercession of Angels

Then, as they gazed down from heaven, Michael, Uriel, Raphael, and Gabriel witnessed much blood being spilt on the ground and complete lawlessness being wrought there. "The earth created without inhabitants cries the voice of their cryings up to the gates of heaven," they murmured to one another in verse two. The souls of mankind are now making their case to you, the holy ones of heaven, saying, "Bring our cause before the Most High." "Lord of lords, God of gods, King of kings, and God of the ages, the throne of Thy glory stands unto all the generations of the ages, and Thy name holy, glorious, and blessed unto all the ages," they cried out to the Lord of the centuries. All things are open and naked in your sight, and since you have power over everything, nothing can hide from you. You created everything, and everything is under your control. You can see what Azazel did, who spread all iniquity on earth and disclosed the everlasting truths that men were attempting to discover in heaven, as well as Samlazaz, whom You have empowered to govern over his friends. And they went to the earth's daughters of men, slept with the women, profaned themselves, and exposed all manner of wickedness to them. And the women gave birth to giants, which resulted in an abundance of blood and injustice on earth. And now, as you can see, the spirits of those who have passed on are wailing as they approach the gates of heaven. Their lamentations have increased and are unabated as a result of the unlawful acts committed on earth. And since you already know everything before it happens, you can observe these things happening while yet tolerating them without telling us what to do about it. The Most High, the Holy and Great One then spoke and sent Uriel to the son of Lamech and told him, "Go to Noah and tell him in my name 'Hide thyself!' and reveal to him the end that is approaching, that the whole earth will be destroyed, and a deluge is about to come upon the whole earth, and it will destroy all that is on it." And now give him instructions so that he can flee and his offspring can survive for all future generations. Once more, the Lord instructed Raphael to bind Azazel from head to toe and hurl him into the darkness. He also instructed Raphael to create an opening in the desert near

Dudael and cast Azazel there. Put hard, sharp boulders on top of him, cloak him in darkness, and leave him there for all time. Cover his face so he can't see the light. And he will be burned alive on the day of the final judgment. So that they can cure the epidemic and prevent all human infants from dying as a result of all the hidden truths that the Watchers have revealed to their sons, heal the earth that the angels have contaminated, and proclaim the healing of the earth. In addition, Azazel is responsible for all sin because of the works he taught people to do. The Lord then addressed Gabriel, saying, "Proceed against the bastards and reprobates, as well as the fornication children, and destroy the children of the Watchers from among humanity. Send them against each other so they can defeat one another in combat because they won't have long days. Since they expect to have an immortal life and that each of them will live for 500 years, no request they make of thee will be fulfilled on their behalf by their dad. Michael received the following order from the Lord: "Go, bind Samlazaz and his friends who have joined with women in order to pollute themselves with them in all their uncleanness. When their sons have killed one another and they have witnessed the death of their loved ones, bind them fast in the earth's valleys for 70 generations, until the day of their judgment and their conclusion, until the everlasting judgment is completed. They will be led away during those times to the lake of fire, the place of agony, and the prison where they will spend the rest of time. And from that point forward, through the end of all generations, everyone who is condemned and destroyed will be tied to them. and exterminate all of the reprobate's spirits as well as the Watchers' offspring because they have mistreated humanity. Destroy all wrongdoing from the face of the earth, put a stop to all bad deeds, and then let the plant of righteousness and truth appear. This will prove to be a blessing, and the works of righteousness and truth will be sown in joy and truth for all time. And after that, all the righteous will be saved and live to have thousands of offspring, spending their entire youth and old age in peace. When this happens, the entire planet will be farmed in righteousness, covered with trees, and brimming with blessings. All suitable trees will be planted there as well as vines, which will provide abundant wine. Of all the seed that will be placed there, each measure will grow a thousand olives and each measure of figs will produce ten presses of oil. And purge the earth of all injustice, sin, oppression, and godlessness. Also, exterminate every uncleanness that has been brought about by human activity on the planet. And when all human beings attain righteousness, all peoples will laud and adore Me, and they will all bow down to Me in worship. The earth will then be freed from all impurity, sin, punishment, and agony, and I will never again send such things upon it from generation to generation and forever. And during such times, I'll let blessings fall from heaven's storerooms onto the land, covering the toil and labor of the children of men. And throughout all of human history and across all human generations, truth and peace will go hand in hand. Enoch was concealed before these things happened, and no one among the children of mankind knew where he was hidden, where he lived, or what had happened to him. His days were spent with the holy ones, and his occupations involved the Watchers. When the Watchers called me, Enoch the scribe, they said to me, "Enoch, thou scribe of righteousness, go, declare to the Watchers of the heaven who have left the high heaven, the holy eternal place, and have defiled themselves with women, and have done as the children of earth do, and have taken unto themselves wives." And as I was blessing the Lord of Majesty and the King of the ages, lo! the Watchers called me. "You have caused great destruction on the earth, and ye shall have neither peace nor pardon for your sins," you should say to them. Inasmuch as they take great pleasure in their offspring, they will witness the murder of their loved ones, weep over the death of their offspring, and pray to eternity, but you will not find mercy and tranquility. Then Enoch went and said to Azazel, "Thou shalt not have peace; for the unrighteousness which thou hast taught, and for all the works of godlessness, unrighteousness, and sin which thou hast shown to men, a severe sentence has gone forth against thee to put thee in bonds; thou shalt not have toleration nor have thy request granted to thee. When I went to speak to them all at once, they were all terrified and shivering with fright. And they pleaded with me to draft a petition asking the Lord of heaven to pardon them and recite their appeal in his presence. For they were ashamed of their misdeeds, for which they had been judged, and could no longer speak with Him or lift their eyes to heaven. I then wrote out each plea, the prayer for their unique spirits, their individual actions, and their requests for mercy and length. I then left and went to the streams of Dan in the Danean land, south-west of Hermon, where I sat down and read their plea until I passed out. I had a dream, sights descended upon me, and I saw images of punishment. Then, a voice told me to tell the sons of heaven about my dream and to correct them. When I awoke, I went to them, and they were all huddled together in Abelsjail, which is located between Lebanon and Seneser, weeping while hiding their faces. I then proceeded to preach words of righteousness and chastise the heavenly Watchers as I described to them all the dreams I had experienced.

Chapter 5: Book of the Words of Righteousness

The book of the words of righteousness and of the eternal Watchers' rebuke in line with the Holy Great One's order in the dream I had. What I shall now utter with a fleshly tongue and my mouth's breath, which the Great One has given to men in order that they may talk with them and comprehend them in their hearts. He formed me and gave me the ability to correct the Watchers, the heavenly children, just as He gave man the ability to understand the word of wisdom when He created him. "I typed up your request, and in my vision it seemed that you would not receive it throughout all of eternity, and that judgment had already been rendered against you. You will not have your request approved. You will no longer be able to ascend into heaven for all of eternity, and a decree has been issued binding you to earthly ties for the duration of the world. And before that happens, you'll have witnessed your beloved sons being killed, and you won't enjoy it; instead, they'll be killed in front of you by the sword. And even if you weep, pray, and speak all the words in the writing I have written, your request on their behalf—or even your own—will not be granted. And the vision was shown to me in the following way: You see, in the vision, clouds and a mist invited me, the stars and lightning sped up and hurried me along, and the winds made me fly and carried me into heaven. I continued on until I was close to a wall made of crystals and encircled by fire tongues, at which point I became frightened. Then I entered the flames and got near to a sizable crystal home, the walls of which resembled a tesselated crystal floor, and the groundwork of which was also formed of crystal. Its ceiling resembled the path of the stars and lightning, with blazing arcs between them. cherubim, and water made up their heaven. The walls were encircled by a burning fire, and its entrances were on fire. When I went inside, the home was as cold as ice and as hot as fire. There were no joys of living there; instead, I was overcome by fear and trembling. Then, as I shook and trembled, I collapsed to the ground and saw a vision; lo, there was a second home, bigger than the first, and the entire doorway was spread out in front of me. It was made of fire flames. It was so superior in every way, including brilliance, splendor, and extent, that I am powerless to adequately convey either to you. Its ceiling was also made of flaming fire, and its floor was made of fire. Above it, lightning strikes and the course of the stars could be seen. And as I turned to gaze, I saw a towering throne with cherubim in vision. The throne's aspect was like crystal, and its wheels glistened like the sun. And streams of burning fire rushed out from behind the throne, obstructing my view. The Great Glory then sat there, and His clothing was whiter than any snow and shone more brilliantly than the sun. Because of His grandeur and splendour, none of the angels could enter and see His face, and no flesh could see Him. There was a big fire before Him and a burning inferno all around Him; no one could get close to Him, and even though there were 10,000 times 10,000 people in front of Him, He didn't need a counselor. I had been lying on my face, afraid, until the Lord beckoned me with His own mouth and said, "Come here, Enoch, and hear my word." And the most holy ones who were close to Him did not leave by night or depart from Him. Then, after one of the holy ones woke me up, I stood up and went to the door, bowing my head in prayer. Then He spoke to me and said, "Fear not, Enoch, thou righteous man

and scribe of righteousness," and I heard Him say this. Come this way and you will hear my voice. You should pray for men, not for men to pray for you, you should go and tell the Watchers of heaven who sent you to do so. Why did you leave the high, holy, and eternal heaven to commit adultery with women, contaminate yourselves with their daughters, take their spouses, act like earthlings, and give birth to giants as your offspring? And yet, despite the fact that you professed to be spiritually pure and to be living an eternal life, you polluted yourself with the blood of women, had children with the blood of flesh, and lusted after flesh and blood like those who die and perish. As a result, I also gave them spouses so they might conceive offspring via them and enjoy all they needed on earth. However, in a previous life, you were spiritual, immortal for all time, and living an eternal life. Due to the fact that the spiritual inhabitants of heaven reside in heaven, I have not appointed brides for you. The giants, who are now created from spirits and flesh, will be referred to as wicked spirits on earth, and they will live there. Given that they were produced from men and that the Watchers were their original and fundamental source, they have evolved into wicked spirits and will be referred to as such on earth. And the ghosts of the giants torment, oppress, demolish, attack, engage in battle, and bring about ruin on earth. Despite not eating, they still experience hunger and thirst and act inappropriately. Because they descended from them, these spirits will rise up against men, women, and their offspring. Until the day of the consummation, when the great judgement in which the age shall be fully consummated over the Watchers and the godless, yea, shall be wholly consummated, the spirits, having gone forth from the souls of whose flesh they have destroyed, shall do so without incurring judgment. And now, when it comes to the Watchers, who have asked you to pray for them and who were previously in heaven, tell them: "You were in heaven, but all the mysteries had not yet been revealed to you, and you knew worthless ones, and these in the hardness of your hearts you have made known to the women, and through these mysteries women and men work much evil on earth." Therefore, tell them: "You have no peace."

Chapter 6: Taken by Angels

Angels abducted me and led me to a world where the inhabitants were like burning fire and could transform into men at will. They then took me to a location of complete darkness and to a mountain whose summit reached the heavens. Then, I beheld the locations of the luminaries, the star treasuries, the thunder, and the deepest recesses, where a blazing sword, a fiery bow, and a quiver of hot arrows were, as well as all the lightning strikes. They then drove me to the living streams and the fire of the west, which is where the sun sets every day. Then I arrived at a river of fire, where the fire flows like water and empties into the vast ocean to the west. I got to the vast river, the great darkness, and the area where no flesh walks after seeing the great rivers. I observed the mountains shrouded in winter's gloom and the source of all the deep waters. I observed the mouths of every river on earth as well as the ocean's opening. I observed the stores of every breeze and observed how He had stocked them with materials to create the entire universe and the stable earth. And I witnessed the foundational element of the earth, the four winds that support the firmament of the heavens. I also observed how the winds are the pillars of heaven, stretching forth the vaults of heaven and stationing themselves between heaven and earth. I

observed the celestial winds that revolve and cause the sun's equator and all the stars to set. I observed the ways of the angels and saw the winds on earth transporting clouds. I observed the firmament of the heavens above at the edge of the earth. I continued on and came to a region that is burning day and night and contains seven mountains made of wonderful stones. There were three heading east and three heading south. The ones to the east were made of colored stone, one of pearl, one of jacinth, and the ones to the south were made of red stone. However, the middle one ascended to heaven like God's throne, which was made of alabaster and had sapphire as its crown. Then I noticed a blazing fire. The end of the huge earth is located beyond these mountains, and it is in this area that the heavens were fully formed. And among them, I saw columns of fire fall that were immeasurable in both height and depth. I also saw a vast abyss filled with heavenly fire columns. And beyond that chasm, I saw a desolate and horrifying area with no firmament of heaven above and no solid earth beneath it. There was no water there, nor were there any birds. When I asked what they were, I saw seven stars there that resembled huge blazing mountains. This is where heaven and earth come to an end, the angel declared. The stars and the company of heaven have turned this into a jail. And because they did not arise at the periods designated by the Lord, the stars that roll through the fire are those who disobeyed his order when they first rose. And He became furious with them and imprisoned them for ten thousand years until the point at which their wickedness would be fully realized. And Uriel replied to me, "These are the angels who have joined with women, and their spirits taking on many various shapes are defiling humans and will lead them astray into offering to demons as gods. They will remain here until the day of the great judgment, when they will be judged until they are no longer needed. And the female members of the wandering angels will turn into sirens. No man will ever see as I have seen since only I, Enoch, saw the vision and the conclusion of everything.

Chapter 7: The Holy Angels

These are the names of the holy angels who keep watch over humans in verse one. Uriel, one of the holy angels in charge of Tartarus and the world. Raphael, one of the heavenly angels in charge of human spirits. Raguel, one of the holy angels who exacts revenge on the luminaries' earth. Michael, one of the holy angels, is in charge of both the orderly portion of humanity and the chaos. Saraqael, a holy angel in charge of the spirits that commit sins of the spirit. One of the holy angels, Gabriel, is in charge of watching over Paradise, serpents, and Cherubim. God appointed Remiel, one of the holy angels, to watch over those who ascend. I then moved on to the chaotic area. And I witnessed something dreadful there: I did not see a stable earth or heaven above, only a chaotic and awful realm. And there, burning with flames like enormous mountains, I saw seven stars of the heaven linked together. After that, I questioned: "For what sin are they

imprisoned, and why were they brought here?" "Enoch, why dost thou ask, and why art thou eager for the truth?" replied Uriel, one of the holy angels who was with me and who was in charge of them. These are among the celestial beings who have disobeyed the Lord's word and are imprisoned here until the ten thousand years required by their sins are fulfilled. After that, I traveled to another location, which was far worse than the first, where I witnessed a terrible event. There was a huge fire there that burned and blazed, and the area was cleared all the way to the bottom due to the abundance of massive fire columns that were descending. I was unable to view it, estimate its size, or even guess at it. After it, I exclaimed, "How terrifying the place is and how horrible to behold!" One of the holy angels who was with me, Uriel, then spoke to me and asked, "Enoch, why hast thou such fear and affright?" To this I said, "Because of this terrifying place and the spectacle of the pain." And he told me, "This place is the prison of the angels, and here they will be imprisoned forever." From then, I traveled to the mountain of hard rock. And inside of it were four smooth, deep, and wide empty spaces. How smooth and deep and dark the hollow areas are to look at. One of the holy angels who was with me responded, "These hollow places have been created for this very purpose, that the spirits of the souls of the dead should gather therein, yea that all the souls of the children of men should gather here," to which I was in response. And these locations have been created to house them until their appointed day of judgment and until that judgment's major consequences. I witnessed a dead guy making up, and his voice was heard making up in paradise. "This spirit that makes suit, whose is it, whose voice goes forth and makes suit to heaven?" I questioned Raphael, the angel who was with me. And in response, he said, "This is the spirit that came from Abel, whom his brother Cain killed, and he makes his case against him until his seed is annihilated from among the seed of men and from the face of the earth." I questioned "Why is one separated from the other?" in relation to it and to all the hollow areas. And when I asked him a question, he replied, "These three have been created so that the spirits of the deceased may be divided. And for the spirits of the righteous, such a separation has been made, wherein is the shining spring of water. And when sinners pass away, are buried in the ground, and no judgment has been brought against them while they were alive, such has been provided for them.In this terrible suffering, their souls will be kept apart until the great day of judgment, punishment, and agony for those who curse forever, as well as vengeance for their spirits. There He will permanently bind them. And such a section has been created for the spirits of individuals who file their claim and disclose information about their demise after having died during the time of the sinners. I praised the Lord of glory and said, "Blessed be my Lord, the Lord of righteousness, who ruleth for ever." From there, I traveled to another location to the west of the ends of the earth, where I saw a burn. Such has been made for the spirits of men who were not righteous but sinners, who were complete in transgression, and of the transgressors they shall be companions, but their spirits shall not be slain in the day of judgement nor" Then Raguel, one of the holy angels who was with me, answered me and said unto me: "This course of fire which thou hast seen is the fire in the west which persecutes all the luminaries of heaven." And from thence I went to another place of the earth, and he showed me a mountain range of fire which burned day and night. And I went beyond it and saw seven magnificent mountains all differing each from the other, and the stones were magnificent and beautiful, magnificent as a whole, of glorious appearance and fair exterior: three towards the east, one founded on the other, and three towards the south, one upon the other, and deep rough ravines, no one of which joined with any other. And the seventh mountain was in the midst of these, and it excelled them in height, resembling the seat of a throne: and fragrant trees encircled the throne. And amongst them was a tree such as I had never yet smelt, neither was any amongst them nor were others like it: it had a fragrance beyond all fragrance, and its leaves and blooms and wood wither not forever: and its fruit is beautiful, and its fruit resembles the dates of a palm. Then I said: "How beautiful is this tree, and fragrant, and its leaves are fair, and its blooms very delightful in appearance." Then answered Michael, one of the holy and honored angels who was with me, and was their leader. And he said unto me: "Enoch, why dost thou ask me regarding the fragrance of the tree, and why dost thou wish to learn the truth?When I replied, "I wish to know about everything, but especially about this tree," he responded, "This high mountain that you have seen, whose

summit is like God's throne, is His throne, where the Holy Great One, the Lord of Glory, the Eternal King, will sit, when He comes down to visit the earth with goodness. No mortal is allowed to touch this fragrant tree until the great judgment, when He will exact justice on everyone and bring it to a permanent conclusion. Then it will be handed to the holy and pious. It will be transplanted to the holy place, to the temple of the Lord, the Eternal King, where its fruit will be used as nourishment for the elect. After that, they will be filled with joy and gladness, enter the holy place, breathe in the aroma of it, and live a long life on earth. Such as thy fathers lived; and in their days shall no sorrow or plague or torment or calamity touch them." Then blessed I the God of Glory, the Eternal King, who hath prepared such things for the righteous, and hath created them and promised to give to them. And I went from thence to the middle of the earth, and I saw a blessed place in which there were trees with branches abiding and blooming. And there I saw a holy mountain, and underneath the mountain to the east there was a stream and it flowed towards the south. And I saw towards the east another mountain higher than this, and between them a deep and narrow ravine:

in it also ran a stream underneath the mountain. And to the west thereof there was another mountain, lower than the former and of small elevation, and a ravine deep and dry between them: and another deep and dry ravine was at the extremities of the three mountains. And all the ravines were deep and narrow, of hard rock, and trees were not planted upon them. And I marveled at the rocks, and I marveled at the ravine, yea, I marveled very much. Then said I: "For what object is this blessed land, which is entirely filled with trees, and this accursed valley between? One of the holy angels who was present with me, Uriel, responded, "This dreadful valley is for people who are cursed for all eternity. All those who speak unclean words against the Lord with their mouths and speak harsh things about His glory will be gathered here as the cursed. They will congregate here, and here will be the location of their trial. In the end days, they will witness a display of just judgment in front of the righteous for all time; in this setting, the merciful will praise the Lord of glory, the Eternal King. In the days of judgement over the former, they shall bless Him for the mercy in accordance with which He has assigned them." Then I blessed the Lord of Glory

and set forth His glory and lauded Him gloriously. And thence I went towards the east, into the midst of the mountain range of the desert, and I saw a wilderness and it was solitary, full of trees and plants. And water gushed forth from above. Rushing like a copious watercourse towards the north-west it caused clouds and dew to ascend on every side. And thence I went to another place in the desert, and approached to the east of this mountain range. And there I saw aromatic trees exhaling the fragrance of frankincense and myrrh, and the trees also were similar to the almond tree. And beyond these, I went afar to the east, and I saw another place, a valley of water. And therein there was a tree, the color of fragrant trees such as the mastic. And on the sides of those valleys I saw fragrant cinnamon. And beyond these I proceeded to the east. And I saw other mountains, and amongst them were groves of trees, and there flowed forth from them nectar, which is named Sarara and Galbanum. And beyond these mountains I saw another mountain to the east of the ends of the earth, whereon were aloe-trees, and all the trees were full of stacte, being like almond-trees. And when one burnt it, it smelt sweeter than any fragrant odor. And after these fragrant odors, as I looked towards the north over the mountains I saw seven mountains full of choice nard and fragrant trees and cinnamon and pepper. And thence I went over the summits of all these mountains, far towards the east of the earth, and passed above the Erythraean sea and went far from it, and passed over the angel Zotiel. And I came to the Garden of Righteousness, and from afar off I saw numerous trees, and these great-two trees there, very great, beautiful, and glorious, and magnificent, and the Tree of Knowledge, whose holy fruit they eat and know great wisdom. That tree is in height like the strangler fig, and its leaves are like the Carob tree, and its fruit is like the clusters of the vine, very beautiful: and the fragrance of the tree penetrates afar. Then I said: "How beautiful is the tree, and how attractive is its look!" Then Raphael the holy angel, who was with me, answered me and said: "This is the tree of wisdom, of which thy father old and thy aged mother, who were before thee, have eaten, and they learnt wisdom and their eyes were opened, and they knew that they were naked and they were driven out of the garden." And from thence I went to the ends of the earth and saw there great beasts, and each differed from the other; and birds also differing in appearance and beauty and voice, the one differing from the other. And to the east of those beasts I saw the ends of the earth whereon the heaven rests, and the portals of the heaven open. And I saw how the stars of heaven come forth, and I counted the portals out of which they proceed, and wrote down all their outlets, of each individual star by itself, according to their number and their names, their courses and their positions, and their times and their months, as Uriel the holy angel who was with me showed me. He showed all things to me and wrote them down for me; also their names he wrote for me, and their laws and their companies. And from thence I went towards the north to the ends of the earth, and there I saw a great and glorious device at the ends of the whole earth. And here I saw three portals of heaven open in the heaven: through each of them proceed north winds: when they blow there is cold, hail, frost, snow, dew, and rain. And out of one portal they blow for good: but when they blow through the other two portals, it is with violence and affliction on the earth, and they blow with violence. And from thence I went towards the west to the ends of the earth, and saw there three portals of the heaven open such as I had seen in the east, the

111

same number of portals, and the same number of outlets. And from thence I went to the south to the ends of the earth, and saw there three open portals of the heaven: and thence there come dew, rain, and wind. And from thence I went to the east to the ends of the heaven, and saw here the three eastern portals of heaven open and small portals above them. Through each of these small portals pass the stars of heaven and run their course to the west on the path which is shown to them. And as often as I saw I blessed always the Lord of Glory, and I continued to bless the Lord of Glory who has wrought great and glorious wonders, to show the greatness of His work to the angels and to spirits and to men, that they might praise His work and all His creation: that they might see the work of His might and praise the great work of His hands and bless Him for ever.

Book 2:
The Parables Chapter 1: The First Parable
The second vision which he saw, the vision of wisdom, which Enoch the son of Jared, the son of Mahalaleel, the son of Cainan, the son of Enos, the son of Seth, the son of Adam, saw. And this is the beginning of the words of wisdom which I lifted up my voice to speak and say to those which dwell on earth: "Hear, ye men of old time, and see, ye that come after, the words of the Holy One which I will speak before the Lord of Spirits. It was better to declare to the men of old times, but even from those that come after we will not withhold the beginning of wisdom." Till the present day such wisdom has never been given by the Lord of Spirits as I have received according to my insight, according to the good pleasure of the Lord of Spirits by whom the lot of eternal life has been given to me. Now three Parables were imparted to me, and I lifted up my voice and recounted them to those that dwell on the earth. The first Parable. When the congregation of the righteous shall appear, and sinners shall be judged for their sins, and shall be driven from the face of the earth: And when the Righteous One shall appear before the eyes of the righteous, whose elect works hang upon the Lord of Spirits, and light shall appear to the righteous and the elect who dwell on the earth, where then will be the dwelling of the sinners, and where the resting-place of those who have denied the Lord of Spirits? It would have been good for them if they had not been born. When the secrets of the righteous shall be revealed and the

sinners judged, and the godless driven from the presence of the righteous and elect. From that time those that possess the earth shall no longer be powerful and exalted: And they shall not be able to behold the face of the holy, for the Lord of Spirits has caused His light to appear on the face of the holy, righteous, and elect. Then shall the kings and the mighty perish and be given into the hands of the righteous and holy. And thenceforward none shall seek for themselves mercy from the Lord of Spirits for their life is at an end. And it shall come to pass in those days that elect and holy children will descend from the high heaven, and their seed will become one with the children of men. And in those days Enoch received books of zeal and wrath, and books of disquiet and expulsion. And mercy shall not be accorded to them, saith the Lord of Spirits. And in those days a whirlwind carried me off from the earth, and set me down at the end of the heavens. And there I saw another vision, the dwelling-places of the holy, and the resting-places of the righteous. Here mine eyes saw their dwellings with His righteous angels and their resting places with the holy. And they petitioned and interceded and prayed for the children of men, and righteousness flowed before them as water, and mercy like dew upon the earth: Thus it is amongst them for ever and ever. And in that place mine eyes saw the Elect One of righteousness and of faith, and I saw his dwelling-place under the wings of the Lord of Spirits. And righteousness shall prevail in his days, and the righteous and elect shall be without number before Him for ever and ever. And all the righteous and elect before Him shall be strong as fiery lights, and their mouth shall be full of blessing, and their lips extol the name of the Lord of Spirits, and righteousness before Him shall never fail. There I wished to dwell, and my spirit longed for that dwelling place, and therefore hath been my portion. For so has it been established concerning me before the Lord of Spirits. In those days I praised and extolled the name of the Lord of Spirits with blessings and praises, because He hath destined me for blessing and glory according to the good pleasure of the Lord of Spirits. For a long time my eyes regarded that place, and I blessed Him and praised Him, saying: "Blessed is He, and may He be blessed from the beginning and for evermore. And there is no stopping in front of Him. He knows before the world was created what is forever and what will be from generation unto generation."

Those who sleep not bless Thee: they stand before Thy glory and bless, praise, and extol, saying: "Holy, holy, holy, is the Lord of Spirits: He filleth the earth with spirits." And here my eyes saw all those who sleep not: they stand before Him and bless and say: "Blessed be Thou, and blessed be the name of the Lord for ever and ever." And my face was changed; for I could no longer behold. And after that I saw thousands of thousands and ten thousand times ten thousand, I saw a multitude beyond number and reckoning, who stood before the Lord of Spirits. And on the four sides of the Lord of Spirits I saw four presences, different from those that sleep not, and I learnt their names: for the angel that went with me made known to me their names, and showed me all the hidden things. And I heard the voices of those four presences as they uttered praises before the Lord of glory. The first voice blesses the Lord of Spirits for ever and ever. And the second voice I heard blessing the Elect One and the elect ones who hang upon the Lord of Spirits. And the third voice I heard prayed and interceded for those who dwell on the earth and supplicate in the name of the Lord of Spirits. And I heard the fourth voice fending off the Satans and forbidding them to come before the Lord of Spirits to accuse them who dwell on the earth. After that I asked the angel of peace who went with me, who showed me everything that is hidden: "Who are these four presences which I have seen and whose words I have heard and written down?" And he told me, "This first is Michael, the merciful and long-suffering; and the second, who is set over all the illnesses and injuries of human children, is Raphael; the third, who is set over all the powers, is Gabriel; and the fourth, who is set over repentance leading to hope for those who inherit eternal life, is named Phanuel." These are the four voices I heard back then as well as the four angels of the Lord of Spirits. And after that, I witnessed all of the mysteries of the heavens, the division of the kingdom, and the method by which human deeds are judged. There, I saw the homes of the elect and the holy, and with my own eyes, I witnessed all of the sinners who reject the Lord of Spirits' name being dragged away from those homes and forced from them. They were unable to endure this punishment because it came from the Lord of Spirits. And while I looked, I observed the origins of the clouds and the dew, as well as how the winds are divided to blow across the world. From these, I was able to determine how the lightning and thunder occur and how they wet the dry earth. And I observed locked chambers from which the winds are divided, including a chamber for hail and winds as well as one for mist and clouds, whose cloud has hovered over the earth since the beginning of time. And I saw the chambers of the sun and moon, from where they come and where they go again, and their glorious return, as well as how one is superior to the other and their stately orbit. I also saw how they do not leave their orbits, adding nothing to them or taking anything away from them, and how they keep faith with one another in accordance with the oath by which they are joined. And initially, in accordance with the Lord of Spirits' decree, the sun rises and moves over the sky; He is called mighty for all eternity. Then I noticed the moon's journey, which she follows in that location both during the day and at night, with each taking a position opposite the other in front of the Lord of Spirits. And they do not stop giving thanks and praising. For to them is their rest in thanksgiving. In the name of the Lord, the moon's course is one of light to the righteous and darkness to the wicked, while the sun frequently changes to be a blessing or a curse. Who, in the

name of His righteousness, separated the light from the darkness, divided men's souls, and boosted the spirits of the virtuous. Because He selects a judge for each of them and judges each of them in front of Him, neither an angel nor a force can stand in the way. When Wisdom was unable to find a place to live, a residence in the skies was allotted to her. Wisdom set out to find a home among the human race, but she was unsuccessful. Wisdom went back to where she had been and sat down next to the angels. Unrighteousness therefore emanated from her quarters; those she didn't seek, she discovered and dwelt with, like rain in a desert and dew on parched ground. I also observed further lightning strikes and celestial bodies, and I witnessed as He called each one of them by name and they all bowed down before Him. I also observed how they are weighed in a just scale based on the proportions of their brightness, the size of their areas, the day of their appearance, and how lightning is produced by their rotation. They are also revolving in accordance with the number of angels, and they maintain their fidelity to one another. And I questioned the angel who accompanied me and revealed what was concealed, "What are these?" The Lord of Spirits has revealed to thee their parabolic meaning: these are the names of the holy who reside on earth and believe in the name of the Lord of Spirits for ever and ever, he said. Another thing I noticed about the lightnings is how some stars change into lightnings and are unable to shed their new appearance.

Chapter 2: The Second Parable

This is the second parable referring to people who disavow the existence of the holy ones' home and the Lord of Spirits. They will neither rise to the heavens nor descend to the earth. The sinners who have disavowed the name of the Lord of Spirits will suffer as a result. for whom the day of hardship and tribulation is thus kept. On that day, My Chosen One will sit on the throne of glory and evaluate each person's deeds, and they will have countless places to rest. When they witness My Elect Ones, their souls will strengthen inside them. And I will cause My Elect One to live among those who have invoked My mighty name. And I will change the world into a blessing and make it an eternal source of blessing and light. I will also cause My Chosen People to live there, but sinners and evildoers won't be allowed to enter. But for the sinners, judgment is coming from Me, and I will wipe them off the face of the earth. I have provided and satisfied My righteous ones with peace and have made them dwell before Me. Then I saw a person with a head of days, whose head was white as wool, and He was accompanied by another being with a man-like countenance who had a gracious face like one of the holy angels. And I questioned the angel who traveled with me and revealed to me all the secrets of that Son of Man, including who he was, where he came from, and why he accompanied the Head of Days. In response, he informed me that I was speaking to the Son of Man, who is righteous. whom virtue resides in and who makes known all the hidden treasures. Because the Lord of Spirits has selected him and has given him priority in righteousness before the Lord of Spirits for all time. And the Son of Man whom you have seen will remove the rulers and powerful people from their positions, loosen the grip of the powerful, and sever the sinners' teeth. They do not humble themselves to realize the source of the kingdom's gift to them, nor do they exalt and praise Him. And he will humiliate the powerful and bring a smile to their face. Worms will serve as their bed and darkness will serve as their home. Because they do not exalt the name of the Lord of Spirits, they will have no chance of getting out of bed. These are the ones who walk on earth and live there while judging the stars of heaven. Every action they take shows their unrighteousness, and their wealth gives them the authority. They reject the name of the Lord of Spirits and place their faith in the gods they have created with their own hands. They attack the believers who hang on to the name of the Lord of Spirits and the homes of His congregations. And before the Lord of Spirits in those days, the prayer of the righteous and their blood from the earth will have ascension. In those times, the holy ones who reside in the skies will sing together in supplication and prayer, praise, and thanksgiving, and will bless the name of the Lord of Spirits in honor of the shed blood of the righteous. And that the virtuous' plea before the Lord of Spirits won't go in vain, that justice will be served to them, and that they won't have to endure suffering forever. During those times, I witnessed the Head of Days as He took a seat on His throne of glory, the books of the living were opened in front of Him, His entire heavenly host, as well as His advisers, gathered around Him. And because the number of the righteous had been offered, their prayers had been heard, and their blood had been needed before the Lord of Spirits, the hearts of the holy were overjoyed. And there, I beheld the never-ending spring of righteousness, surrounded by numerous other springs of wisdom. All those who were thirsty drank from them, became wiser, and lived among the righteous, holy, and elect. And at that time, the Son of Man was given a name before the Head of Days and in front of the Lord of Spirits. In fact, His name was given before the Lord of Spirits before the creation of the sun, the signs, or the heaven's stars. He will serve as a support for the upright so that they won't stumble, as well as the light for the Gentiles and the glimmer of hope for those who are distressed in spirit. All those who live on earth will kneel in adoration before Him, praising and blessing Him, and joyfully rejoicing in the Lord of Spirits. And it is for this reason that He has always been chosen by Him and kept concealed from view. Because they have hated and despised this world of unrighteousness and all its works and ways in the name of the Lord of Spirits, they are saved, and it has been in accordance with His good pleasure in regard to their life, according to verse . And the wisdom of the Lord of Spirits has revealed Him to the holy and righteous, for He has preserved the lot of the righteous. Because of the labors of their hands, the kings of the earth and the powerful people who hold the land will now have a gloomy demeanor. Because they won't be able to defend themselves on the day of their suffering and sorrow, I will turn them over to My Elect. They will burn before the face of the holy like straw does in a fire, and they will sink before the face of the righteous as lead does in water, leaving no trace behind. In addition, on the day of their suffering, the earth will be at rest, and those in front of them will fall and not rise again. They have refused the Lord of Spirits and His Anointed One, thus no one will be able to resurrect them with his hands. Be thankful for the name of the Lord of Spirits. For grandeur does not wane before Him forever, and wisdom is poured out like water. Because He is powerful in all the ways of righteousness, injustice will vanish like a shadow and cease to exist. Due to the fact that the Elect One is standing before the Lord of Spirits, whose splendor endures forever and whose power transcends all generations. Additionally, He is the home of the spirit of wisdom, the spirit of insight, the spirit of understanding and power, the spirit of those who have passed away in righteousness, as well as other spirits. Since He is the Elect One in the eyes of the Lord of Spirits according to His good will, no one will be able to speak a lie in front of Him when He judges the hidden things. A transformation will occur for the Holy and Elect during those days, and the Light of Days will continue to shine upon them, bringing glory and honor to the Holy. On the day of suffering when evil will have been kept in reserve against sinners. The Lord of Spirits will grant victory to the righteous in His name, and He will make the other witnesses so that they will turn from their sins and abandon their human endeavors. They will not be honored by the name of the Lord of Spirits, but they will be saved by it, and the Lord of Spirits will have compassion on them because of the depth of His mercy. He is also righteous in His judgment, and when He judges, unrighteousness cannot continue in the face of His glory. When He judges, the unrepentant will perish in front of Him. And going forward, I won't show them any kindness, declares the Lord of Spirits. The planet will also return what has been given to it throughout those times. Hell and Sheol will each return what they owe and what they have received, respectively. For in those times the Elect One will appear and He will pick out of them the righteous and holy. For the time has come for their deliverance. Then, when the Elect One is seated on My throne, the Lord of Spirits will grant Him all the knowledge of wisdom and counsel and will exalt Him in doing so. The hills and mountains will also skip like lambs full of milk during those days, and the faces of the angels in heaven will be beaming with delight. The world will rejoice, the righteous will live there, and the elect will walk on it. And after those days in that location where I had witnessed all of the concealed sights, for I had been taken in a whirlwind and they had carried me in the direction of the west. There, in front of my eyes, were all the future secrets of heaven, including a mountain made of lead, a mountain of soft metal, a mountain of soft metal, a mountain of copper, a mountain of silver, and a mountain of gold. And I asked the angel who went with me, saying, "What things are these which I have seen in secret?" And he said unto me: "All these things which thou hast seen shall serve the dominion of His Anointed that He may be potent and mighty on the earth." And that angel of peace answered, saying unto me: "Wait a little, and there shall be revealed unto thee all the secret things which surround the Lord of Spirits. And these mountains which thine eyes have seen, the mountain of iron, and the mountain of copper, and the mountain of silver, and the mountain of gold, and the mountain of soft metal, and the mountain of lead. All these shall be in the presence of the Elect One as wax before the fire, and like the water which streams down from above and they shall become

powerless before his feet. And it shall come to pass in those days that none shall be saved either by gold or by silver and none be able to escape. And there shall be no iron for war. Nor shall one clothe oneself with a breastplate. Bronze shall be of no service, and tin shall not be esteemed, and lead shall not be desired. And all these things shall be destroyed from the surface of the earth." And I looked and turned to another part of the earth, and saw there was a deep valley with burning fire. They then started casting the monarchs and the powerful into this deep valley after bringing them there. And there, in front of my eyes, I witnessed how they crafted these massive iron chains that served as their tools. Then I questioned the angel of peace who was traveling with me, "For whom are these chains being prepared?" And he replied, "These are being prepared for the hosts of Azazel, so that they may take them and cast them into the abyss of complete condemnation, and they shall cover their jaws with rough stones as the Lord of Spirits commanded." And on that great day, Michael, Gabriel, Raphael, Phanuel, and Michael shall take hold of them. And in those days, the Lord of Spirits will bring judgment, and He will let all the fountains below the ground and the chambers of waters above the heavens open. And all waters will be linked together; the feminine water is that which is beneath the ground, and the masculine water is that which is above the heavens. And they will exterminate everyone who resides on earth and in the lower reaches of the sky. They will perish as a result of these when they realize the injustice they have brought about on earth. The Head of Days then remorsefully declared, "In vain have I destroyed all who dwell on the earth." And He vowed by His great name, "Therefore I will not do so to all who dwell on the earth, but I will write a sign in the heaven, and it shall be for a token of good faith between Me and them for ever, so long as heaven is above the earth, and this is according to My command. When I have desired to seize them, the Ye powerful kingdoms of the earth must see My Elect One, according to Isaiah How He judges Azazel and all of his allies in the name of the Lord of Spirits while seated on the throne of glory. Then I witnessed the armies of the punishment angels moving there while brandishing iron and metal chains and scourges. And I questioned the angel of peace who accompanied me, "To whom are these who hold the scourges going?" And he replied, "To their elect and beloved ones, that they may be cast into the chasm of the abyss of the valley." And at that point, that valley would be filled with their elect and beloved, and their days would be over, and the days of their leading people astray would no longer be counted. And in those times, the angels would come back and attack the Parthians and Medes from the east. They will cause the kings to become restless and awaken them from their thrones so that they can emerge like lions from their dens and like ravenous wolves amid their herds. And they will advance and trod on the territory of His chosen people, but the city of the righteous will hinder their horses. They will then start fighting among themselves, and they will have a powerful right hand. And until there are no more corpses from their slaughter and their punishment is not in vain, a man will not know his brother, nor will a son know his father or mother. They will be sucked into Sheol during those times when its jaws will be opened. Their annihilation will come to an end. Sheol shall devour the sinners in the presence of the elect." And it came to pass after this that I saw another host of wagons, and men riding thereon, and coming on the winds from the east, and from the

west to the south. And the noise of their wagons was heard, and when this turmoil took place the holy ones from heaven remarked it, and the pillars of the earth were moved from their place, and the sound thereof was heard from the one end of heaven to the other, in one day. And they shall all fall down and worship the Lord of Spirits. And this is the end of the second Parable.

Chapter 3: The Third Parable

And I began to speak the third Parable concerning the righteous and elect. Blessed are ye, ye righteous and Elect for glorious shall be your lot. And the righteous shall be in the light of the sun and the elect in the light of eternal life. The days of their life shall be unending and the days of the holy without number. And they shall seek the light and find righteousness with the Lord of Spirits. There shall be peace to the righteous in the name of the Eternal Lord. And after this it shall be said to the holy in heaven that they should seek out the secrets of righteousness, the heritage of faith. For it has become bright as the sun upon earth and the darkness is past. And there shall be a light that never ends and to a limit of days they shall not come. For the darkness shall first have been destroyed and the light of uprightness established for ever before the Lord of Spirits. In those days my eyes saw the secrets of the lightning, and of the lights, and the judgements they execute, and they lighten for a blessing or a curse as the Lord of Spirits willeth. And there I saw the secrets of the thunder, and how when it resounds above in the heaven, the sound thereof is heard. And He caused me to see the judgements executed on the earth, whether they be for well-being and blessing, or for a curse according to the word of the Lord of Spirits. And after that, all the secrets of the lights and lightning were shown to me, and they lighten for blessing and for satisfying. In the year 500, in the seventh month, on the fourteenth day of the month in the life of Enoch. In that parable I saw how a mighty quaking made the heaven of heavens to quake, and the host of the Most High, and the angels, a thousand thousands and ten thousand times ten thousand were disquieted with a great disquiet. And the Head of Days sat on the throne of His glory, and the angels and the righteous stood around Him. And a great trembling seized me, and fear took hold of me, and my loins gave way, and dissolved were my reins, and I fell upon my face. And Michael sent another angel from among the holy ones and he raised me up, and when he had raised me up my spirit returned; for I had not been able to endure the look of this host,

and the commotion and the quaking of the heaven. And Michael said unto me: Why art thou disquieted with such a vision? Until this day lasted the day of His mercy; and He hath been merciful and long -suffering towards those who dwell on the earth. And when the day, and the power, and the punishment, and the judgement come, which the Lord of Spirits hath prepared for those who worship not the righteous law, and for those who deny the righteous judgement, and for those who take His name in vain, that day is prepared, for the elect a covenant, but for sinners an inquisition. When the punishment of the Lord of Spirits shall rest upon them, it shall rest in order that the punishment of the Lord of Spirits may not come in vain, and it shall slay the children with their mothers and the children with their fathers. Afterwards the judgement shall take place according to His mercy and His patience." And on that day were two monsters parted, a female monster named Leviathan, to dwell in the abysses of the ocean over the fountains of the waters. However, the male is known as Behemoth, and he inhabited a barren desert by the name of Duidain on the eastern side of the garden, where the elect and the righteous live, where my grandpa was carried up, the seventh from Adam and the first man that the Lord of Spirits created. And I pleaded with the other angel to demonstrate to me the power of those monsters, how they were split in two and cast, one into the depths of the sea and the other onto dry land in the wilderness, in a single day. The other angel who accompanied me and revealed what was concealed told me what is first and last in the heavens in the height, and beneath the earth in the depth, and at the ends of the heavens, and on the foundation of the heavens. And he said to me: "Thou son of man, herein thou dost seek to know what is hidden." And the chambers of the winds, how the winds are divided, how they are weighed, and how the wind portals are calculated, each according to the strength of the wind, the strength of the moonlight, and the strength that is appropriate; and the divisions of the stars according to their names and how all the divisions are divided. And the thunder in accordance with the locations where it occurs, together with all the divisions formed in the lightning so that it can illuminate, and their host so that they can immediately comply. Because lightning and thunder are not one and the same, they travel together through the spirit and do not separate, even if the thunder has

designated resting spots while it waits for its peal. Because the stock of their peals is like sand, each one is reined in with a bridle as it peals, turned back by the power of the spirit, and pushed forward in accordance with the various quarters of the earth. When the lightning strikes, the thunder utters its voice, and the spirit enforces a pause during the peal and divides equally between them. The spirit of the sea is male and powerful, and he uses a rein to drive it back and forth and disperse it among all the mountains on earth in accordance with the might of his strength. Additionally, the spirit of the hail is a beneficent angel, and the spirit of the hoarfrost is his personal angel. Due to his might, the snow spirit left his lairs. There is a unique spirit there, and Frost is its name; the spirit that rises from it is like smoke. The mist spirit, however, is not merged with them in their chambers; rather, it has a separate chamber since an angel resides there and the mist spirit's course is lovely both in the light and the dark, in the winter and the summer. The spirit of the dew dwells at the extremities of the heavens, is linked to the chambers of the rain, and runs in the winter and the summer. Its clouds are linked to the clouds of the mist, and the one feeds the other. The angels appear to open the chamber where the rain's spirit is kept and lead it outside. Once it has spread throughout the entire earth, it joins the water there. Likewise, whenever it mixes with earthly water. Because the waters are food for the earth from the Most High, who is in heaven, they are for those who live there. As a result, there is a measure for the rain, and the angels are in charge of it. And I observed these things as they related to the Righteous Garden. And I saw in those days how long ropes were given to those angels, and they took to themselves wings and flew, and they headed towards the north. This is what the angel of peace who was with me said to me: "These two monsters, prepared conformably to the greatness of God, shall feed." And I asked the angel, saying unto him: "Why have those angels taken these cords and gone off?" And he said unto me: "They have gone to measure." And the angel who went with me said unto me: "These shall bring the measures of the righteous and the ropes of the righteous to the righteous. That they may stay themselves in the name of the Lord of Spirits for ever and ever. The elect shall begin to dwell with the elect, and those are the measures which shall be given to faith and which shall strengthen

righteousness. And these measures shall reveal all the secrets of the depths of the earth. And those who have been destroyed by the desert, and those who have been devoured by the beasts, and those who have been devoured by the fish of the sea. That they may return and stay themselves on the day of the Elect One; for none shall be destroyed before the Lord of Spirits, and none can be destroyed." And all who dwell above in the heaven received a command and power and one voice and one light like unto fire. And with their very first words, they wisely blessed, praised, and lauded that One. They also had a wise demeanor and a vibrant energy. The Elect was then seated on the throne of glory by the Lord of Spirits. And he will evaluate all the holy works that have been done in the heavens above and judge them. The Lord gave the following instructions to the kings, the powerful, the exalted, and the people of the earth: "Open your eyes and lift up your horns if ye are able to recognize the Elect One." The Lord of Spirits then seated him on the throne of His glory and the spirit of righteousness was poured out upon Him. All sinners are put to death by the word of his mouth, and all the unjust are exterminated in front of his face. And on that day, all the kings, the powerful, the exalted, and the rulers of the earth will stand up, and they will see and recognize how He sits on the throne of His glory. And before him, righteousness is evaluated, and untruthful words are never said. When that happens, they will experience discomfort similar to that of a woman giving birth or going through labor. And when they see the Son of Man seated on the throne of his glory, a portion of them will turn to look at the other and they will be horrified, dejected, and overcome with agony. And He Who Rules Over All, Who Was Hidden, Shall Be Blessed And Glorified And Exalted By The Kings And The Mighty And By All That The Earth Possess. The Son of Man was concealed from the beginning, but the Most High preserved Him in the midst of His power and made Him known to the elect. On that day, all of the elect will stand before him as the congregation of the elect and holy is sown. All kings, the powerful, the elevated, and those in positions of authority on earth will bow down before Him on their faces, adore the Son of Man, place their hope in him, and beseech him for forgiveness. However, the Lord of Spirits will exert such pressure on them that they will immediately leave His presence, their faces will be filled with humiliation, and the blackness will spread more across their features. And He will hand them over to the angels for punishment in order to get revenge on them for oppressing His elect and His children. And they will be a display for the just and His elect, who will exult over them because the Lord of Spirits' wrath has been poured out on them and His sword has been drenched in their blood. And on that day, the elect and righteous will be saved, and they will never again see the sinners and ungodly. They will dine, sleep, and rise with the Son of Man for all of eternity under the rule of the Lord of Spirits. And the elect and virtuous will have ascended from the ground and lost their faces of gloom. And they will have been dressed in robes of glory, which are the garments of life given by the Lord of Spirits. Your clothing will not deteriorate. Nor will your brilliance fade in the presence of the Lord of Spirits. During those times, the powerful and the monarchs who rule the globe would beg the Lord of Spirits to grant them a brief reprieve from the punishment angels to whom they were given so that they can kneel before Him and adore Him and confess their misdeeds. And they shall bless and glorify the Lord of Spirits, and say:

"Blessed is the Lord of Spirits and the Lord of kings, and the Lord of the mighty and the Lord of the rich, and the Lord of glory and the Lord of wisdom, and splendid in every secret thing is Thy power from generation to generation, and Thy glory for ever and ever. Deep are all Thy secrets and innumerable, and Thy righteousness is beyond reckoning. We have now learnt that we should glorify and bless the Lord of kings and Him who is king over all kings." And they shall say: "Would that we had rest to glorify and give thanks and confess our faith before His glory! And now we long for a little rest but find it not. We follow hard upon and obtain not, and light has vanished from before us, and darkness is our dwelling−place for ever and ever. For we have not believed before Him nor glorified the name of the Lord of Spirits but our hope was in the scepter of our kingdom, and in our own glory. And in the day of our suffering and tribulation He saves us not and we find no respite for confession that our Lord is true in all His works, and in His judgements and His justice, and His judgements have no respect for persons. And we pass away before His face on account of our works and all our sins are reckoned up in righteousness." Now they shall say unto

themselves: "Our souls are full of unrighteous gain, but it does not prevent us from descending from the midst thereof into the burden of Sheol." And after that their faces shall be filled with darkness and shame before that Son of Man, and they shall be driven from his presence, and the sword shall abide before his face in their midst. The Lord of Spirits then declared, "This is the ordinance and judgement with respect to the mighty and the kings and the exalted and those who possess the earth before the Lord of Spirits." And other forms I saw concealed there, as well.

Book 3:
The Book of Noah Chapter 1: Birth of Noah

And after some days my son Methuselah took a wife for his son Lamech, and she became pregnant by him and bore a son. I heard the voice of the angel saying, "These are the angels who descended to the earth, and revealed what was hidden to the children of men and seduced the children of men into committing sin." His physique was as white as snow and as red as a rose in blossom, and his long locks and head of hair were as white as wool. His eyes were also lovely. When he opened his eyes, he illuminated the entire house like the sun, making it extremely brilliant. After that, while still in the midwife's care, he stood up, spoke, and engaged the Lord of righteousness in conversation. His father Lamech fled in fear and eventually found his father Methuselah. And he said to him, "I have begotten a strange son, different from and unlike man, resembling the sons of the God of heaven; and his nature is different and he is not like us, his eyes are as the rays of the sun, and his countenance is glorious; and it seems to me that he is not sprung from me but from the angels, and I fear that in his days a wonder may be wrought on the earth. And I said unto him: "Behold, here am I, my son, wherefore hast thou come to me?" And he answered and said: "Because of a great cause of anxiety have I come to thee, and because of a disturbing vision have I approached. And now, my father, hear me: unto Lamech my son there hath been born a son, the like of whom there is none, and his nature is not like man's nature, and the color of his body is whiter than snow and redder than the bloom of a rose, and the hair of his head is whiter than white wool, and his eyes are like the rays of the sun, and he opened his eyes and thereupon lighted up the whole house. And he arose in the hands of the midwife, and

opened his mouth and blessed the Lord of heaven. And his father Lamech became afraid and fled to me, and did not believe that he was sprung from him, but that he was in the likeness of the angels of heaven; and behold I have come to thee that thou mayest make known to me the truth." And I, Enoch, answered and said unto him: "The Lord will do a new thing on the earth, and this I have already seen in a vision, and make known to thee that in the generation of my father Jared some of the angels of heaven transgressed the word of the Lord. And behold they commit sin and transgress the law, and have united themselves with women and commit sin with them, and have married some of them, and have begot children by them. And they shall produce on the earth giants not according to the spirit, but according to the flesh, and there shall be a great punishment on the earth, and the earth shall be cleansed from all impurity. Yea, there shall come a great destruction over the whole earth, and there shall be a deluge and a great destruction for one year. And this son who has been born unto you shall be left on the earth, and his three children shall be saved with him: when all mankind that are on the earth shall die he and his sons shall be saved. And now make known to thy son Lamech that he who has been born is in truth his son, and call his name Noah; for he shall be left to you, and he and his sons shall be saved from the destruction which shall come upon the earth on account of all the sin and all the unrighteousness, which shall be consummated on the earth in his days. And after that there shall be still more unrighteousness than that which was first consummated on the earth; for I know the mysteries of the holy ones; for He, the Lord, has shown me and informed me, and I have read in the heavenly tablets. And I saw written on them that generation upon generation shall transgress, till a generation of righteousness arises, and transgression is destroyed and sin passes away from the earth, and all manner of good comes upon it. And now, my son, go and make known to thy son Lamech that this son, which has been born, is in truth his son, and that is no lie." And when Methuselah had heard the words of his father Enoch—for he had shown to him everything in secret—he returned and showed to him and called the name of that son Noah; for he will comfort the earth after all the destruction.

Chapter 2: Calling Enoch

During those times, Noah noticed that the earth had sunk and that its destruction was imminent. He then got up, traveled to the far reaches of the planet, and called out to his great-grandfather Enoch. I asked Noah, "Tell me what is falling out on the earth, that the earth is in such evil plight and shaken, lest perhaps I shall perish with it," and he replied, "Tell me what is falling out on the earth." Noah then cried out three times in a resentful voice, "Hear me, hear me, hear me," and I fell to the ground. And Enoch my grandfather came and stood by me, and said unto me: "Why hast thou cried unto me with a bitter cry and weeping? A command has gone forth from the presence of the Lord concerning those who dwell on the earth that their ruin is accomplished because they have learnt all the secrets of the angels, and all the violence of the Satans, and all their powers, the most secret ones. And all the power of those who practice sorcery, and the power of witchcraft, and the power of those who make molten images. For the whole earth: And how silver is produced from the dust of the earth, and how soft metal originates in the earth. For lead and tin are not produced from the earth like the first: it is a fountain that produces them, and an angel stands therein, and that angel is preeminent." And after that my grandfather Enoch took hold of me by my hand and raised me up, and said unto me: "Go, for I have asked the Lord of Spirits as touching this commotion on the earth. And He said unto me: "Because of their unrighteousness their judgement has been determined upon and shall not be withheld by Me for ever. And these, they have no place of repentance for ever because they have revealed what was hidden, and they are the damned: but as for thee, my son, the Lord of Spirits knows that thou art pure, and guiltless of this reproach concerning the secrets; and He has destined thy name to be among the holy and will preserve thee amongst those who don't destroy the earth and those who dwell upon it. And the Lord of Spirits gave orders to the angels that were leaving, telling them to keep the waters from rising and to keep the powers of the rivers under control. After that, I left Enoch's presence.

Chapter 3: Judgement of Angels

And in those days, the word of the Lord came to me, saying, "Noah, thy lot has come up before Me, a lot without blame, a lot of love and uprightness. And now the angels are working; when they have finished their task, I will place My hand upon it and preserve it, and there shall come forth from it the seed of life, and a change shall come so that the earth shall not remain without inhabitant. And Then I noticed the valley where the streams and a big convulsion were both happening. And after all of this, a sulfurous smell emanated from the burning molten metal and from its convulsion in that location. It was associated with those waters, and the valley of the angels that had been misled burnt beneath that area. And streams of fire travel across its valleys, punishing the angels who had misled those who live on earth. However, those waters will be used in those days for the benefit of kings, the powerful, the exalted, and those who live on earth. They will be used to heal the body, but will also be used to punish the spirit because their spirit is currently consumed by lust. Despite frequent reminders of their punishment and their denial of the Lord of Spirits, they refuse to trust in His name. And as the severity of their physical burning increases, a matching transformation in their spirits will occur forever; because no idle word shall be spoken before the Lord of Spirits. As a result of their belief in their physical lust and denial of the Lord's Spirit, they will face judgment. And in those days, the same waters will experience a change; for when those angels are punished in the waters, the temperature of the springs will change, and when the angels ascend, the temperature of the springs' water will change and turn cold. As Michael responded, I overheard him say: "This judgement wherewith the angels are judged is a testimony for the kings and the mighty who possess the earth. Because these waters of judgement minister to the healing of the body of the kings and the lust of their body, they will not see and will not believe that those waters will change and become a fire which burns forever. And on that day Michael answered Raphael and said: "The power of the spirit transports and makes me tremble because of the severity of the judgement of the secrets, the judgement of the angels: who can endure the severe judgement which has been executed, and before which they melt away?" And Michael answered again, and said to Raphael: "Who is he whose heart is not softened concerning it, and whose reins are not troubled by this word of judgement that has gone forth upon them because of those who have thus led them out?" And it came to pass when he stood before the Lord of Spirits, Michael said thus to Raphael: "I will not take their part under the eye of the Lord; for the Lord of Spirits has been angry with them because they do as if they were the Lord. Therefore all that is hidden shall come upon them for ever and ever; for neither angel nor man shall have his portion, but alone they have received their judgement for ever and ever." And after this judgement they shall terrify and make them tremble because they have shown this to those who dwell on the earth. And look at the names of those angels: the first is Samjaza, the second is Artaqifa, the third is Armen, the fourth is Kokabel, the fifth is Turael, the sixth is Rumjal, the seventh is Danjal, the eighth is Neqael, the ninth is Baraqel, the tenth is Azazel, the eleventh is Armaros, the twelve is Batarjal, the thirteen is Busasejal And these are the names of their greatest angels, who rule over hundreds, fifties, and tens of angels. The first Jeqon's name, or the one who brought the sons of God to earth, led them astray, and did so using human women as his conduits. The second, known by the name Asbeel, gave the holy sons of God bad advice and misled them, causing them to contaminate their bodies with the daughters of men. The third was called Gadreel, and he is the one who led Eve astray and presented all the weapons of death to the human race, including a shield, a mail coat, a combat blade, and other deadly implements. And starting that day and continuing forever, they have waged war on people who live on earth. The fourth was known as Penemue, and he imparted to human children both the bitter and the sweet as well as all of their wisdom's secrets. And he taught people how to write on paper and with ink, which led to numerous sins from all of time into the present. Men weren't made to use pens and ink to use pen and ink to demonstrate their good faith. Because mankind were created in the same manner as angels, with the intention that they should remain morally upright, death, which destroys everything, could not have gripped them. Instead, it is men's knowledge and power that are causing them to perish. The fifth was given the name Kasdeja; he is the one who revealed to human children all the evil works of spirits and demons, the smiting of the unborn child so that it may perish, the serpent's bites, and the smitings that befall the serpent's son Tabaet during the noonday heat. And this is Kasbeel's assignment; the chief of the oath, whose name is Biqa, which he displayed to the holy ones when he was seated high above in splendor. This angel asked Michael to divulge the concealed name so that he might use it in the oath and cause those who revealed everything that was kept secret to the children of humanity to shudder in the presence of that name and oath. And this is the strength of this oath, because it is strong and powerful, and he gave Michael this oath, Akae.

Book 3: The Book of Noah, Ch. 4: Secrets of the Parables A.I.

These are the oath's secrets, and his oath makes them powerful: Before the world was made, and for all time, the heaven was suspended. And because of it, the earth was based on water, and since the beginning of time and forever, magnificent rivers have flowed from the hidden valleys of the mountains. As a result of that oath, the sea was created, and He used the sand to serve as its foundation, preventing it from expanding into eternity from the time of the world's creation. And because of that oath, the depths are fixed in place from eternity to eternity and do not move. And because of that oath, the sun and moon finish their journey and adhere to their prescribed path from eternity to eternity. Through that pledge, the stars finish their journey, and when He addresses them by name, they respond to Him forever and ever. Furthermore, this oath has great power over them, preserving their courses and keeping them on course. And because the name of that Son of Man had been made known to them, there was great gladness among them, and they blessed, glorified, and praised God. And while He sat on the throne of His glory, the Son of Man received the whole measure of judgment. He then caused the sinners to perish and be wiped off the face of the earth, along with those who have misled the world. All of their works will be wiped off the face of the earth, and they will be imprisoned in their assembly place of destruction while they are tied in chains. There will no longer be anything corruptible since the Son of Man has appeared and ascended to the throne of His glory. All evil will cease in front of His face, and the Son of Man's speech will be spoken freely before the Lord of Swords.

Book 4
Chapter 1: Enoch is Taken to Heaven

And it so happened that among those who live on earth, his name was lifted up to that Son of Man and to the Lord of Spirits throughout his lifetime. He was then carried upward on spiritual chariots, and among them his name disappeared. From that point on, I was no longer included in their number, and He placed me between the two winds, between the North and the West, where the angels took the cords to measure for me the area reserved for the elect and the righteous. And I witnessed the first fathers and the virtuous who have lived in that location from the beginning. After this, my spirit was translated and it rose into the sky, where I beheld the holy sons of God. They were treading on fire; their faces sparkled like snow, and their clothes were white. I saw two streams of fire and their light sparkled like hyacinth, and I immediately fell to the ground before the Lord of Spirits, falling to my right. Then, the angel Michael took hold of my right hand, hoisted me up, and guided me into all the secrets, revealing to me all the ways of righteousness. And he revealed to me every detail of the heaven's outermost regions, as well as every star's interior chamber and every luminary's route to the holy ones' faces. He then sent my spirit to the skies itself, where I beheld what appeared to be a building made of crystals with living fire tongues protruding from the crystals. And I perceived in my spirit the girdle that surrounded the burning building, which was surrounded by streams of blazing fire on all four sides. Around them were Seraphin, Cherubic, and Ophannin; they are the ones who never sleep and keep watch over His seat of glory. And I witnessed an uncountable number of angels. Around that mansion, a million times a million and ten thousand times ten thousand. The heavenly angels that reside above the sky, including Michael, Raphael, Gabriel, and Phanuel, enter and exit that building. And they left that home along with Michael, Gabriel, Raphael, Phanuel, and countless other heavenly angels. And also the Head of Days, Whose clothing is beyond description and Whose head is as white and clean as wool. I then collapsed to the ground, and as my entire body relaxed, my spirit was transformed. I then sobbed aloud in the spirit of power, blessing, extolling, and praising God. And these blessings that I uttered were highly acceptable to the Head of Days. And the Head of Days arrived alongside Michael, Gabriel, Raphael, and Phanuel, along with an uncountable number of other angels. Then He came and spoke to me, saying, "This is the Son of Man who was born into righteousness, and righteousness abides over Him, and the righteousness of the Head of Days does not forsake Him." And he told me, "He preaches unto thee peace in the name of the world to come; because out of this peace has proceeded since the creation of the world, and thus it shall be unto thee for ever and for ever and ever. And since virtue has never abandoned Him, everyone will follow in his footsteps. They will share their homes and heritage with Him, and they won't be apart from Him forever and ever and ever. Thus, the Son of Man will live a long time, and in the name of the Lord of Spirits, the virtuous will enjoy eternal peace and an upright path.

Chapter 2: The Luminaries of Heaven

The holy angel Uriel, who was with me and is their guide, revealed to me the book of the courses of the luminaries of heaven, the relations of each according to their classes, their jurisdiction and their seasons, according to their names and places of origin, and according to their months. And he revealed to me all of their laws in exact detail, along with how they apply to all of time—both now and forever—until the new creation, which lasts for all of eternity, is complete. The sun, a luminary, rises in the eastern portals of heaven and sets in the western portals, according to the first law of luminaries. And I saw the leaders of the stars and those they lead, as well as six portals in the east and six in the west, each following the other precisely in corresponding order. I also saw many windows to the right and left of these portals, as well as six portals in which the sun rises and six portals in which the sun sets. And first, the great luminary known as the sun emerges. His circumference is equal to that of the heavens, and he is completely filled with fire that both illuminates and warms the world. The wind propels the chariot on which he ascends, and the sun descends from heaven and travels back through the north to reach the east. He is so led that he arrives at the proper portal and beams in the face of heaven. He awakens in the great doorway, which is the fourth, in this manner in the first month. A flame will emanate from each of the twelve window holes at the fourth portal, which is where the sun rises in the first month. The sun rises in the heavens through the fourth portal for thirty mornings in a row before setting precisely in the fourth portal in the western hemisphere. During this time, the night gets shorter every night until the morning of the thirty-first day, and the day gets longer every day. On that day, the day is exactly ten parts long while the night is only eight parts long, making the

day nine parts longer than the night. And the sun rises from that fourth portal, sets in the fourth, then rises from and sets in the fifth portal of the east thirty mornings later. After then, the day lengthens by two parts to become eleven parts, while the night shortens to become seven parts. And because of its sign, it turns again toward the east and enters the sixth gate, rising and setting there every one and thirty mornings. On that day, the day doubles in length compared to the night, the day is divided into twelve parts, and the night is cut in half, becoming divided into six parts. As the day becomes shorter and the night grows longer, the sun returns to the east, passes through the sixth portal, rises from it, and sets thirty mornings later. And after thirty mornings have passed, the day has shrunk by exactly one part to eleven, and the night has shrunk to seven. After leaving the sixth western portal, the sun travels to the east, where it rises in the fifth portal for thirty mornings before setting in the west once more in the fifth western portal. On that day, the day is reduced by two parts to 10 parts, while the night is reduced to eight parts. After rising in the fourth portal for one hundred and thirty mornings as a result of its sign, the sun departs from that fifth portal and sets in the fifth portal of the west. On that day, the day and night are equalized; the night is equal to nine parts of the day, and vice versa. The sun rises from that portal and sets in the west before rising thirty mornings later in the third portal and setting in the west in the third portal before turning around and setting in the east. And starting that day, the night becomes longer than the day, the day grows shorter than the day, and so on until the thirty-first morning, when the night is exactly ten parts long and the day is eight parts long. And the sun rises from that third portal, sets in the third portal in the west, then moves back to the east, rising in the second portal in the east for thirty mornings before doing the same in the second portal in the west. And on that day, there are seven parts of the day and eleven parts of the night. And on that day, the sun rises from that second portal and sets in the west in the second portal before returning to the east and entering the first portal for an additional thirty mornings before setting in the west of the heavens. And on that day, the night lengthens to exactly twelve parts and the day to six, making up the double of the previous day's length. The sun also travels across the divisions of his orbit before turning around and entering that portal thirty mornings later. It likewise sets in the west across from it. That night, the night shrank by a ninth of its original length, growing to eleven parts, while the day shrank by seven. The sun has since come back, entered the second portal in the east, and has been rising and setting on those portions of his orbit for thirty mornings. And on that day, the night gets shorter; it is divided into 10 parts, while the day is divided into eight. On that day, the sun rises from that portal, sets in the west of the heavens, and then rises from the third portal for one hundred and thirty mornings before setting in the east. On that day, the night shortens to nine parts, the day shortens to nine parts, the night is equal to the day, and the year is exactly equal to its 364 days. Through the movement of the sun, distinctions are formed between the length of the day and the night, as well as the shortness of the day and the night. The result is that its course lengthens everyday and shortens at night. This is also the rule governing the course of the sun, which rises and sets endlessly and makes sixty separate trips around the earth. The great luminary is what rises, and it is given that name based on how it appears, as the Lord directed. He rises and sets at the same time, does not diminish or rest, but continues to move throughout the day and night. His brightness is seven times brighter than the moon's, although their sizes are identical. And following this law, I noticed another one that dealt with the Moon, a smaller nebula. In addition, her chariot, which she travels in, is propelled by the wind, and she receives light in proportion to the size of the heavens. Additionally, her rising and setting times vary every month, and her days are similar to those of the sun. When her light is consistent, it equals the seventh of the sun's light. She rises in this way. The moon's first phase in the east begins on the thirty-first morning, and on that day she becomes visible and, for you, coincides with the sun in the gateway where the sun rises on the thirty-first day. With the exception of one-seventh of it, the fourteenth part of her light, the other half of her exits by a seventh part, leaving the rest of her circumference vacant and without light. And her light equals one seventh part plus the other half when she obtains one seventh part of the other half. In that night at the start of her morning at the beginning of the lunar day, the moon sets with the sun, becoming invisible that night with the fourteen parts and the half of one of them. When the sun rises, the moon rises with him and receives the half of one part of light. And she rises on that day with precisely a seventh part, then emerges and moves away from the sun's rising, gaining thirteen parts of brightness throughout the course of her remaining days. And I observed another method, a rule for her, and how, in accordance with that rule, she carries out her monthly revolution. The holy angel Uriel, who is the commander of them all, then revealed to me each of these things, along with their locations. I noted each location as he gave it to me, as well as the months and the appearance of each light until the fifteen days had passed. She completes all of the light in the east in a single seventh part and all of the darkness in the west in a single seventh part. Additionally, she changes her settings occasionally and takes her own unique course occasionally. In those two middle portals—the third and fourth—the moon sets with the sun every two months. After seven days of travel, she returns through the portal where the sun rises, completes her mission and moves away from the sun. After eight days, she enters the sixth portal, which is where the sun sets. When the sun emerges from the fourth portal, she does so for seven days until she emerges from the fifth and, after returning to the fourth portal after seven days, uses up all of her light. In eight days, she recedes and enters the first portal. And she enters the fourth portal, where the sun emerges, to return once more after seven days. As a result, I observed their location, the moons' rising and setting phases at the time. And if five years are added together, the sun has a surplus of thirty days, giving it a total of 364 days when each of those five years is complete. And the excess of the sun and the stars is six days; in five years, six days a year add up to thirty days; and the moon lags behind the sun and the stars by a period of thirty days. The years are brought in exactly by the sun and the stars, who also complete them in 364 days with perfect justice. This prevents them from moving forward or backward in time throughout eternity by even a single day. There are 1,092 days in a year, 1,820 days in five years, and 2,912 days in eight years. In 3 years, there are 1,062 days for the moon alone. In 5 years, she is 50 days behind the total and must add 5 more days, for a total of 62 days. Considering that there are 1,770 days in every 5 years, the moon has 21,832 days every 8 years. Since she is 80 days behind in eight years, the total number of days she is behind is 80. And the year is precisely finished in accordance with the sun's stations, which rise from the portals through which it rises and sets 30 days, as well as their global stations. And the leaders of the heads of the thousands, who are in charge of the entire creation and all the stars, are also involved in the four intercalary days because they are integral to their roles in the calendar year and perform duties on the four days that are not included in the calendar year. They actually serve on the world stations, one in the first portal, one in the third portal of heaven, one in the fourth portal, and one in the sixth portal, and the accuracy of the year is achieved through each of the three hundred and sixty-four stations separately. As a result, men make mistakes there. Because the angel Uriel, whom the Lord of glory has set over all the luminaries of the heaven, in the heaven and in the world, showed them to me, they should rule over the face of the heaven, be seen on the earth, and be leaders for the day and the night, as well as all the ministering creatures that rotate in all the chariots of the heaven. Similar to this, Uriel revealed to me twelve openings in the perimeter of the sun's chariot in the heavens, through which the sun's rays emerge and from which, when they are opened at their designated times, warmth is disseminated across the globe. As well as for the winds and dew's spirit when they are opened, standing wide at the ends of the heavens. The sun, moon, stars, and all the creations of heaven in the east and the west emerge through the twelve gates in the heaven at the ends of the world. There are many windows open to their left and right, and each window produces warmth according to the season, much like the doors from which the stars emerge in accordance with His commands and where they settle in accordance with their number. Then I noticed chariots in the sky racing above the world's gateways where the stars that never set orbit. And one is bigger than the others, and it is that one that travels around the entire planet. And at the ends of the world, I noticed twelve portals that were wide open to every direction the winds come from and blow across the planet. Three of them are visible on the sky's surface, including three in the west, three to the heaven's right, and three to its left. The three first are from the east, followed by three from the north, three from the south's left, and three from the west. When these winds are sent, they bring disaster to the entire earth, the water on it, the people who live there, and everything that is in the water and on the land. Through four of them, winds of blessing and prosperity come, and from those eight, winds of harm. The first portal, which is in the east and leans toward the south, is where the so-called east wind, which is the first wind to emerge from those portals and brings with it desolation, drought, heat, and destruction, enters the world. The second gate in the middle also brings what is appropriate, bringing rain, fruitfulness, prosperity, and dew; the third door, which faces north, brings cold and drought. And after these, three portals in the south bring forth winds; the first of them brings forth a hot breeze that is inclined to the east. And there come forth sweet odors, dew and rain, wealth and health from the middle doorway next to it. And by the third doorway, which is to the west, locusts, rain, and desolation burst forth. And after these, the north winds, which bring rain, locusts, and devastation from the seventh doorway in the east. The third portal in the west brings cloud, hoarfrost, snow, rain, dew, and locusts, while the center portal brings health, rain, dew, and prosperity in a straight line. Following these four are the west winds, which blow through the first portal next to the north and bring with them dew, hoarfrost, cold, snow, and frost. And through the final gate, which is adjacent to the south, come forth dryness and desolation, as well as burning and destruction; and from the middle portal come forth dew and rain, prosperity, and blessing. I have revealed to you, my son Methuselah, all of the laws, all of the plagues, and all of the blessings of the twelve gateways of the four regions of heaven. And because it is the first, the first quarter is known as the east. The second is the south, where the Most High will descend in a very unique way as the One who is blessed for all time. Because all of the heaven's luminaries wane and dim there, the west quarter is also known as the reduced quarter. The fourth quarter, which is known as the north, is divided into three sections: the first is designated for human habitation; the second contains watery seas, abysses, woods, rivers, darkness, and clouds; and the third section is designated for the garden of righteousness. I saw seven mountains that were higher than all other mountains on earth. From these mountains, hoarfrost emerges, and days, seasons, and years pass by. I observed seven rivers on Earth that were greater than all other rivers, one of which empties into the Great Sea from the west. These two then travel from the north to the sea and pour water into the eastern Erythraean Sea. Of the remaining four, two depart for the Erythraean Sea and two enter the Great Sea before discharging themselves there and, according to some, into the desert. The other two remain on the side of the north. Two on the mainland and five in the Great Sea make up the seven large islands I spotted in the water and on land. The first is Orjares, and the second is Tomas, are the names of the sun. The moon also goes by four names: Asonja, Ebla, Benase, and Erae. Asonja is the first name given to the moon. These are the two big luminaries, and both of their circumferences are the same size and are similar in shape to the heaven's. There are seven areas of light around the sun's circle that are contributed to it more than the moon, and this process continues until the seventh area of the sun is completely used up. They then prepare and enter the western portals, turn about to the north, and emerge from the eastern portals on the surface of the heavens. And as the moon rises, a quarter of it may be seen in the heavens; at that point, she has completed her light for the fourteenth day. And until her light is complete on the fifteenth day, according to the year's sign, fifteen parts of light are transmitted to her, while the moon expands by one-fourth of a part. And in her waning, decreases on the first day to fourteen parts of her light, on the second day to thirteen parts of her light, on the third day to twelve, on the fourth day to eleven, on the fifth day to nine, on the sixth day to eight, on the eighth day to seven, on the ninth day to six, on the tenth day to five, on the eleventh day to four, on the thirteenth day to two, on the fourteenth day to the half of a seventh, and all   Additionally, the month can occasionally have twenty-nine days and once   twenty-eight.   Uriel also demonstrated to me another law, namely the direction and timing of the sun's transmission of light to the moon. When the moon is opposite the sun for fourteen days, she achieves her light in the heavens for the entire time she is developing in brightness, and when she is fully illuminated, she achieves her light in the heavens fully. She is referred to as the new moon on the first day because that is when the light shines upon her. She rises from the east at night and gets full precisely on the day the sun sets in the west. The moon shines throughout the entire night till the sun rises over her

and may be seen over against the sun. Again, she dwindles until all of the moon's light is gone, all of the month's days have passed, and her circumference is empty and devoid of light on the side where the moon's light emerges. She also creates three thirty-day months, three twenty-nine-day months, and three months at her time, during which she completes her fading in the first period of time and in the first portal for one hundred and seventy-seven days. And during the period of her departure, she makes three appearances of thirty days each, followed by three appearances of twenty-nine days each. She has a twenty-day cycle of appearing as a man at night and as heaven during the day, with only her light existing within her. The law governing every star in the heavens has now been fully revealed to you, my son. And he revealed to me all of the laws governing these for each day, each season for the production of rule, each year for its departure, and each month's and week's prescribed order: And the moon's waning, which occurs in the sixth gateway since it is here that her light is completed. After that, the waning begins, commencing in the first portal of its season, and lasts until one hundred seventy-seven days—counted in weeks, twenty-five and two days—have passed. She lags behind the sun and the constellations by precisely five days during the course of a time, and after this location that you can see has been explored. Uriel the archangel, who is their leader, showed me a photo and a drawing of each luminary.

Chapter 3: Heavenly Tablets
The angel Uriel responded to me at that moment and said, "Behold, I have showed thee everything Enoch and I have revealed everything to thee that thou shouldst behold this sun and this moon, and the leaders of the stars of the

heaven and all who turn them, their assignments, times, and departures. In addition, the years will be shorter and the seed of the sinners' lands and farms will come late. The rain will be held back by the heavens, and everything on earth will change and fail to manifest in its proper time. Additionally, the fruits of the trees will not ripen when they should and the fruits of the soil will be delayed during those seasons. The moon will also change her schedule and stop appearing when she should. And during those times, the sun will be seen. He will travel in the west at dusk on the end of the large chariot and shine brighter than is consistent with the natural order of light. And many commanders of the stars will break the rules, changing their orbits and assignments and failing to show up at the times that were set out for them. And the entire arrangement of the stars will be hidden from sinners, and everyone on earth will have incorrect ideas about them. And they will change in all of their ways. Yes, they will misunderstand and believe they are gods. And they will experience increased evil, and they will get punishment that will completely destroy them. Then He commanded me, saying, "Observe, Enoch, these heavenly tablets and read what is written thereon, and mark every individual fact." I then observed the celestial tablets, read everything that was written and understood it, and read the record of all human acts and all fleshly descendants who would ever live on earth down to the farthest generations. The moment I realized that the great Lord, the King of glory for all time, had created all of the world's works, I praised Him. And I praised the Lord for His forbearance and gave thanks to Him for humankind's descendants. Then I continued by declaring: "Blessed is the man who dies in righteousness and goodness concerning whom no book of

unrighteousness is written and against whom no day of judgment shall be found." And when they brought me, they laid me down on the ground in front of my door and commanded me, "Declare everything to your son Methuselah, and demonstrate to all of your offspring that there is no flesh that is righteous in the eyes of the Lord, for He is their Creator. For a year, we will leave you with your son so that you can instruct your children, keep a record for them, and witness to all of your offspring. The second year, they will remove you from their midst. Be courageous because the good will proclaim the righteousness of the good; the righteous will rejoice with the righteous and will congratulate one another. But sinners will perish with sinners, and apostates will perish with apostates. And those who uphold righteousness will perish as a result of human actions and be removed as a result of the actions of the godless. And during those times, they stopped speaking to me, so I went to my people and praised the Lord of the universe.

Chapter 4: One Year to Record
And now, my son Methuselah, I'm telling you about and recording all of these things for you! So, my son Methuselah, keep the books in your father's possession and see to it that you deliver them to the world's generations. I have given wisdom to thee and to thy children and thy children that shall be to thee, that they may give it to their children for generations, this wisdom that passeth their understanding. And those who comprehend it won't go to sleep; instead, they'll listen with their ears to learn this wisdom, which will make people who consume it more appetizing than good food. Those who follow the path of righteousness and refrain from sinning like sinners are blessed, as do all the righteous. In the counting of all their days

when the sun travels across the sky, entering and leaving the portals for thirty days with the heads of thousands of the order of the stars, along with the four that are intercalated which divide the four portions of the year, who lead them and enter with them four days. Because of them, men will be at fault for failing to precisely identify them and account for them in the year's total reckoning. One in the first portal, one in the third, one in the fourth, and one in the sixth are genuinely recorded for all time and the year is through in 364 days, therefore they all count toward the tally of the year. Because Uriel has disclosed and revealed the luminaries, months, festivals, years, and days to me, who the Lord of the entirety of creation of the world has submitted the host of heaven to, the account of it is precise and the recorded reckoning of it is exact. In addition, he has control over the sun, moon, stars, and all other celestial bodies that move in circular chariots, as well as over night and day in the heavens, causing the light to shine on people. And these are the constellations' orders, which correspond to the seasons, holidays, and months in which they are set. These are the names of the people who are in charge of making sure that they arrive at the appropriate times, according to the prescribed orders, seasons, months, periods of dominion, and positions. Their four leaders who divide the four parts of the year enter first, followed by the twelve leaders of the orders who divide the months, heads over thousands for the three hundred and sixty who divide the days, and the leaders who divide the four intercalary days. These heads over thousands are sandwiched between one leader and the next, each hiding behind a station, but it is their leaders who choose how they are divided. The four halves of the year are divided by these leaders, whose names

are Milkiel, Helemmelek, Melejal, and Narel. There are three people who follow the leaders of the orders, Adnarel, Ijasusael, and Elomeel, and one person who follows the three people who follow the leaders of the stations that split the year's four halves. Melkejal, also known as Tamaini and the Sun, rises first and takes the throne at the beginning of the year, and he rules for a total of ninety-one days. And these are the days' signs that will be evident on earth during his reign: sweat, heat, and calms; all trees bear fruit; all trees produce leaves; the harvest of wheat; rose blooms; and all the flowers that appear in the fields. However, the trees that are in bloom during the winter season wither. The days of their domination are coming to an end, and these are the names of the leaders who are beneath them: Berkael, Zelebsel, and another who is added as a head of a thousand, called Hilujaseph. After him comes Helemmelek, also known as the brilliant sun, whose reign lasted ninety-one days in total. In the days of his dominion, the earth will experience glowing heat and dryness, the trees will ripen their fruits and produce all of their ripe and ready fruit, the sheep will pair up and become pregnant, all of the earth's fruits will be gathered in, everything in the fields will be harvested, and the winepress will be in operation. Gidaljal, Keel, and Heel, as well as the name of the head of a thousand who is joined to them, Asfael, are the names, orders, and leaders of those heads of thousands. The days of his dominance are coming to an end.

Chapter 5: Visions

And now, my son Methuselah, I will narrate all of the visions I have had for you to behold. Before I married, I had two visions, one of which was very different from the other. The first time was while I was learning how to write; the second time was just before I abducted your mother. And I prayed to the Lord about them. I had just fallen asleep in my grandfather Mahalaleel's home when I had a vision of the heaven collapsing, being carried away, and hitting the ground. And as it hit the ground, I witnessed how the earth was engulfed in a massive chasm, mountains were hung on top of one another, hills descended on top of one another, and tall trees were severed from their stems and sent downward into the chasm. At that point, I let out a word that caused me to lift up and shout, "The earth is destroyed!" My grandfather Mahalaleel woke me up as I was lying next to him and asked me, "My son, why do you cry so much and why do you make such lamentation?" I told him what I had seen in the vision, and he replied, "My son, what thou hast seen is a horrible thing, and of grave matter as to the secrets of all the wickedness of the earth: it must descend into the depths and be destroyed with a vast destruction. And now, my son, stand up and ask the Lord of glory—since you are a believer—to save some of His people from the destruction of the entire planet. My son, all of this will descend from heaven and the planet will experience an enormous catastrophe. After that, I got up, pleaded, begged, and wrote down my prayer for all future generations. I'll show everything to you, my son Methuselah. Then, after I descended to the earth's surface and saw the heavens, the sun rising in the east, the moon setting in the west, a few stars, the entire earth, and everything as He had known it in the beginning, I praised and blessed the Lord of judgment for having caused the sun to rise from the east, as well as for having caused Him to ascend and rise on the face of the heavens and set out on the path that had been revealed to Him. And I extended my hands in righteousness to bless the Holy and Great One while speaking out loud using the flesh tongue that God created for children of the flesh of men so they could speak with it. God gave them breath, a tongue, and a mouth so they could speak. Blessed be You, O Lord, King, Great and Mighty in Your Greatness, Lord of the entire creation of the heavens, King of kings, and God of the entire earth. All the heavens are Thy throne for all time, and the whole earth is Thy footstool for all time; and Thy power, monarchy, and greatness abide for ever and ever, as well as Thy reign throughout all generations. Since You created everything and Rule Everything, There Is Nothing Too Hard For Thee. Wisdom does not leave the location of Thy seat or turn away from it. Nothing is hidden from You since You see everything, and you know, see, and hear everything. The angels of Thy heavens have now committed a transgression, and Thy wrath remains on human flesh until the great day of judgment. And now, O God, Lord, and Great King, I plead and beg Thee to grant my request and not grant the destruction of all human flesh and the making of the planet inhabitable in order to bring about an eternal destruction. And now, O Lord, eliminate from the face of the earth the flesh that has provoked Thy wrath, but establish the flesh of righteousness and uprightness as a plant of the eternal seed, and do not hide Thy face from the prayer of Thy servant. And after that, I had another dream, which I will now disclose to my kid in its entirety. Then Enoch rose and addressed his son Methuselah, saying, "To thee, my son, will I speak: hear my words; bend thine ear to the dream; incline thine eye to the vision of thy father. Prior to taking your mother Edna, I had a dream in which I saw a white bull emerging from the ground, followed by a heifer and then two more bulls—one black and the other red—all emerging simultaneously. After the black bull gored the red one and chased him across the ground, I was unable to see the red bull any more. But as the black bull matured and the heifer followed him, I noticed that many other oxen followed and looked like him. And that cow, the first one, left the first bull's presence to look for the red one, but she was unsuccessful. She then searched for him and wept bitterly. I watched until the first bull approached her and calmed her down; after that, she stopped crying. And after that, she gave birth to a second white bull, followed by numerous other bulls and black cows. Then, while I was sleeping, I watched the white bull develop into a large white bull and give birth to numerous other white bulls that looked just like him. They then started to give birth to several white bulls that resembled them, one after the other. Then, while I dozed off, I once again saw with my own eyes the heavens above and noticed a star that had fallen from them and was now eating and grazing among those oxen. Then I noticed the big, black oxen; lo and behold, they all started interacting with one another and changing their stalls, pastures, and livestock. And once more, as I watched the vision and turned to face the sky, I saw a great number of stars come tumbling down to the first star, where they transformed into bulls and pastured alongside the cattle. Then I turned to look at them and noticed that they were all letting out their private parts like horses and starting to cover the oxen's cows. Eventually, all of them conceived and gave birth to elephants, camels, and asses. As a result of their dread and fright, all of the oxen started to bite, devour, and cause pain with their horns. In addition, they started eating those oxen, at which point all of the inhabitants of the earth started to fear and shudder in their presence and run away. Then I once more witnessed how they started to consume and gore one another, which caused the earth to scream loudly. Then I lifted my eyes once more to the sky, and I saw in the vision that entities that resembled white men were emerging from heaven. Four of these beings left the area, and three more followed them. And those three who were the last to appear grabbed hold of my hand, lifted me beyond the generations of the earth, and showed me a tower that was elevated far over the landscape, with all the hills being lower. Then someone said to me, "Remain here until you see everything that happens to those elephants, camels, and asses, as well as the stars and the oxen, and everything else." Then I saw one of the four individuals who had emerged first capture the first star to fall from the sky, bind it from head to toe, and toss it into a chasm. That chasm was now small, deep, horrifying, and dark. Then one of them pulled out a sword and handed it to the elephants, camels, and asses. When they started slashing each other, the entire earth trembled in response. And as I was watching the vision, behold, one of the four who had down stoned the beings from heaven, gathered and took all the large stars, whose privy members resembled that of horses, chained them all hand and foot, and flung them all into the depths of the earth. One of those four went to that white bull and taught him a secret without making him afraid; he was born a bull, became a man, and built a large vessel on which to live, in which three bulls also lived and were covered. Then I looked up again and noticed a towering roof with seven water torrents that were pouring a lot of water into a confined area. Then I looked again, and I saw that the fountains had been opened on the top of the large enclosure, and the water had started to rise and fill the surface. I then saw the enclosure completely filled in water. And as the water, the darkness, and the mist grew thicker around it, I noticed that the water's level had risen over that of the enclosure and was now spilling over it as it stood on the ground. The entire herd of cattle in that corral was collected up until I witnessed their sinking, being sucked up by the sea, and dying there. However, that ship remained afloat as every animal—including all the oxen, elephants, camels, and horses—sank to the bottom. I was unable to see the animals any more, and since they were unable to swim away, they perished and fell to the bottom of the sea. I continued to see in the vision up until the water torrents from the high roof were stopped, the earth's chasms were leveled off, and additional abysses were made accessible. As the earth became apparent, the water started to flow into these, but when that vessel touched the ground, the blackness vanished and light broke through. But the white bull that had changed into a man emerged from the jar together with the other three bulls, one of which was white like the white bull, another was red like blood, and the third was black; the white bull then left them. Then they started giving birth to various kinds of animals and birds, including wolves, dogs, hyenas, wild boars, foxes, squirrels, pigs, falcons, vultures, kites, eagles, and ravens. A white bull was also born among them. They started biting each other, but the white bull that was born among them also sired a wild ass and another white bull, which led to an increase in the number of wild asses. However, the bull that was born from him produced a white sheep and a black wild boar, the latter of which produced twelve more sheep than the former. When the twelve sheep reached adulthood, they abandoned one of them to the asses, who then abandoned it once more to the wolves, where it raised its young. And the Lord took the eleven sheep and placed them among the wolves to pasture with them, where they multiplied and grew into numerous flocks of sheep. Then the wolves started to dread them, and they tormented them until they were destroyed, making them scream aloud for their children and bring complaints to their Lord. And a sheep that had been rescued from wolves fled and made its way to some wild asses. I watched the sheep as they wept and pleaded with their Lord with all of their might until the Lord of the sheep came to them and pastured them in response to the sheep's cries from a lofty abode. The sheep that had escaped the wolves was called, and He spoke to it about the wolves so that it would warn them not to touch the sheep. According to the Lord's word, the sheep walked to the wolves, where another sheep met it and followed. The two sheep then went into the group of wolves and spoke with them, warning them not to touch the sheep in the future. After then, I witnessed the wolves brutally tormenting the sheep with all of their might as the animals cried out in pain. When the Lord arrived, the sheep started to be struck by the wolves, who then started to weep, but the sheep immediately stopped crying out and went silent. I watched the sheep till they disappeared from the wolves, but the wolves' eyes had been blindfolded, so they had to flee in hot pursuit of the sheep. And the Shepherd of the Sheep walked with them as their leader, and all of His Sheep followed Him; and it was a horrible thing to see the face of the Shepherd of the Sheep. But the wolves got after those sheep and followed them until they came to a sea of water. Their Lord guided them and stood between them and the wolves as the sea was split, with the water standing on one side and on the other in front of their faces. Then, because the wolves had not yet noticed the sheep, the sheep moved into the middle of the sea, and the wolves followed them and dove into the water after them. When they came face to face with the Shepherd of the Sheep, they turned to run, but the sea gathered itself together and returned to its original state, swelling and rising until it engulfed the wolves. And I saw as all of the wolves that were pursuing those lambs died and drowned. But the sheep managed to get away from that water and ventured into a wilderness where there was neither water nor grass. As they started to open their eyes and see, the sheep started to lead them and I observed the shepherd tending to them and providing them with food and drink. The Lord of the Sheep then sent the sheep to them after it reached the top of the tall cliff. Then I saw the Sheep Lord standing in front of them; He had a huge, terrifying, and magnificent aspect, and when the sheep saw Him, they were terrified in front of His face. As a result of His presence, they all grew frightened and shook, and they called out to the flock that was present, "We are not able to stand before our Lord or to behold Him." When they reached the top of the rock, the sheep that had been leading them back down began to become blinded and to stray from the path he had shown them, but it was unaware of this. When the sheep realized that the sheep's Lord was furiously angry with them, they descended from the top of the rock and went to the sheep, where they discovered that the majority of them had become blinded and separated from the flock. When they first saw it, they shuddered in terror and yearned to go back to their folds. Then, when it approached the sheep who had broken away, it brought other sheep with it and started to kill them. The sheep were terrified of its approach, and as a result, the sheep that had broken away were brought back and returned to their folds. I continued to see this vision until the sheep turned into a man, built a home for the sheep's Lord, and then brought all the sheep inside.

And I watched until the sheep that had encountered the one that had led them passed out. I also watched until all the large sheep died and the little ones rose in their place, and they eventually arrived at a pasture and began to walk toward a body of water. When their leader, a sheep who had transformed into a man, departed from them and fell asleep, all the sheep went in search of it and wept bitterly over it. And I watched as they stopped pleading for that sheep and crossed the watery stream, at which point the two sheep that had been leading them before they fell asleep suddenly reappeared as their leaders. And I watched until the sheep arrived in a beautiful location in a peaceful and wonderful land, and I watched until those sheep were full, at which point the house stood amid them in the peaceful land. And occasionally, their eyes were opened, and other times, they were blinded, until another sheep got up and led them all back, at which point, their eyes were opened. When the Lord of the Sheep raised up another sheep, a ram from their midst, who led them, the dogs, foxes, and wild boars started to devour those sheep. And that ram started to butt those dogs, foxes, and wild boars on either side until he had eliminated them all. And when a sheep's eyes were opened, it saw the ram among the sheep and abandoned its splendour to start butting the sheep, trampling on them, and acting in an unsightly manner. Then, in place of the ram that had abandoned its glory, the Lord of the Sheep sent the lamb to another lamb and reared that lamb to become a ram and the shepherd of the sheep. It then went to it and spoke to it alone, promoted it to the status of a ram, and appointed it as the sheep's prince and leader. Throughout this entire process, however, the dogs continued to mistreat the sheep. The second ram got up and ran away in front of the first ram as it was being pursued, and I watched until the first ram was killed by the dogs. And that second ram got up and started leading the young lambs. These sheep increased in number, but all the dogs, foxes, and wild boars were terrified of it and fled before it. The ram then attacked and killed the wild animals, removing their dominance over the 49 sheep and preventing further theft. That ram produced numerous sheep before passing away, and a small sheep took its place as ram, serving as the sheep's prince and leader. The house grew to be quite large and was constructed for the sheep. The Lord of the sheep had a towering and large tower constructed on his lowly dwelling, and when the tower was elevated and lofty, the Lord of the sheep stood atop it while they laid a full table before Him. And once more, I observed those sheep as they made the same mistakes, moved in different directions, and abandoned their home. The sheep's Lord then sent out some of the sheep, but the sheep started killing them. One of them was saved and not killed; it fled quickly and screamed out over the sheep. They tried to kill it, but the Shepherd of the Sheep delivered it up to me and made it live there. He also sent numerous other sheep to those sheep to bear witness to them and weep for them. Then I saw how they completely fell away when they abandoned the Lord's house and His tower, and their eyes became completely blind. I also witnessed how the Shepherd of the Sheep carried out great murder among them in their herds until those sheep invited that killing and violated His position. And He turned them over to all the wild animals, including wolves, lions, tigers, foxes, and hyenas. These animals then started tormenting the sheep by tearing them to pieces. Then I saw that He abandoned their dwelling and tower and sent them to the lions, who tore them

to pieces and devoured them, as well as the hands of all the wild animals. I then started to wail loudly with all my might, calling out to the Shepherd's Lord and telling Him that the sheep had been eaten by every wild animal. Even though He was aware of it, He did nothing but enjoy that they were eaten, swallowed, and taken, and He left them for all the animals to eat. He then gathered seventy shepherds and gave them the sheep so they might tend to them. He then addressed the shepherds and their companions, saying, "Let each of you tend the sheep from this point forward, and do whatever I shall order you. And I will hand them over to you after properly counting them, telling you which ones need to be destroyed so that you can then do so. And He handed those sheep over to them. "Observe and mark everything that the shepherds will do to those sheep, for they will kill more of them than I have commanded them," He then called another and addressed him. Record every excess and the destruction brought about by the shepherds, including how many they kill at my direction and how many at their own whim. List all the destruction brought about by each individual shepherd. And count out in front of me the number of people they kill and give away for destruction so that I can use this as evidence against them. I also need to be aware of everything the shepherds do so that I can understand what they are doing and determine whether they are following the instructions I have given them. However, they won't be aware of it, and you shouldn't tell them or warn them about it; instead, just keep track of every instance of destruction the shepherds cause and present it to me. And I observed until the time came for those shepherds to graze, at which point they started killing and destroying more animals than was required of them, handing those sheep over to the lions. And the lions and tigers ate and gobbled up the majority of those sheep, along with the wild boars; they also burned down the tower and tore down the home. Because the sheep's housing was destroyed and I was unable to determine whether the sheep had entered it thereafter, I became incredibly upset over the tower. The shepherds and their associates then gave those sheep to all the wild animals for them to devour, and each one of them received a specific number in his or her turn. It was recorded by the other in a book how many of them each destroyed. Each one killed and ruined far more sheep than was necessary, and I started to cry and grieve for those animals. And so, in the vision, I witnessed the writer as he meticulously recorded each animal that the shepherds had sacrificed to destruction, carried it up to the Lord of the Sheep and laid it down there, and then actually showed him the entire book, detailing everything the shepherds had done, taken, and sacrificed. After the book was read in front of the Shepherd Lord, He took it from him, read it, sealed it, and set it aside. I immediately noticed that the shepherds had been grazing for a full twelve hours when I noticed that three of the sheep had turned around, returned, entered, and started to rebuild the parts of the home that had collapsed. The wild boars attempted to stop them, but they were powerless to do so. They started construction once more and raised the tower, giving it the name "high tower." They also started setting up a table in front of the tower, but everything on it was contaminated and unclean. In regards to this, the sheep's eyes were blindfolded so that neither they nor their shepherds could see. They then sent the sheep to their shepherds in great numbers for slaughter, who then tramped on them with their feet and ate them. When all the sheep had been scattered

across the field and had mixed with them and no one had been able to preserve them from the hands of the monsters, the Lord of the Sheep remained motionless. And the author of the book brought it before the Shepherd of the Sheep and read it, presented it to Him, and begged Him on their behalf as he displayed all the actions of the shepherds and testified in front of Him against all of them. After taking the actual book, he set it down next to Him and left. And I watched as 35 shepherds took on the pasturing in this way, finishing their times separately as did the first, before being taken in by others to graze them for their periods, each shepherd in his own period. Then I saw in a vision all the birds of heaven, including eagles, vultures, kites, and ravens, arriving. The eagles led the other birds as they started to pick out the sheep's eyes and eat their flesh. Then the sheep screamed out as the birds ate their flesh, and I looked and wept in my sleep over the shepherd who was tending the sheep. And I watched as those sheep were consumed by dogs, eagles, and kites, who stripped them of all their flesh, skin, and sinew until only their bones remained. As a result, the number of sheep decreased as a result. And I watched until twenty-three had started the pasturing and finished it fifty-eight times during their various durations. However, those white sheep were now carrying lambs, and the lambs started to open their eyes, see, and call out to the other sheep. Indeed, they shouted out to them, but they were utterly deaf and blind, and they paid no attention to anything they said. In the vision, I witnessed how the ravens attacked the lambs, stole one of the lambs, tore the sheep to pieces, and then ate them. And I saw as the horns on those lambs developed and the ravens threw down their horns. I also watched as one of those sheep's large horns sprouted and their eyes were opened. When it gazed at them, their eyes opened, and it screamed out to the sheep. When the rams saw this, they all rushed to the crying sheep. And despite all of this, the eagles, vultures, ravens, and kites continued to tear apart the sheep, swoop down on them, and devour them. The sheep continued to be silent, but the rams wept and cried out. And those ravens fought and struggled with it, trying to bring down its horn, but they were powerless to do so. All of the eagles, vultures, ravens, and kites were collected together, and they brought all of the field sheep with them. In other words, they all came together and assisted one another in breaking the ram's horn. I watched as all the animals and birds of the sky fled in fear as the sheep attacked all the animals in the field with a large sword that had been given to them. And I observed the author of the book who had followed the Lord's instructions until he had revealed how much more harm the twelve last shepherds had brought about before the Lord of the sheep than their forefathers had. And I saw as all the creatures and all the birds of heaven fell from among those sheep and were sucked up in the earth, which then covered them, as the Shepherd of the Sheep approached them and grasped the rod of His fury in His hand. And I saw as the sheep Lord sat on a throne that had been set up in the lovely region, and the other person took the sealed books and unlocked them in front of the sheep Lord. The Lord then referred to those individuals as the "seven first white ones" and told them to bring before Him all the stars with visible members resembling those of horses, starting with the first star that led the way. They did so. Take those 70 shepherds to whom I delivered the sheep and who, taking them on their own power, murdered more than I commanded them, He said to that man who wrote before

Him, who was one of those seven white ones. They were all standing before Him and I saw that they were all shackled. The stars were judged first, and after being found guilty, they were sent to the place of condemnation where they were flung into a pit that was engulfed in flames and fire pillars. And after being judged and found guilty, those 70 shepherds were condemned and put into the blazing pit. At that time, I witnessed the opening of a similar, blazing pit in the middle of the ground. They then brought the blinded sheep, judged and found them all guilty, and then flung them into the abyss where they burnt. And I witnessed the burning of those sheep's bones. And I got up to watch as they folded up the old home, taking all the pillars, beams, and decorations with them as they did so. They then transported the old house away and buried it somewhere in the south of the country. And I observed until the Sheep Lord brought a new house greater and loftier than the first and erected it in the location of the first that had been folded up; all of its pillars were new, and its ornaments were larger and newer than those of the first, the old one that He had removed, and all the sheep were inside. Then I witnessed every remaining sheep, along with every animal on the planet and every bird in the sky, bowing down to the remaining sheep, praying to them, and doing everything in their might to please them. Following their capture of my hand, which they had already taken up, and the hand of that ram also catching hold of me, the three who were dressed in white then lifted me up and placed me among the sheep before the judgment. Additionally, the wool of those sheep was plentiful and clean, and they were all white. All of the previously destroyed and dispersed things, together with all of the wild animals and avian species, gathered in that building, and the Lord of the Sheep was ecstatic that they were all good and had come back to His abode. I watched until the sword that had been given to the sheep was put down and taken back into the house, where it was sealed in the sight of the Lord. All of the sheep were then invited inside, but the house was unable to accommodate them. There was not a single person in the group who did not see the good when their eyes were enlightened by this. Then I noticed how big, wide, and packed the house was. And I witnessed the birth of a white bull with prominent horns, whom all wild animals and birds of the air terrified and constantly prayed to. The first of them changed into a lamb, and that lamb grew to be a large beast with enormous black horns on its head. The Lord of the sheep delighted over it and over all the oxen. And I watched until all of their generations were transformed, and they all became white bulls. I dozed out in the middle of them, woke up, and took in everything. I dreamed of this vision, and when I awoke, I praised the Lord of righteousness and gave Him glory. When I saw, they flowed because of what I had seen; all will come to pass and be accomplished, and all the deeds of men in their order were shown to me. I sobbed then with a tremendous crying, and my tears did not stay until I could no longer bear them. That evening, I had a flashback of my first dream, which caused me to cry and feel uneasy because I had witnessed that vision.

Book 5:
Enoch's Epistle
Chapter 1: Enoch's Instructions

Now, my son Methuselah, bring all of your brothers and mother's sons to me. The word has called me, and the spirit has been poured forth upon me so that I may tell you everything that will happen to you in the future. Methuselah then went and gathered his family and sent for all of his brothers. "Hear, ye sons of Enoch, all the words of your father, and hearken rightly to the voice of my mouth, for I exhort you and say unto you, beloved: Love uprightness and walk therein," he said to all the offspring of righteousness. And do not approach righteousness while harboring a double heart. Do not associate with individuals harboring a double heart. Instead, my sons walk in righteousness. And it will lead you down the correct roads, and righteousness will walk alongside you. Because I am aware that there will be an increase in violence on earth, as well as a severe chastisement, which will put an end to all iniquity and cut it off at the source, destroying its entire framework. And injustice will once more come to fruition on earth. And all acts of injustice, aggression, and violation will succeed to a greater extent than before. And when sin, wickedness, and blasphemy abound, along with all forms of violence, apostasy, trespass, and uncleanness, All of them will get severe punishment from heaven, and the holy Lord will show his wrath and chastisement in order to bring about justice on earth. During those times, dishonesty and the roots of injustice will both be uprooted, and they will both be destroyed from the foundations of the earth. All pagan idols will be abandoned, their temples will be set ablaze, and they will be removed from the entire planet. They will then be condemned to eternal destruction by fire and perish in its wrath. And the wise will awaken and be handed to the righteous, bringing them out of their sleep. Then the roots of unrighteousness will be cut off, the sinners will be put to death by the sword, and blasphemers will be put to death everywhere. Those who plan acts of violence and those who blaspheme will also be put to death by the sword. And now, my boys, I'll explain you and demonstrate the differences between the violent and righteous paths.

Yes, I'll show them to you once more so you can see what will happen. And now, heed my advice, my sons, and choose the upright way rather than the violent one, for everyone who follows the former will die for all time.

Chapter 2: Wisdom of Enoch

The book that Enoch wrote For all of my children who will live on the planet, Enoch did in fact write this comprehensive doctrine of wisdom, admired by all mankind and a judge of the entire earth. And for the generations still to come who will uphold righteousness and peace. "Do not let the times bother your spirit; for the Holy and Great One has determined the times for everything. The righteous person will awaken from sleep, walk in the ways of righteousness, and engage in all activities with an attitude of unfailing goodness and grace. He will be kind to the just and grant him eternal uprightness. He will also give him strength so that he will be with goodness and righteousness. And he will move in unending light. And sin will vanish forever into darkness and never again be visible after that day. Then Enoch gave and started recounting from the books. And Enoch said, "I will explain these things concerning the offspring of righteousness, concerning the elect of the world, and concerning the plant of uprightness. Yes, I Enoch will declare to you, my sons: According to what I saw in the heavenly vision, what I learned from the heavenly tablets, and what I learned from the word of the holy angels. Enoch then started retelling the story from the books, saying: "I was born on the seventh day of the first week, while judgment and righteousness were still in effect. And following me, in the second week, there will be a huge rise in wickedness and deceit, and that is where the first end will come. And a man will be rescued through it; once it is through,

however, wickedness will rise and a law will be made for sinners. And after that, at the conclusion of the third week, a man will be chosen to serve as the seed of just judgment, and his descendants will serve as the plant of righteousness forever. Then, at the conclusion of the fourth week, visions of the righteous and holy will be seen, and a law for all generations as well as an enclosure will be constructed for them. Then, at the end of the fifth week, the mansion of glory and dominion will be constructed forever. And after that, in the sixth week, everyone who lives there will become blind and abandon wisdom in a godless manner. And a man will rise in it; at its conclusion, the house of dominion will be consumed by fire, and the entire chosen root race will be scattered. And after that, in the seventh week, a generation of apostates will emerge, whose acts will be many and wholly apostate. And at its conclusion, the elect righteous of the eternal plant of righteousness will be chosen, and they will be given sevenfold teaching about all His creation. Who among all human beings is able to hear the voice of the Holy One without becoming disturbed? Who is capable of thinking His thoughts? Who is present who is able to observe all the activities of heaven? How would one be able to see the heavens, and who is there who could comprehend their workings, see a soul or a spirit, and tell of such, or ascend and see all their purposes, conceive them, or act in accordance with them? Who among all men is able to determine the dimensions of the earth's breadth and length, and to whom has the total distance between them been revealed? Or is there anyone who can determine the size of the heaven, its height, the material on which it is built, the quantity of stars, and the location of all the luminaries? So now I say to you, my sons, embrace righteousness and walk in it since the roads of unrighteousness will be abruptly destroyed and gone while the paths of righteousness are deserving of acceptance. And certain men of a generation will learn the paths of bloodshed and death, and they will keep their distance from them and refuse to pursue them. And now I say to you who are upright: Do not walk in the ways of evil or in the ways of death, and do not approach them, lest you perish. But seek and make a decision for yourself to live a righteous and elect life, and follow peaceful paths, and you will live and flourish. And keep my words close to your hearts and do not allow them to be forgotten. This is because I am aware that sinners will try to persuade people to seek wisdom for evil purposes in order to prevent her from flourishing and to make all temptations stronger. Woe to those who establish injustice and oppression and use deception as a basis; they will be abruptly overturned and will not find peace. Woe to those who built their homes on iniquity for they will be destroyed from all of their foundations and brought low by the sword. Those who obtain gold and metal in judgment will perish suddenly. Woe to you, rich people, for putting your reliance in your wealth and departing from it because you forgot to remember the Most High while you were affluent. You have sinned and done wrong, and you have prepared yourself for the day of the great judgment, the day of the slaughter, and the day of darkness. Accordingly, I speak and proclaim to you that your Creator will overcome you, and he or she will take pleasure in your demise rather than feel pity for you. And in those days, your virtuous people will be a disgrace to sinners and atheists. Oh, that my eyes were a cloud of waters so that I could mourn over you and let my tears fall as a cloud of waters, so that I may find relief from my heart's suffering. Who has given you permission to act in a reproachful and malicious manner? As a result, you sinners will experience judgment. Do not be afraid of the sinners, you upright; for the Lord will again release them into your hands so that you may judge them as you see fit. Woe to you who fulminate anathemas that cannot be reversed: Because of your misdeeds, healing shall be far from you. Woe to you if you treat your neighbor unfairly; you will be held accountable for your actions. Woe to you, dishonest witnesses, and those who weigh unjustly, for you will perish suddenly. Woe to you, sinners, for you oppress the just; for you will be handed over and oppressed because of injustice, and its yoke shall be heavy upon you. Have hope, you righteous people; sinners will suddenly perish in front of you, and you will rule them as you choose. And on the day of the tribulation of the ungodly, your offspring will mount and soar like eagles, and your nest will be higher than the vultures. You will ascend and enter the cracks in the ground and the fissures in the rock for all eternity as coneys before the ungodly, and the sirens will sigh and weep because of you. Consequently, do not be afraid, you who have endured suffering, for recovery will be your lot, and you will be illuminated by a bright light and hear the voice of rest coming from heaven. Woe to you, you sinners; your wealth makes you seem like the righteous, but your hearts accuse you of sin, and this truth will be used as evidence against you as a reminder of your wrongdoings. Woe to you who consume the finest of the wheat, sip wine from huge bowls, and violently tramp the weak. Woe to those of you who ingest water from every source; for suddenly you will perish and fade away because you have abandoned the source of life. Woe to you who practice wickedness, deceit, and blasphemy; it will serve as a reminder of your wrongdoing. Woe to you, powerful people who use their power to oppress the good; the day of your ruin is near. On the day of your judgment, the righteous will experience many and good days.

Chapter 3: Wisdom of Enoch

Believe, ye upright, that the sinners will perish in the day of unrighteousness and become a disgrace. Know that the Most High is conscious of your ruin and that the angels of heaven rejoice in it. When the voice of the righteous' prayer is heard on the day of judgment, what will you do, you sinners, and where will you run? In fact, you will fare similarly to those people to whom the statement "You have been in company of sinners" will be used as evidence. And then the days of your judgment will come, and the prayers of the righteous will be heard by the Lord. Your faces will be covered in humiliation when all of your wicked remarks are read out in front of the Great Holy One, who will also reject any work based on unrighteousness. Woe to you, ye sinners, who dwell in the middle of the sea and on dry land and whose memory brings misfortune upon you. Woe to those of you who acquire silver and gold dishonestly and boast that they have obtained all of their desired assets and wealth. And now, let's carry out our plan since we have collected silver and have many husbandmen living in our homes. And our grain bins are overflowing with grain. Indeed, your lies will disappear like water, and your wealth won't cling to you; rather, it will quickly ascend from you because you obtained it all via unrighteousness and will be subjected to a severe curse. And now, both the clever and the ignorant, I make a vow to you, for you will have a variety of experiences on earth. For you men will dress more elaborately than women and wear more colorful clothing than virgins; in majesty, grandeur, and power, as well as in silver,

gold, and purple, splendor, and food, they will be poured out as water. As a result, they will lack teaching and insight, and they will perish along with their belongings as a result. And their spirits will be tossed into the flaming furnace with all of their brilliance and splendor, as well as in humiliation, slaughter, and extreme poverty. I have sworn to you, you sinners, that a mountain has never been made a slave, and a hill has never been made a woman's handmaiden. Nevertheless, sin was not thrust upon the earth; rather, it was brought about by man, and those who practice it will suffer a severe curse. And the woman has not been granted barrenness; rather, due to the actions of her own hands, she passes away childless. I swear to you, ye sinners, by the Holy Great One, that all your wicked deeds are made known in the skies and that none of your oppressive deeds are covered up and kept secret. Furthermore, do not believe or claim in your heart or mind that you are unaware of the fact that every transgression is daily recorded in heaven in the sight of the Most High. As of now, you are aware that every act of injustice you commit will be recorded daily until the day of your judgment. Woe to you, you fools, because you will perish as a result of your foolishness; additionally, you have sinned against the wise, and therefore good fortune will not be your part. Finally, be aware that you are ready for the day of judgment: Sinners, do not expect to live; rather, expect to depart and die; for you have no knowledge of a ransom; for you have been made ready for the day of the great judgment, for the day of suffering, and for the day of much anguish for your spirits. Woe to you, obstinate heartless ones, who practice evil and consume blood: How did you get delicious stuff to eat, drink, and fill you up? You won't have peace because of all the beautiful things that the Most High

Lord has abundantly provided on earth. Woe to you who adore the works of injustice: Why do you hope for good to come to you? Be aware that when the righteous receive you, they will kill you and cut off your necks without showing any mercy. Woe to you who take pleasure in the suffering of the righteous; no grave will be prepared for you. Woe to you, for you have no chance of survival if you disregard the teachings of the righteous. Woe to those of you who record godless and dishonest speech because they do it so that others can hear their lies and act inhumanely toward their neighbors. As a result, they won't experience any tranquility and will pass away suddenly. Woe to you who promote godlessness and dishonesty and exalt them; you will perish and have no joyous existence. Woe to those who twist the words of righteousness, disobey the eternal law, and change from what they were to sinners! They will be crushed to death on the ground. In those days, get ready to lift up your prayers as a memorial and present them before the angels as a testimony so that they may bring the sin of the sinners before the Most High as a memorial. During those times, the families of the nations will rise up on the day of destruction, stirring up the nations. And in those days, the poor will leave their children behind and take them away, causing their children to perish as a result. In fact, they will abandon their infants and not come back, showing no compassion for their cherished ones. Once more, I promise to you sinners, sin is ready for a day of nonstop murder. Those who worship stones, grave statues made of gold, silver, wood, or clay, as well as impure spirits, devils, and other unknowable idols, won't receive any assistance from them. And as a result of their heartlessness, they will become godless, and their hearts' terror and dreams'

visions will cause them to become blind. As a result of this, they will become afraid and godless because they will have done all of their work in deception and worshiped a stone. As a result, they will perish in an instant. But at those times, blessed are those who hear the words of wisdom, comprehend them, follow the Most High's instructions, do what is right, and avoid becoming like the godless. They will be rescued. Woe to you, who sow discord among your neighbors; you will perish in Sheol. Woe to you who take dishonest and fraudulent steps and who sow discord on the land; For they will be completely consumed in the process. Woe to you who construct your homes using the painful labor of others, using only the sinful bricks and stones as your building materials; I assure you that you will not find peace. Woe to those whose spirits follow after idols and who reject the standard and eternal inheritance of their fathers; for they shall not find rest. Woe to those who promote injustice, support oppression, and murder their neighbors up until the day of the final judgment. For He will demolish your glory, inflict suffering on your hearts, stir up His ferocious wrath, and slaughter you all with the sword; and all the holy and righteous will recall your transgressions. And during those times, all of the fathers and their sons will be killed in one location, and brothers will die one after the other until the rivers overflow with their blood. For from dawn until dusk they shall kill one another; a man shall not spare his sons, and his sons' sons; and the sinner shall not spare his honorable brother. The chariot will be drowned up to its height, and the horse will walk up to its breast in the blood of sinners. During those times, angels will enter secret locations and bring all individuals who brought iniquity into the world together in one location. The Most High will then rise on the day of judgment to carry out severe punishment on sinners. And over all of the righteous and holy, He will choose watchmen from among the holy angels to watch over them as the apple of His eye until He puts an end to all evil and all sin, so that even if the righteous sleep a long slumber, they have nothing to fear. And the earth's inhabitants will witness the wise in safety, comprehend every word in this book, and realize that no amount of wealth will be able to shield them from the consequences of their actions. Woe to you, Sinners, on the day of great distress, you who afflict the upright and burn them with fire: You will receive recompense for your deeds. Woe to you, obstinate heartless ones, who keep watch to plan evil: terror shall fall upon you, and none shall deliver you. Woe to you, ye sinners, for the words you have spoken and the works you have done in the name of your godlessness. You will burn in raging flames that are worse than fire. And now, be aware that He will seek information about your actions in heaven from the angels, as well as about your misdeeds from the sun, moon, and stars since you judge the righteous on earth. Every cloud, mist, drop of dew, and drop of rain will be called to account for you before the Lord, as they will all have refrained from falling upon you due to your transgressions. And now, offer gifts to the rain and the dew so that none of them will be prevented from falling onto you after receiving gold and silver from you. You won't be able to stand before them in those days when the hoarfrost, snow, and all of the snowstorms with their calamities fall upon you.

Chapter 4: Wisdom of Enoch

"Observe heaven, you children of heaven, and all that the Most High does, and fear Him, and do not transgress in His sight." What will you do if He shuts the heavens' windows and prevents rain and dew from falling on the land because of you? You will not find peace if He pours His wrath onto you as a result of your actions because you spoke arrogantly and impudently against His righteousness. And do you not observe how the sailors on board the ships are in great peril as their vessels are thrown about by the wind and waves? As a result, they are afraid because all of their valuable possessions are lost in the water with them. They also harbor deep-seated fears that the sea will engulf them and cause their deaths. Didn't the Most High create the entire sea, all of its waters, and all of its motions? Additionally, didn't He set boundaries for the sea's actions and completely enclose it in sand? At His correction, it becomes terrified and dries up, killing all the fish and everything else in it; but you earthly sinners have no fear of Him. He created the heavens, the earth, and everything on it. Who is it that has given knowledge and wisdom to every living thing on land and in the sea? The sea is not feared by the ship's crew? Yet the Most High is not feared by sinners. Where will you go and where will you find relief in those days when He has set a terrible fire upon you? And when He unleashes His Word against you, won't you be alarmed and terrified? Additionally, the entire earth will be terrified, shaking, and alarmed, as well as all the luminaries. The children of Earth will tremble and quiver, and all the angels will carry out their instructions and try to hide from the Great Glory. You sinners will be condemned for all time, and there will be no rest for you. Do not be afraid, you righteous souls, and have hope, you who have died in righteousness. And do not be sad if your soul has fallen into Sheol in sorrow and that your body has not fared in life according to your goodness; instead, prepare for the day of sinners' judgment and the day of curses and chastisement. However, when you pass away, sinners will say over you: "As we pass away, so pass the upright; what reward do they receive for their deeds? They pass away in sorrow and darkness, just like we do, and what do they have more of than we have? We are on this point equal. What will they receive and witness forever, then? They have all passed away, and they will never again see the light. You sinners are happy to eat, drink, steal, sin, strip men of their clothing, amass fortune, and live happy lives, I tell you. Have you observed how the just finish up? Is there no violence detected in them until they pass away? Nevertheless, they died and lost all existence, and their souls suffered a terrible descent into Sheol.

Chapter 5: Wisdom of Enoch

Enoch also composed a book for his descendants, including Methuselah, who will uphold the law in the end times. You who have done good must wait for those times until those who do evil and the power of transgressors are put a stop to. And wait until sin is no longer an issue; otherwise, their names will be struck out of the Book of Life and the Holy Books, their descendants will perish for all time, their spirits will perish, they will weep and mourn in a barren wasteland, and they will burn in the fire because there is no earth there. Because of its depth, I was unable to see over it, but I saw what appeared to be an invisible cloud there. I also saw a bright fire flame and what appeared to be dazzling mountains orbiting and moving in all directions. I then enquired of one of the holy angels who was present: "What is this shining thing? Since there is no heaven there, all that can be heard there is the sound of wailing, crying, lamenting, and intense suffering. Then he told me, "This place that you see is where the spirits of sinners and blasphemers, as well as those who practice wickedness and those

who pervert everything the Lord has revealed through the mouths of the prophets—the things that shall be—are cast." Because some of them are written and etched above in the heavens, the angels can read them and learn what will happen to sinners, the spirits of the humble, and those who have suffered physical suffering and received retribution from God. And of those who were humiliated by evil people: those who loved God but did not desire riches, silver, or any other wonderful things in the world, but instead submitted their bodies to torment. Who, from the moment of their creation, had no need for nourishment from the soil and lived as such; the Lord put them to a great test and found their spirits to be clean, enabling them to praise His name. And I have detailed in the books all the blessings that were meant for them. And he has given them their due compensation since it was discovered that they were those who valued heaven more than their lives on earth. Despite being humiliated by bad people and suffering their abuse and revulsion, they still praised Me. And now, I'll call upon the souls of the righteous from the generation of light, and I'll change those who were born in darkness and weren't treated with the respect that their fidelity merited. I will also reveal those who have cherished My holiness, and I will place each on the throne of his or her honor. And they will be glorious for countless times to come because God will judge the world in righteousness and provide faithfulness to the faithful in the abode of honest paths. They will witness those who were born into darkness being driven deeper into it, but the righteous will be radiant. And when the sinners see them radiant, they will scream aloud, and they will go to the places where the appropriate days and seasons are.

Chapter 6: Revelation of Enoch

I swear to you that the angels in heaven will remember you for good before the great one's glory, and that the great one will write your names there. Have hope; in the past, sickness and affliction put you to shame; nevertheless, in the future, you will shine like the lights of heaven, be seen, and have the doors of heaven opened for you. And as you cry out for justice, it will manifest itself to you; all of your suffering will be visited on the authorities and on everyone who supported those who pillaged you. Be optimistic and don't give up on your dreams because you will experience great delight like the heavenly angels. What are you need to do? You won't need to hide on the day of the great judgment, and you won't be exposed as sinners. The eternal punishment will be distant from you for all future generations. And now, do not be alarmed, ye righteous; when ye see the wicked flourishing and gaining strength in their deeds, do not associate with them; rather, keep a safe distance from their violence; for you shall associate with the hosts of heaven. And despite the claims of sinners that their transgressions won't be looked up and recorded, all of your transgressions will be recorded daily. Now I'll demonstrate to you how all of your faults are visible to light and darkness, day and night. Do not be godless in your minds; do not lie; do not modify the words of uprightness; do not accuse the Holy huge One of lying; do not make an account of your idols; for all your lying and all your godlessness result in huge sin rather than righteousness. Now that I'm aware of it, it's a wonder to me that sinners will twist and corrupt the words of righteousness in a variety of ways, spout lies, engage in serious deception, and even write volumes about their statements. But when they accurately translate all of my statements into their native tongues, without adding or deleting anything, they will be doing exactly what I first affirmed about them. After that, I am aware of another mystery: books will be given to the upright and wise so that they may be a source of joy, uprightness, and great wisdom. After they receive the books, believe in them, and rejoice over them, all the righteous who have learned from them and followed all the paths of uprightness will get compensation. The Lord commanded to call the children of earth to account for their wisdom at that time, saying, "Show unto them; for ye are their leaders and a recompense over all the earth. Because I and My son will always be with them on the righteous paths of their lives, you will enjoy peace. Rejoice, you children of righteousness.   Amen."

Evidence of Giants (Nephilim, the offspring of unholy fallen angels & earthly women)

Massive human skeletal fossils have been discovered all over the world. Many of them, who range in size, have also been discovered to be equipped with enormous weaponry, armor, and weird objects known as OOPARTS (Out of Place objects). According to evolution, the worldview model for humans does not support the creation of a massive human race. These giant prehistoric humans were revered in many different global faiths, many of which have stories about them defeating dragons. It is significant to note that Sir Edward Owen changed the word "dragon" to "dinosaur" in 1871. According to the ontology of the word change connections involved, any mention to dragons in ancient literature is therefore a reference to dinosaurs. The following is a brief summary of gigantic fossilized human remains that have been discovered; the majority of these remains are now in the private collections of society's elite, with the exception of a few number that have ended up in museums around the globe. Although many of these museums have sold these artifacts to private individuals recently for hefty sums of money, the discoveries made by these researchers remain well-documented and beyond doubt. Consider the proof for yourself before deciding whether "Giants were on the earth in those days." - Gen. 6:4.

Crete is possibly the greatest place to start when presenting proof of the existence of enormous humans. Arcadia was the previous name for Crete. According to Eustathius, a historian mentioned by the Greek historian Herodotus, Arcadia was previously known as Gigantis, or "The Land of Giants," since giants once resided there. It was also referred to as the Garden of Eden in Greek. Given that the Arcadians frequently lived to be 300 years old, according to 4th century Roman author Servius in his Commentary on the Eneid, the connection between Arcadia, giants, and the Garden of Eden makes sense.

Land of the Giants "Nephilim," a Hebrew word, translates to "giants."

These descriptions of giants, gods, and the island of Crete are supported by some of history's most significant writers. To name a few, there was Diodorus Siculus, Pliny, Strabo, Plutarch, and Plato. There are historical stories from some of the most respected sources in the world, as well as scientific evidence from actual enormous bones discovered on the Greek island of Crete. In fact, the largest bones ever unearthed were located on this very same island, supporting the theory that it was the real Land of Giants.

The Book of Enoch is indeed an ancient religious text that includes various accounts of heavenly angels and fallen angels, but the description you provided contains some inaccuracies and misconceptions.

The Book of Enoch is a collection of several apocryphal writings attributed to the biblical figure Enoch, who was considered to be the great-grandfather of Noah. It is not a part of the traditional Hebrew Bible or the Christian Old Testament, but it is considered canonical by the Ethiopian Orthodox Church and the Eritrean Orthodox Church.

The book touches on relationships between fallen angels and humans, including how fallen angels instruct ladies in the use of cosmetics and witchcraft and how they instruct man in the use of magic, weapon making, and astrology. The Book of the Watchers, a section of the Ethiopian Book of Enoch, contains most of the information you described regarding fallen angels corrupting people by teaching them various abilities. According to these tales, a band of angels commanded by Azazel—who had been teaching humanity various prohibited talents and forbidden knowledge. Additional details and stories about fallen angels teaching humans various forms of knowledge, including makeup, weapons of war, magic, witchcraft, and astrology.

In these narratives, the fallen angels are depicted as corrupting human society by sharing knowledge and practices that were considered illicit and against divine will. The interactions between these fallen angels and humans lead to a state of moral decline and corruption, culminating in the rise of the Nephilim, the offspring of the angels and human women, who were believed to be giants.

In the Book of Enoch, fallen angels, also referred to as Watchers, do come to Earth and interact with humans. They are believed to have taught forbidden knowledge to humanity, such as the use of metals, weaponry, and other technologies. They also engaged in relationships with human women, leading to the birth of hybrid beings called Nephilim. These Nephilim were considered giants and are mentioned in the biblical book of Genesis as well.

The Book of Enoch primarily focuses on themes of righteousness, judgment, and the heavenly realms. It contains visions and prophecies attributed to Enoch, as he was said to have been taken up to heaven and shown various mysteries.

It's important to note that the Book of Enoch is not widely regarded as a historically accurate account and is not part of the biblical canon for most Christian denominations. Different religious groups interpret the book differently, and its significance varies across cultures and religious   traditions.

The Art Gallery

155

170

172

175

177

215

268

269

287

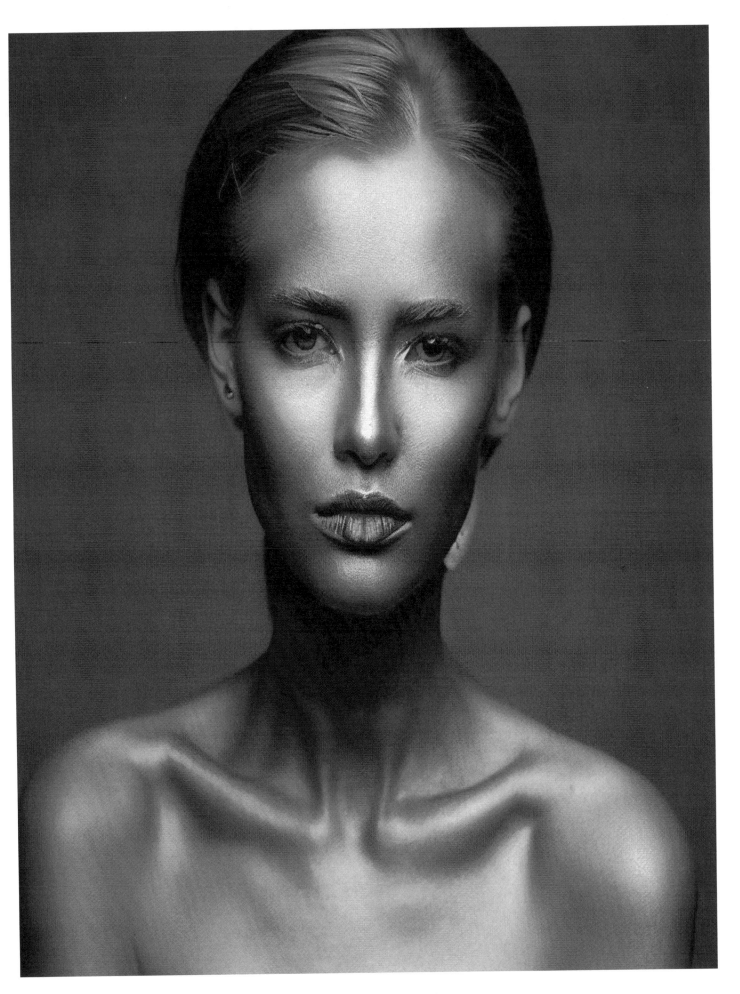

291

292

303

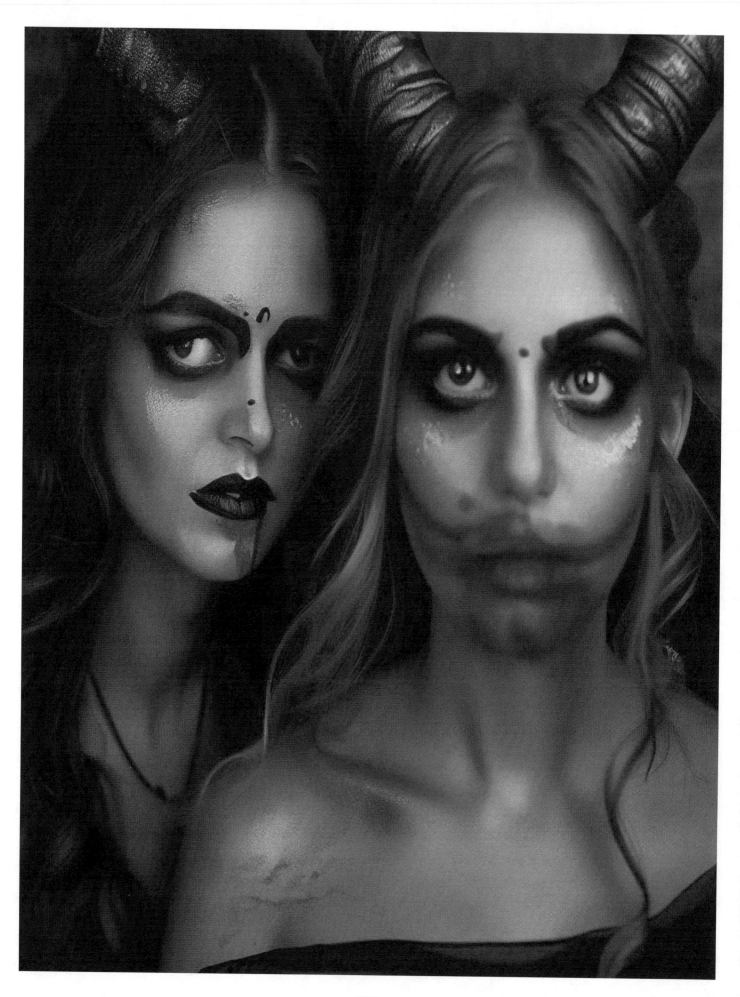

319

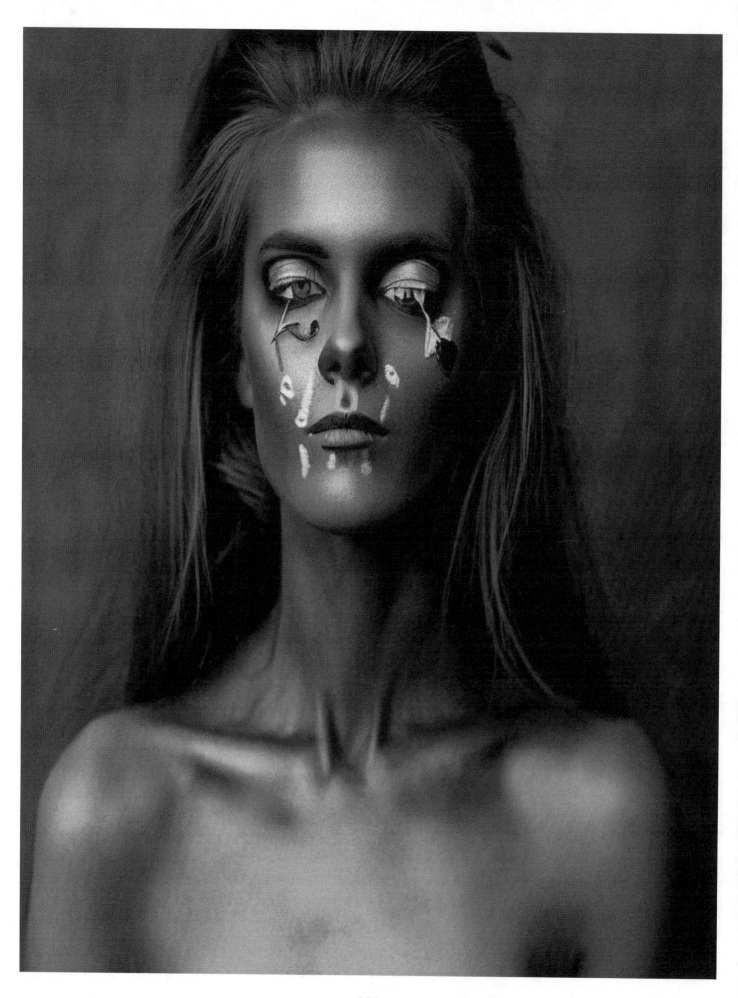

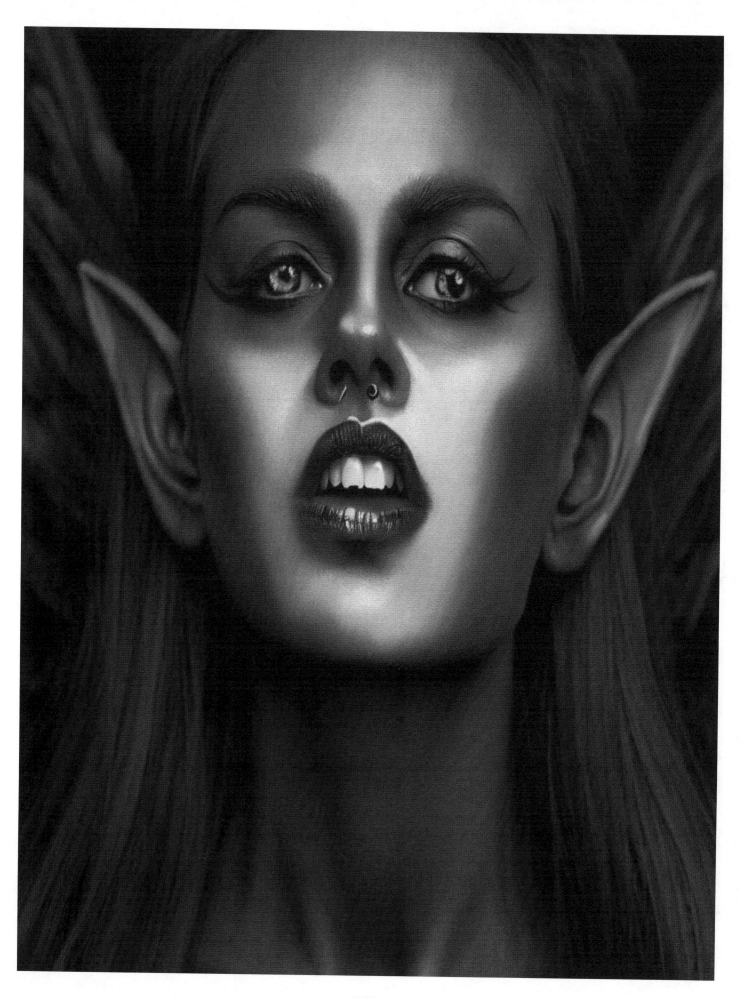

333

338

347

356

363

367

379

400

409

412

444

451

455

460

464

466

468

478

480

491

506

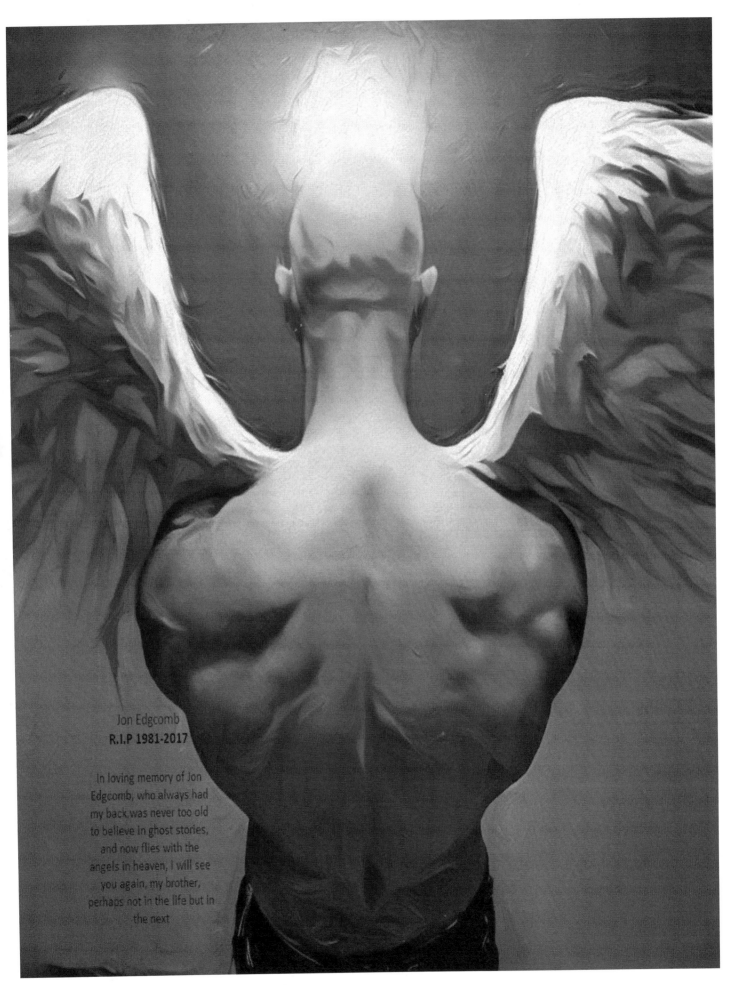

Jon Edgcomb
R.I.P 1981-2017

In loving memory of Jon
Edgcomb, who always had
my back, was never too old
to believe in ghost stories,
and now flies with the
angels in heaven, I will see
you again, my brother,
perhaps not in the life but in
the next